IMMORTAL VALOR

OSPREY
PUBLISHING

T0035364

Dedication

This book is dedicated to the seven Medal of Honor recipients. They showed what "above and beyond the call of duty" truly means.

And to my children, Micky, Chloe, Joshua, and James, the four bright lights in my life. It is tough to imagine any father could love his children more.

★ ★ ★ ★ ★ ★ ★ ★

IMMORTAL VALOR

THE BLACK MEDAL OF HONOR
RECIPIENTS OF WORLD WAR II

★ ★ ★ ★ ★ ★ ★

ROBERT CHILD

OSPREY PUBLISHING
Bloomsbury Publishing Plc
Kemp House, Chawley Park, Cumnor Hill, Oxford OX2 9PH, UK
29 Earlsfort Terrace, Dublin 2, Ireland
1385 Broadway, 5th Floor, New York, NY 10018, USA
E-mail: info@ospreypublishing.com
www.ospreypublishing.com

OSPREY is a trademark of Osprey Publishing Ltd

First published in Great Britain in 2022

© Robert Child, 2022

Robert Child has asserted his right under the Copyright, Designs and Patents
Act, 1988, to be identified as Author of this work.

This paperback edition was first published in Great Britain in 2023 by
Osprey Publishing.

For legal purposes the Acknowledgments on pp. 260–262 constitute an
extension of this copyright page.

All rights reserved. No part of this publication may be reproduced or
transmitted in any form or by any means, electronic or mechanical, including
photocopying, recording, or any information storage or retrieval system,
without prior permission in writing from the publishers.

A catalog record for this book is available from the British Library.

ISBN: HB 978 1 4728 5285 4; PB 978 1 4728 5284 7; eBook 978 1 4728 5286 1;
ePDF 978 1 4728 5287 8; XML 978 1 4728 5288 5

23 24 25 26 27   10 9 8 7 6 5 4 3 2 1

Plate section image credits are given in full in the List of Illustrations (pp. 8–9).
Index by Alan Rutter

Typeset by Deanta Global Publishing Services, Chennai, India
Printed and bound in Great Britain by CPI (Group) UK Ltd, Croydon
CR0 4YY

Osprey Publishing supports the Woodland Trust, the UK's leading woodland
conservation charity.

To find out more about our authors and books visit www .ospreypublishing
.com. Here you will find extracts, author interviews, details of forthcoming
events and the option to sign up for our newsletter.

Contents

Author's Note

Throughout this book the terms "colored" and "negro" appear as part of historic quotes and as original military unit designations reflecting the segregation of the United States military. For example, the 326th Service Battalion QMC (Colored). The "N word" appears in a few direct quotes reported from the time and which clearly illustrate the racism that permeated society and the military at the time.

List of Illustrations

The American infantry in this photo are facing similar terrain and weather conditions as they encountered at Climbach. (Signal Corps/NARA)

Charles Thomas being awarded the Distinguished Service Cross in 1945. (Allene Carter)

Vernon Baker with Edward Carter III, who is holding the Medal of Honor awarded to his father Edward Carter Jr., at the White House in 1997. (Allene Carter)

Sandra Holiday and Vernon Baker at the White House in 1997. (Allene Carter)

Vernon Baker from *Ebony* magazine. At the time this photo was taken he was the only soldier in the 92nd Division to be awarded the DSC. (Allene Carter)

Soldiers from an 81mm mortar platoon from the 92nd Infantry Division, Vernon Baker's division, in action against targets in northern Italy, 1944. (NARA)

Valcenie James with President William J. Clinton at the White House in 1997. (Allene Carter)

A sketch commissioned by the James family of Willy James Jr. (Allene Carter)

Valcenie James with the sketch the family commissioned of her husband. She guided the art from her memory. No photographs exist of Willy James Jr. (Allene Carter)

Edward Carter Jr. (on right) with other soldiers at Fort Benning in 1942. (Allene Carter)

Another photo of Edward Carter Jr. at Fort Benning in 1942. (Allene Carter)

A third view of Edward Carter Jr. at Fort Benning in 1942. (Allene Carter)

In this photograph printed in *Ebony* magazine in the 1940s, Edward Carter Jr. shows his sons Edward and William his Distinguished Service Cross. (Allene Carter)

Russell Blair (Sgt. Carter's World War II commander) and Allene Carter (Sgt. Carter's daughter-in-law). (Allene Carter)

The White House Medal of Honor ceremony in 1997. (Allene Carter)

Edward Carter Jr. receiving his Distinguished Service Cross in Los Angeles. (Allene Carter)

William Carter, his wife Karen, Russell Blair, and Edward Carter III at Sgt. Carter's reinternment at Arlington National Cemetery, 1997. (Allene Carter)

Allene Carter and Mildred Carter (Sgt. Carter's wife) at Arlington National Cemetery. (Allene Carter)

The Hall of Heroes event at the Pentagon in 1999 where the Army formally apologized to Sgt. Carter. Left to right: Allene Carter; General John Keane, Army Vice Chief of Staff; Mildred Carter; Edward Carter III; and William Carter. (Allene Carter)

Sgt. Carter's grandchildren Santalia and Corey Carter at the Pentagon. (Allene Carter)

This photograph of George Watson, taken before World War II, appeared in *Ebony* magazine. (Allene Carter)

The cargo transport USNS *Watson* (T-AKR-310), named for George Watson. (Allene Carter)

Sergeant Major of the Army Gene C. McKinney accepting the Medal of Honor on behalf of George Watson in 1997. (Allene Carter)

Ruben Rivers was the only one of the seven Medal of Honor recipients not to be awarded the Distinguished Service Cross. (Joe Wilson Jr.)

Ruben Rivers with another soldier from World War II. (Joe Wilson Jr.)

Ruben Rivers' draft card. The card can also be viewed on Ancestry.com. (NARA)

The 761st Tank Battalion in France in one of their new Sherman tanks. (Signal Corps/NARA)

David Williams in combat gear during World War II. (Joe Wilson Jr.)

On April 25, 1945, M5A1 Stuart tanks of Company D, 761st Tank Battalion park in the town square of Coburg, Germany. Sgt. Ruben Rivers was in Company A. (NARA)

David Williams at the White House in 1997. (Joe Wilson Jr.)

John Fox. This photo of him has only been published once in *Braided in Fire* by Solace Wales. (© Copyright and Courtesy, Sandra Fox / 2021.)

Otis Zachary, John Fox's friend who had to obey the order to fire the artillery on John's position. (Photo courtesy of Solace Wales)

Sandra Fox, Cassandra Charles (John Fox's granddaughter), and Arlene Fox (John Fox's wife) in Sommocolonia, Italy, in 2000, with the La Rocca tower, where John Fox called in the artillery strikes, in the background. (© Copyright and Courtesy, Sandra Fox / 2021. Photo taken by Solace Wales)

Arlene Fox and President Clinton at the White House in 1997. (© The White House / 1997. Courtesy of the White House)

Arlene Fox, Grace Rivers (Ruben Rivers' older sister), Valcenie James (Willy James Jr.'s wife), and Mildred Carter in 1999. (Allene Carter)

May 27, 1942: Admiral Chester W. Nimitz, Commander-in-Chief Pacific Fleet, pins the Navy Cross on Steward's Mate 3rd Class "Dorie" Miller at a ceremony in Pearl Harbor, Hawaii. There is currently a petition supporting Miller being awarded the Medal of Honor. (NARA)

Edward Carter Jr.'s granddaughter Ashli Carter with five out of the seven Medals of Honor in 2015 at the Honor Deferred Exhibit at The National World War II Museum in New Orleans. (Allene Carter)

The Honor Deferred Exhibit at The National WWII Museum in New Orleans, organized by Allene Carter in 2015. (Allene Carter)

*"Shame on the nation that has no military heroes,
but much more shame on the nation that has heroes and
does not honor them."*

PERICLES, GREEK STATESMAN
AND GENERAL, 450 BC

Introduction

*"Few inventions could be more happily calculated to diffuse the
knowledge and preserve the memory of illustrious characters and
splendid events than medals."*

THE CONTINENTAL
CONGRESS, 1787

The tradition of awarding medals for military merit in the United
States began with General George Washington in August 1782. In
his headquarters at Newburgh, New York, he established the Badge
of Military Merit. The award was the first military decoration
to apply to enlisted men and was retroactive to the American
Revolution. Earlier, the Congressional Gold Medal generally
applied only to officers.

Unfortunately, as it came a year after the British surrender at
Yorktown, awareness of the new medal was not widespread. There
are only four confirmed recipients of the Badge of Military Merit
for service during the Revolutionary War. The award fell into
disuse for 150 years until it was revived in 1932 by the Army's then
Chief of Staff, Douglas MacArthur, on the 200th anniversary of
Washington's birth. The War Department, in christening the new
medal, also gave it a new name and announced:

By order of the President of the United States, the Purple
Heart, established by Gen. George Washington at Newburgh,

New York ... is hereby revived out of respect to his memory
and military achievements.

Congress kept the Badge of Merit's original shape of a "purple
heart" as the medal's theme, adding a new insignia containing
Washington's likeness and his coat of arms. "For Military Merit"
appears on the reverse in reference to the original enlisted man's
military honor.

The medal that we know today as the United States' highest
award for military valor in action, the Medal of Honor, did not
come into being until the Civil War. In 1861 President Abraham
Lincoln signed legislation proposed in Congress by Iowa Senator
James W. Grimes, creating the first Medals of Honor for heroic
Naval service actions. Congress followed up in 1862, devising the
Army's first Medal of Honor specifically for "noncommissioned
officers and privates who distinguished themselves by their gallant
actions." Later it grew to include officers.

Of the nearly 3,500 Medals of Honor awarded to date, a
disproportionately small number of African Americans have
received the decoration. Less than 3 percent or 89 Medals of
Honor have been awarded to 88 African Americans, with one
sailor, Robert Sweeny, receiving two during peacetime, both
times for rescuing fellow sailors from drowning in the late 1800s.

After the close of the Civil War, 25 African Americans were
deemed worthy of the coveted award for their gallant actions, and
subsequently, six passed the test following the end of the Spanish–
American War. In each case, awards were conveyed shortly after the
close of both conflicts.

As the 20th century dawned, it became an entirely different
story in awarding the Medal of Honor to worthy African American
servicemen. It was not until 1991 that the first black serviceman
from World War I, Freddie Stowers, was awarded the Medal of
Honor 73 years after being killed in action. The second black World
War I recipient, William Henry Johnson of the 369th Infantry
Regiment, was awarded his Medal of Honor posthumously by
President Barack Obama in 2015.

The lateness in awarding the nation's highest military honor to World War I African American soldiers is shocking enough. But it was in what many consider America's "Greatest War" fought by America's "Greatest Generation" that systemic racism within the military delayed and almost denied deserving African Americans from receiving their country's highest award for bravery.

Out of the nearly 500 Medals of Honor awarded for conspicuous gallant action during World War II, only seven black Americans have received the award – the men whom you will meet in this book. This minute number of recipients is in stark contrast to the more than 1 million African Americans who served and a total of 16 million Americans in uniform during the war.

Yet sadly, this is not surprising given the world black Americans grew up in prior to World War II. Despite the inequalities that still exist in modern America, the United States during this time is one that is difficult to recognize today. Many black families in the south were only a few generations away from being former slaves. Black soldiers who served in the war knew only segregation from the white population and, of course, segregation inherently meant inequality. Schools for black children were consistently underfunded compared to schools for white children. Access to the voting booth was also significantly curtailed for black citizens both officially with the institution of poll taxes and literacy requirements and unofficially with widespread intimidation of potential black voters. Segregation had become so prevailing that it was ingrained in society and this carried over into the military. Despite this, hundreds of thousands of African Americans would clamor to serve in America's hour of need. Initially black Americans were restricted to service or rear echelon roles. This would ultimately change in late 1944 but no service was without risk. Many young black men, however, began to ask the question that needed to be asked: "Should I sacrifice to live 'half American'?"

James G. Thompson, a black soldier from Kansas, asked that exact question in a letter to the *Pittsburgh Courier* in late January 1942, which became the catalyst for the Double V Campaign:

victory abroad and at home. Victory at home, of course, meant equality and full citizenship after the war for the sacrifice asked of African Americans.

✳✳✳

This book will introduce you to the seven extraordinary African Americans whose World War II acts of courage broke through the barrier of racism that conspired to silence their accomplishments. They are as different from one another as one could imagine, but they all share a common thread: devotion to the mission and sacrifice above and beyond the call of duty.

Four gave the ultimate sacrifice while three returned home to civilian life and a country little changed from when they had left. In all cases in writing this book, I found the men to be wise and humble heroes who felt they were simply doing their jobs to the best of their ability. They gave credit to the soldiers who surrounded them, especially those left behind on the battlefield. The overriding motivation in all cases was not fighting for God and country, although they were all patriotic. When it came right down to it, they were fighting for each other. The men did not want to let down their brothers-in-arms.

They stepped forward to provide us all an example of what true heroism and sacrifice for one's fellow man, regardless of skin color, looks like. The delay in receiving the recognition they deserved does not diminish their heroic acts of valor; in my view, it elevates them, especially when you consider how different the world was in the 1940s. But as we celebrate the lives and the achievements of these men in this book, we shouldn't forget how their heroic acts continued to remain unrecognized for over 50 years after the war's end. Only with the continuous efforts of determined individuals, from family members to historians to Congressional lawmakers, did the wheels finally start turning on an official investigation into the brave acts of black soldiers during World War II.

During America's "Greatest War," racism was acute, pervasive, and entrenched in American society. Yet, these men answered to a higher call, rising above the injustice and discrimination that surrounded them. Fighting a war under these conditions, in my opinion, places them into a class all by themselves. It has been an honor and a privilege to get to know these men and to have the opportunity to tell their stories.

Within these pages, you will hopefully come to know these remarkable heroes better than you ever have before, even if you have long been a student of World War II. That was my objective in the research and writing of this book. Hopefully, you will agree that this has been achieved when you arrive at the final page.

Robert Child
July 2021

PART ONE

Charles L. Thomas

Chapter 1

Graduation Day

Charles Leroy Thomas, tall, soft-spoken, and mild-mannered with close-cropped hair, stood beaming on the auditorium stage in his green graduation gown with his fellow seniors in the class of 1938. He was in the third row back on the cramped stage at Cass Tech, a technical high school in midtown Detroit. His parents Essie, 42, and Horace, 46, flanked by his two sisters Alice, 15, and Lena, 19, looked on in admiration as the principal called Charles's name. The new graduate made his way to the podium to accept his diploma.

Charles had excelled in his studies and, growing up, loved books and had a great interest in planes and electronics. He anticipated attending nearby Wayne University, where he had been accepted and would be majoring in Mechanical Engineering in the fall.

The Thomases were originally from Birmingham, Alabama. Horace had married Essie Albertha Byrd 21 years earlier in Montgomery in 1917. Horace shipped out the following year with D Company of the 326th Service Battalion QMC (Colored) for service in World War I. He returned from the war in late June 1919. After Horace's return from the service, Charles was born, and the family decided to relocate north in 1920, seeking a better life with waves of other African Americans during the Great Migration.*

Although they rented at first in Detroit's 7th Ward, they eventually became homeowners of their two-story bungalow-style home at 5877 Beechwood Avenue, a leafy, tree-lined street on Detroit's west side. The family epitomized the black middle-class economic boom experienced by the city in the early part of the 20th century.

In the auditorium, watching his son graduate, Horace had a surprise announcement he'd been saving for after the ceremony. As the principal finished thanking all for attending the graduation, Horace waved his son over. Charles arrived smiling, and his father asked him how it felt to be a graduate.

The diploma-clutching senior said it was a relief, and he looked forward to his summer break. His father, however, had other plans. Horace, bursting at the seams with his surprise, asked Charles if he planned to lie around all summer and goof off. Charles laughed and said he wasn't sure yet.

Horace glanced over at Essie then told his son that he wouldn't have much idle time. He had pulled some strings and gotten the boy a job as a molder at Ford's Rouge Factory Complex in Dearborn, where Horace worked as a machinist.

The complex, a self-contained city spanning over 1,000 acres, churned out a finished automobile every 28 hours. In the late 1930s, Henry Ford provided well-paying jobs to black citizens at the massive factory complex, which enabled a burgeoning black middle class to prosper in Detroit. Ford factory workers also benefited from the recent passage of the Wagner Act, which led to the creation of powerful industrial trade unions, including the United Auto Workers, in August 1935.

---

* The Great Migration was the movement of over 6 million African Americans from rural Southern states to the Northeast, Midwest, and West. It began during World War I. Some historians differentiate between a first Great Migration (1910–40) and a second (1940–70). In both instances it was a desire to escape the Jim Crow laws and economic realities.

Realizing what the opportunity at Ford meant for his future, Charles was thrilled but thought his father was kidding as he hadn't even graduated college yet. Horace assured him that it was no joke and that his son could work full time during the summer and scale back when classes started. Charles's mother kissed him on the cheek and told him how proud they both were of him. Both his sisters moved in for a hug.

Charles began working at the Ford plant in June, learning the ropes and becoming a skilled molder. As fall classes began at Wayne University, Charles found them more challenging than anticipated. He had to scale back his hours at the Dearborn Complex more than he had expected, to keep up with his studies. Supporting Charles's decision, his father encouraged him to focus on school as the job would always be there.

Thousands of miles away from Detroit, at this same time, the global winds of war were escalating to a gale. Germany's invasion of Austria in March 1938 incorporated the formerly sovereign nation into the growing German Reich. A torrent of violence followed against Jews in Vienna and other cities by the totalitarian regime during the summer and fall.

By the fall of 1941, the United States was getting dragged into the European quagmire. On September 4, 1941, the USS *Greer* was fired upon by a German U-boat, even though the United States remained a neutral power. Less than a week later, President Roosevelt ordered the US Navy to shoot any ship or convoy if threatened on the high seas in preparation for the formal launch of Allied supply "Liberty Ships."

The first Liberty Ship, the SS *Patrick Henry*, was launched on September 27 as Charles was beginning classes in his junior year at Wayne. Thomas had been doing well and felt he'd gotten a handle on his academic workload. He was also able to pick up more hours at the plant. He felt everything was falling into place for his future. As his studies isolated him somewhat from global politics and Hitler's continuing conquest of swathes of Europe, Charles still naively believed, as most Americans did, that the war was a distant European problem that wouldn't impact his life. But, as he looked forward to passing the mid-year mark in his junior year at Wayne, his entire world would change less than three months later.

One wintery Sunday, Essie, who had just finished cleaning up lunch, walked into the family parlor and switched on the wood-paneled Philco radio. She relished stealing a few minutes listening to the symphony before Horace insisted on switching to the football game. The radio tubes warmed, and soon the Thomas's parlor was filled with the New York Philharmonic's Symphony No. 1 in F minor by Russian composer Shostakovich. Then, a few minutes past 3 p.m., the radio suddenly went silent as a network reporter broke in with a breaking news announcement.

> This is John Daly speaking from the CBS newsroom in New York. Here is the far east situation as reported to this moment. The Japanese have attacked the American Naval Base at Pearl Harbor, Hawaii, and our defense facilities at Manilla, capital of the Philippines. The first disclosure of this news was made by Presidential Secretary Stephen Early by telephone at approximately 2:25 in Washington.[1]

Essie shouted for Horace, and he came running into the parlor. Charles was upstairs studying for midterm final exams, which were in less than two weeks. Horace listened to the radio for a moment, then walked to the bottom of the stairs and called for his son to come down right away; Charles asked what was wrong as he descended the stairs trailed by his younger sister Alice. Charles and Alice arrived beside their parents with questioning expressions. Horace pointed to the radio and said, "listen." The somber newscaster continued that an announcement was expected from President Roosevelt at any moment. Essie glanced over to her son, put a hand to her mouth, and rushed from the room.

Charles asked his father a question he already knew the answer to: *was the country going to war?* His father, who knew war all too well from his service during World War I, replied with an acknowledging nod followed by a sigh. There was no doubt.

Charles Thomas was drafted into the Army just over a month later, on January 20, 1942. On his draft registration, he listed his height as 5ft 11in., and his weight as 162lb. As most Michigan residents did, Thomas started his military journey at Fort Custer just outside of Battle Creek, 130 miles west of Detroit. The fort sprawled over 16,000 acres, with an additional 2,000-acre artillery training ground. Its facilities held quarters for 1,279 officers and 27,553 enlisted men. However, black troops were segregated into their own barracks and mess halls. The fort served as home for the 184th Field Artillery, part of the 5th Division, entirely composed of African American soldiers and officers.[2]

Fort Custer was the reception center for all Michigan inductees, except for those from the Upper Peninsula. Each recruit would spend an average of three to four days at the reception center being evaluated under a classification system administered by Army psychologists. First, the draftee would provide information in regard to his education and employment. Then, each recruit would be personally interviewed by an officer who was trained to assign recruits. Despite his academic background and mechanical aptitude, Thomas drew the infantry and began basic training in late January.

Several days after Thomas began basic training, on January 31, 1942, a letter was published by an African American GI, James G. Thompson, in a black-owned newspaper, the *Pittsburgh Courier*. Thompson's letter publicly asked the questions on all African American recruits' minds as they began service and sacrifice to their country.

Being an American of dark complexion and some 26 years, these questions flash through my mind: "Should I sacrifice my life to live half American?" "Will things be better for the next generation in the peace to follow?" "Would it be demanding too much to demand full citizenship rights in exchange for the sacrificing of my life?" "Is the kind of America I know worth defending?" "Will America be a true and pure democracy after this war?" "Will colored Americans still suffer the indignities that have been heaped upon them in the past?" These and other questions need answering. James G. Thompson.[3]

Thompson's letter galvanized the discussion around equality and resulted in the launch of the Double V Campaign: Victory for democracy at home and abroad. The newspaper officially launched the Double V campaign a week later, on February 7, and thereafter Double V articles appeared weekly well into 1943.

The effort, which drew widespread popular support, especially among black service members, provided additional incentive for them to push their absolute limits on the battlefield. Fighting hard and winning against a foreign foe, they believed, meant that the victory of equality was drawing ever closer at home.

In basic training, Thomas met and befriended fellow Detroiter, Chris Sturkey. A year older than Thomas, Sturkey hadn't finished high school and had been working as a chauffeur in civilian life before being drafted. He had a gregarious personality, was streetwise, and spoke his mind, which Thomas, much more reserved, enjoyed.

In April 1942, they were both transferred to Camp Wolters, Texas, for additional infantry training in the new tank destroyer (TD) battalions that were forming. On November 21, 1941, General George C. Marshall had activated the new Tank Destroyer Force (TDF), which was developed by Army Ground Force's General Leslie J. McNair and implemented by General Andrew Bruce at Camp Hood, Texas. They were charged with the mission to Seek, Strike, and Destroy enemy tanks.[4]

The new main self-propelled tank destroyer was primarily built on a Sherman chassis but didn't have the tank's armor. Its five-man crew, however, commanded higher speed, visibility, and maneuverability and at least equaled the Sherman's firepower. The Defense Department could produce one battle-ready tank destroyer for materially less than the cost of a tank and in far less time. And by employing tank destroyers, Shermans, Stuarts, and, later, Pershings and other tank models were freed up to pursue mechanized offensive missions, including close infantry support, cavalry support, and artillery support.[5]

One forward-thinking component of the new TDF was that, as a fully fledged independent branch, it was required by War Department policy to establish units staffed by African Americans. The War Department subsequently exerted pressure on the Army to ensure that black soldiers operated a significant number of combat units.[6]

Thomas became the beneficiary of two new Army policies, both implemented in 1942, that directly impacted African American recruits. First, the aforementioned push to form black combat tank destroyer battalions, and second, the Officer Corp mandate to train more black officers. Thomas stood out among his peers with his mechanical engineering aptitude and several years of college behind him. Along with his friend Chris Sturkey and several others, Thomas was chosen as a candidate for officer training in early 1943.

Sturkey, however, had an acute attack of appendicitis after becoming a candidate, which required surgery, delaying his entrance. Thomas visited him just before he left for Camp Carson, Colorado, where black officers were training in preparation for deployment with the 614th Tank Destroyer Battalion. Sturkey, lying in his hospital cot, told Thomas that he was right behind him and to "learn slow" so he'd have a chance to catch up when he got there. The comment made them both laugh.

The 614th TD Battalion had been officially formed the previous year on July 25, 1942 at Camp Carson, Colorado, as a self-propelled battalion. Its primary weapon was the M1897 75mm field gun mounted on an M3 (half-track). The outfit had five white officers, but the field commanders, including company commanders, were all African American. Charles Thomas became "Charlie" (C) Company commander, which included a headquarters detachment, a medical detachment, and three tank destroyer platoons with approximately 50 men.

Commissioned as a 2nd Lieutenant in March 1943, Thomas transferred to Camp Hood in Texas with the 614th. The tank destroyer battalion was making Hood its permanent home. The unit was also reorganized as a towed battalion in May of the same year when it gained new M5 3-inch guns pulled by the M3 half-tracks.

Chris Sturkey never made it to Officer Candidate School (OCS) at Camp Carson. In the interim, he transferred to Camp Hood and completed enlisted man training, and rose in rank to Staff Sergeant. When Thomas arrived back, he was now Sturkey's superior which, despite his disappointment, didn't fill Sturkey with envy, only pride.

Camp Hood was one of the most extensive training facilities for American soldiers during World War II. It encompassed more than 160,000 acres with a population of close to 80,000 officers and men. Meat requirements alone totaled 1.5 million pounds a month, and the kitchen facilities baked 25,000 loaves of bread every day.[7]

Upon arrival, newly commissioned officers like Thomas trained in a week-long battle-conditioning obstacle course alongside enlisted men. They lived in the same clothes for the entire week, sliding under barbed wire, climbing walls, rappelling down ropes, crossing water hazard streams, and scaling mountains and hills. Each man had to cover the obstacle course three times daily.

Settling into his new role at Camp Hood, Thomas noticed one immediate and stark difference between the African American 614th and the white tank destroyer outfits. Thomas's battalion and other black units were forced to use older, less efficient equipment that frequently needed repairs.[8]

Chris Sturkey, now a Staff Sergeant in 1st Platoon, and never one to hold back, approached Thomas on a scorching June afternoon to complain about the battered equipment. Sturkey conveyed his disgust as Thomas patiently listened, knowing there wasn't much he could do. Sturkey reported that half their equipment was old and constantly breaking down and being patched up. He asked his friend and his superior what they would do when they needed to rely on it during a battle. Thomas had no answer for him.

Added to the older equipment they were forced to use, black soldiers at Camp Hood did not enjoy the same privileges as white soldiers. Recreational facilities were nonexistent, and they often received a chilly reception when venturing off base. One weekend on liberty traveling into Killeen with friends, Thomas came upon the Old Chesapeake hotel surrounded by a high stockade fence. Glen Miller swing music filtered into the street from a live band at the hotel, and drew Thomas, Sturkey, and the group's attention.

As they approached the hotel, a gruff doorman immediately held out his hand, saying there was no admittance to Negros. Sturkey, angered, started approaching the doorman, but Thomas grabbed his shoulder and pulled him back. He whispered to his friend it wasn't worth getting brought up on charges or worse. All the men could do was peer through the slats in the fence at white people inside, dancing, having a ball.

During the summer of 1943, Thomas got to know all his men in 3rd Platoon much better. He felt the closeness was necessary to build trust. He wanted the men to rely on each other when the going inevitably got rough. Working together as a team, Thomas knew they had a better chance of surviving. His platoon leader and second in command was 1st Lieutenant George W. Mitchell, a capable commander from Gary, Indiana. Mitchell was a graduate of Morehouse College. Thomas also got to know Corporal Pete Simmons from farming country in Saluda County, South Carolina. The men called him "old man" because of his ripe old age of 32. Then there was 1st Lieutenant Floyd Stallings whom Thomas knew from OCS at Camp Carson. Stallings was their sole west coast man hailing from San Francisco. Thomas considered the men a great bunch of motivated soldiers who excelled at what they did.

In October 1943, the 614th experienced a change of commanding officers. Lieutenant Colonel Frank S. Pritchard, a Michigan man like Thomas and Sturkey, took over for Lieutenant Colonel Blaisdell C. Kenon on October 16, 1943. Pritchard had served in World War I as an Artillery Sergeant and would command the 614th through the remainder of the war into November 1945.

In early February 1944, word arrived that the battalion would soon be on the move. Their turn came to join the Army training exercises known as the Louisiana Maneuvers near Camp Polk. Thomas was notified of the orders early one morning, and his first thought was of the natural hazards. Louisiana was one of the few places more rustic than Texas, and bayous and swamps would only add to the unpleasantness. Chris Sturkey was deathly afraid of snakes and figured the snakes *had* to be more numerous in bayous and swamps than in Texas. He was right.

The Louisiana Maneuvers were grueling large-scale military exercises in that state's bayous and snake-infested swamplands that had begun in 1941. They were held every year through 1944 until the invasion of Normandy. In Colonel Robert S. Allen's book, *Lucky Forward*, he described the area as "a 40 by 90 mile sparsely settled, chigger and tick-infested bayou and pitch pine section between the Sabine and Red Rivers."[9] Thomas and the 614th joined the maneuvers in late February and trained through March 21, 1944.

The 614th was initially expected to be part of the D-Day landings in June 1944, but at the last moment those orders were canceled, sending morale into a tailspin. The 614th had been rated as "combat ready" for Europe by late May. But many of the black soldiers in the ranks believed that white commanders purposefully wanted them left out of the war. At least that's the way it appeared to them.

Thomas expressed his frustrations privately to fellow field officers about the endless rounds of training throughout the summer, which only seemed to diminish their combat readiness. The unit spent several weeks in indirect fire training, which saw the mood lift for a short period when Staff Sergeant John Weir destroyed a Texas outhouse with only two rounds at 9,000 yards. His accuracy on that target became the talk of the battalion for the remainder of July as the men lingered, awaiting orders to finally ship out.

Chapter 2

Last Stop USA

Entering August, the Tank Destroyer Force received the long-awaited word that the Army needed their services on the front line. The 614th loaded men and equipment on trains at Killeen, and on the 10th set out on a 1,700-mile, three-day journey north. Their destination was Rockland County, New York, and Camp Shanks, better known to the GIs as "Last Stop USA."

Camp Shanks, 20 miles northeast of New York City, spread out over 2,000 acres. The military installation saw 1.3 million soldiers pass through, including 75 percent of the soldiers who took part in the D-Day invasion. The camp had its own baseball team, orchestra, and newspaper, and being so close to New York City, activity organizers often wrangled celebrities to make the trip up to "entertain the boys." Frank Sinatra, Jimmy Durante, Joe Louis, and Joe DiMaggio frequently made appearances on the nightly bill.[10]

Arriving at Camp Shanks on August 13, Thomas and the men spent much of their free time exploring Manhattan for a "last fling," as they termed it, before crossing the Atlantic.

Chris Sturkey felt he was in his element, loved the fast pace and bright lights, and wanted to stay. Before long, however, the fun and games were over. The 614th, along with the 761st Tank Battalion, including future Medal of Honor recipient Ruben Rivers, embarked for England on August 27, 1944 on the SS *Esperance Bay*.

A former 1920s-era Australian luxury liner, the ship was heavily used for American troop transport and featured an ingenious type of camouflage. On her port and starboard sides, the military painted a white profile of a Royal Navy Hunt-class destroyer as a ploy to discourage enemy submarine attacks.[11]

Thomas, the 614th, and the 761st Tank Battalion arrived in England at Avonmouth near Bristol on September 7 after an uneventful 12-day voyage. Thomas, peering out from the top deck with hundreds of other American soldiers, smiled as they were welcomed by scores of attractive female Red Cross volunteers waving greetings. The soldiers appreciated the smiles as much as the Red Cross donuts and hot coffee.

The train to take the battalion to the staging area was waiting on tracks near the docks so the men wouldn't have far to walk with their gear. The 614th's destination was a temporary tent camp at Burley, England, 100 miles to the southeast. Once settled in, they would continue training and wait for their equipment to catch up with them.

At this stage in the war, September 1944, the Allies were making headway, pushing toward Germany. On September 13, American troops reached the Siegfried Line, the formidable defense system known as the *Westwall* in German. A major Allied offensive was also just days away on the 17th. On that date, the British-led Operation *Market Garden*, the largest airborne assault until that point in the war, would commence. Unfortunately, as history would record, the operation was not the success the Allies had anticipated.

The 614th's tank destroyer equipment reached Burley in late September, and the battalion left camp on October 2 on a 25-mile motor march toward Southampton, their point of embarkation for France.

They shivered in formation at Southampton on windswept docks, waiting to board the LSTs for the channel crossing. Northern gales accompanied by driving rain mixed to create the perfect atmosphere of gloom.

Even Sturkey, who often had a smile on his face, was dismayed. The chop in the English Channel was a fury of whitecaps, and Sturkey had severe doubts the flat-bottomed LSTs could even stay afloat. In fact reasonably seaworthy, the LSTs were nicknamed "Low Slow Targets" by Allied troops for the seemingly perfect target they presented to enemy aircraft.

Pritchard, the 614th CO (commanding officer), who appeared surprisingly cheerful or, as the men believed, entirely out of touch, attempted to lift morale, calling the downpour "liquid sunshine." Pritchard concluded his pre-voyage pep talk by recommending they relax and enjoy the short boat ride to France. Sturkey whispered aloud, "Yeah, if we make it." Hearing the comment, Thomas looked back to Sturkey and laughed.

The 614th would not soon forget the five-day channel crossing as the flat-bottomed boats pitched and rolled in the high seas and men heaved. Midway through the voyage, two M5s broke loose from their mounts and careened into several motorcycles and an armored car. Above the crashing waves and lurching artillery, a singular, straining voice beseeched the heavens. That voice belonged to Chaplain Harvey Johnson, whom the men described as "kicking his praying into high gear."[12]

All the LSTs arrived none the worse for wear on Utah beach between October 8 and 10. Disembarking troops were confronted with yet another weather-related hazard: the ankle-deep Normandy mud. It covered everything and eventually everyone as they traveled 25 miles east from Cherbourg to a temporary home in a saturated field near Surtainville. Here they bivouacked for the next 30 days, trying to keep dry. Unfortunately, during their stay, only on four days did it not rain.

Stuck in tents most of the time due to the ever-present deluge, the men passed the time passing around flasks of their new favorite indulgence, calvados, the revered Normandy apple cider brandy. The drink, distilled in the region since 1553, flowed like water and the troops humoredly referred to it as "the juice of the apple that made strong men gasp."

Thomas seldom imbibed but enjoyed the laughter and camaraderie with his platoon. He saw that these men had spirit and drive. The majority of the 614th were hard-working farmhands from rural North and South Carolina. They even referred to themselves as the "614th Gamecocks." There were many who were illiterate, but Thomas believed that although they were unschooled, they were not ignorant men, and he felt proud to serve alongside them.[13]

Enjoying a respite from the rain one afternoon, Thomas walked through the camp on his way to the Command Post (CP) for a meeting. En route, he reflected that the road ahead would not be easy. The battalion had passed miles of destroyed and abandoned German armor and remnants of furious engagements, including shell-torn roads and countless blown bridges. Village after nameless village had been reduced to unrecognizable piles of rubble, and refugees were omnipresent.

At the CP, Lt. Col. Pritchard's aide pulled a tent flap aside, allowing him into the meeting. Entering, Thomas saluted the Colonel, who was just putting out a cigarette. Pritchard informed him that they had finally received their orders to move out.

The 614th was now attached to the 95th Infantry Division, heading to Metz, in northeastern France, to link up with Third Army. Thomas knew serving under Patton was quite an honor for the unit, and had no doubt that his men would rise to the challenge. Pritchard provided more details then closed the meeting by directing Thomas to prepare his company to move out.

They reached Metz by the third week of November, but only the reconnaissance platoons saw action here. Those platoons were employed to protect the right flank of the division in woods where commanders suspected an enemy force lurked. Third Army had a full complement of tanks and tank destroyer units already on hand, and more than they could utilize. From Metz they were ordered to Perl, Germany, on the Moselle River on the left flank of XX Corps and the Third Army. Upon arrival, the battalion became a part of Task Force Polk and Third Cavalry. Here, on November 22, the men would see their first action and their first combat decorations.

Near Mittel, Germany, on the 22nd, 1st Lieutenant Walter S. Smith of Bonner Springs, Kansas, commander 1st Platoon, Charlie

Company, led his unit across open, exposed terrain when suddenly, 100 yards behind them, a German shell landed and exploded, killing Private First Class (PFC) Clarence Clark of Jacksonville, Florida. Confused and frightened by the ambush, several men in 1st Platoon panicked and ran for shelter in nearby trees.

Sturkey, seeing them flee, started to follow, then stopped and looked out at the towed guns exposed in the open. He knew the German artillery would soon target them. Climbing out of the half-track, Lt. Smith had the same thought.

He shouted to Sturkey over the enemy artillery fire that they had to get the men back and keep moving forward. Sturkey, not having a better idea, put two fingers in his mouth and blew as hard as he could. His shrill whistle cut through the artillery fire and stopped the men dead in their tracks. Sturkey then waved them back. Smith did the same, rallying the platoon, shouting that they had to keep moving and couldn't leave the guns exposed.

Men looked to one another embarrassed by their cowardice in the first contact with the enemy. They did an about-face and sprinted back through the smoke and exploding shells and machine gun fire. Several men hauled PFC Clark's body into the rear half-track, and the remainder climbed back in the other vehicles shouting, "Go, go, go!"

Upon hearing 1st Platoon under fire and in trouble, Thomas, further back in the column with the 3rd Platoon, had started forward. He arrived with several men from his platoon to help secure the guns and get the convoy moving. Sturkey, seeing Thomas, shouted to him that he'd been missing all the fun. In the interim, Baker Company had emplaced their M5s and threw indirect fire into the German positions covering First Platoon's evacuation.

This initial engagement tested the mettle of the men, and Thomas demonstrated his fearlessness in running toward the fight. His actions were not lost on anyone and would prove critical in the days to come.

For their gallant actions and cool-headedness under fire, Lt. Smith and Staff Sgt. Sturkey were both awarded the Silver Star for valor. Sturkey's citation read in part:

Perceiving that the valuable pieces of equipment must be immediately moved if they were to escape total destruction, he braved the bombardment and, by courageous example, encouraged the men to return to their vehicles and resume the march. By his action, he brought all weapons and men to safety. Sturkey's gallantry and leadership reflect the highest credit upon himself and the Army.

The 614th then returned to France and arrived in Luneville on December 4, bivouacking in a demolished race track. They quickly found a better location for the encampment and spent time on maintenance and repairs to equipment.

On December 7, the battalion left Luneville and proceeded to Kuttolsheim, near the border with Germany, where, upon arrival, they came under the command of the 103rd Infantry Division and were relieved from attachment to XX Corps. Able Company was attached to Task Force Forest made up of the 103rd Reconnaissance Troop, a company of the 756th Tank Battalion, and a company of the 409th Infantry. One platoon of Baker Company became part of the Palace Guard at the Division CP, and Charlie Company, led by Thomas, was attached to the 411th Infantry Regiment.

The 411th had been activated on November 15, 1942 at Camp Claiborne, Louisiana, under Colonel Donovan P. Yeuell and formed part of the 103rd Infantry Division commanded by Brigadier General Charles C. Haffner.

The 103rd Division was in the process of relieving the 45th and 79th Divisions in a sector on the west bank of the flooded Zintzel du Nord River. Beginning on December 8, as elements of the 103rd moved into the line, companies of the 614th started to provide supporting fire. Charlie Company, commanded by Thomas, knocked out an enemy observation post in a church steeple, destroyed a machine gun emplacement, and delivered harassing fire on German troops.[14]

Thomas's company continued to impress the advancing infantry with their accuracy in Griesbach and Pforzheim. In both towns,

German observation posts in church steeples were knocked out by the 614th's guns.

But as American forces reached the Siegfried Line, German resistance stiffened considerably. The strategy behind the German defensive line was to cause attacking forces to sustain such heavy losses that they would simply have to give up the attack and fall back.[15]

Thomas was called to the CP for a high-level meeting on December 13. The 411th's Executive Officer, Lieutenant Colonel John P. Blackshear, with subordinate commanders gathered, announced a reorganization of units into a small task force under his command. Blackshear, hovering over a map, pointed out their objective, storming the enemy-held town of Climbach and cutting off communications between it and Lembach.

The Colonel further conveyed that intelligence had reported three Panzer IV tanks had been spotted in the area. Thomas asked about the terrain. Blackshear frowned and said Climbach was situated on a 1,600ft-high ridge overlooking a valley surrounded by woods. They had only one road in, and the approach to the town was in all likelihood well defended.

This was grim news; it wasn't the ideal scenario to go on the offensive. Then Blackshear outlined his attack strategy. The bulk of the 411th Infantry would commit to a flanking attack on the town once the tanks had engaged the German defenders. The task force had the firepower to take Climbach with Sherman tanks from the 47th Armored, a platoon of F Company (riding on tanks) from 411th Infantry, a heavy weapons platoon, and C Company's 3rd Platoon from the 614th. They just had to advance over the worst possible terrain fighting uphill.

In early December, intelligence received from captured German POWs reported the battle-hardened 21st Panzer Division were defending Climbach. The division had spent the previous two years fighting under Erwin Rommel in North Africa. They had settled into Climbach for the winter, and their orders were to hold the town at all costs.

Thomas exited the meeting side by side with the infantry commander of the 411th. Thomas, not familiar with the officer, tried to break the ice. The reaction was less than favorable, bordering on hostile. The infantry commander reportedly warned Thomas that his coloreds had better damn well do their jobs 'cause his men's lives depended on it. The 411th was composed of soldiers mainly from Arkansas and other parts of the South who didn't appreciate the fact their supporting artillery was a unit of "Negros."[16]

Thomas returned to his platoon. With the formation of the task force, he now had 250 men under his command. He met with the 3rd Platoon, his tank destroyers, which he would take into battle to outline the mission. Their equipment consisted of four M5 3-inch howitzers towed by M3 half-tracks with a "pulpit mount" M49 .50 caliber machine gun.

The M3s were contemptuously referred to as "purple heart boxes" by soldiers for the vehicle's thin armor, which could be pierced easily by enemy machine gun fire. The M3 also lacked a roof to protect soldiers from air-burst shrapnel. Thomas would lead the platoon in his M20 command vehicle, which featured a center-mounted single .50cal Browning M2 heavy machine gun, which was about to come in very handy.

Chapter 3

A Hell of Fire

December 14 dawned damp and overcast with low-hanging fog. A scattered covering of snow remained from a storm several days earlier. H Hour was scheduled for 0800, but Lt. Col. Blackshear had been hard at work since 0215 when C Company of the 328th Engineer Battalion reported to him. He ordered the 328th to clear any roadblocks on the way to Climbach.

By 0330, Blackshear sent a detailed message to the commanding officer of the tank platoon, which consisted of four Shermans. Blackshear communicated, "1 Platoon of tanks to attack from NW and break enemy defenses. Tanks to attack at 0800, seize Climbach and the high ground surrounding the town. Taskforce to consist of 1 platoon tanks, 1 full-strength company (Co. F), and 1 platoon of TD." This message *was* the battle plan as recorded in the 411th's unit journal. Still, the famous adage, *No battle plan ever survives contact with the enemy*, first attributed to the legendary Prussian Field Marshal Helmuth von Moltke, certainly would apply to the battle that eventually unfolded at Climbach, France on this day in December 1944.

At 0422, Blackshear put his infantry into motion and sent the following message to the CP: "Send ten trucks to Co F, strengthened to full strength of 187 men, to transport point (069-438) and follow tanks N on road from that point."

Three minutes later, Blackshear sent his first order at 0425 to Charles Thomas in command of the tank destroyer platoon: "T.D. will follow Inf N on road from (069-438), help seize Climbach and surrounding high ground."

At 0446, Blackshear sent a follow-up order to Thomas assigning his vehicle and his position in line: "Have one M-20 lead the column."

By 0540, with dawn breaking, hints of potential problems began to unfold as the Communications Officer reported to the S-3,* "Roadblock still on road to Climbach. Engrs have not started removing it. Cannot get wire thru to O.P. Will take wire jeeps with tank force so they will have communication."

The task force would soon learn that not one but two separate roadblocks impeded all movement on the only road into Climbach. At 0600, Lt. Col. Blackshear ordered the S-3 to notify all task force commanders to "Stay in position and await orders to move."

Two hours later, at 0816, the CO of 1st Battalion informed the S-3 that, "The engineers had demolished the first roadblock but left without reducing the 2nd."

One minute later, at 0817, the S-3 sent the message to "demolish the 2nd roadblock immediately." One can still sense the exasperation in that order all these years later.

By 0846, the engineers were back at work on the 2nd roadblock and reported that "they expected to have it blown by 1000."

By this time, Task Force Blackshear had been sitting in the cold, in a single column for nearly three hours waiting to move. The tanks that Blackshear expected to lead the brunt of the initial attack were way back in the line, mired in mud. An hour and a half after the 0846 message, the Assistant S-3 noted in the unit journal at 1023 that "TF Blackshear had left the C.P."[17]

---

* The S-3 officer is in charge of operational planning and training at the battalion and brigade level.

As noon approached, Lt. Col. Blackshear, who had been leading the task force through the foggy, narrow, wooded road, reached the entrance to the valley and gave orders to halt. Visibility was next to nonexistent.

Puzzled why Lt. Col. Blackshear had halted, Thomas, in his M20 command car carrying four other soldiers, drove forward in the line and came up beside Blackshear. He found the Colonel inexplicably hesitant and told the commander, "he'd take it," meaning he'd volunteer to take his guns forward.[18] In interviews after the war, Thomas did not know why Blackshear had stopped, and he was given no explanation at the time.

All Thomas knew was that his guns were the only match for the German Mark IV tanks reported in the area. He suspected that the road into town would be mined and covered by German 88mm artillery, but intelligence had not confirmed that.

Thomas directed two of his guns forward to follow his armored scout car into the valley. He also ordered platoon leader Lt. Mitchell to hold in reserve with the two remaining guns. Blackshear watched as the African American unit moved forward to lead the attack, entering the fog-covered valley with visibility less than 300 yards.

Thomas's M20 rounded a curve that led up the winding slope toward Climbach, approaching the town from the southeast near La Schleife hill. As Thomas and his two M3s towing the guns ascended the hill, the German artillery arrayed on the surrounding heights had Thomas's antitank guns targeted in their sights. Sporadic small arms and automatic weapons fire began to flash from the ridges.

With the fog lifting near 1400 hours, Thomas saw the edge of the town come into view 300 yards distant with enemy tanks and artillery another 700 yards beyond that. Then, suddenly in the scout car, he and his crew felt a concussion from the vehicle's front right as it buckled. They'd struck a buried mine in the road. Seconds later, with men scrambling out, the M20 was hit again *hard* by a German 88mm shell splintering armor, sending shrapnel everywhere and throwing Thomas and another soldier to the ground.

Thomas got to his feet in a momentary daze, bleeding from several wounds to his legs and arms with his ears ringing. He helped others out of the scout car as it was then raked by murderous machine gun fire. Several rounds caught Thomas across the chest.

Wounded severely, Thomas ordered his two gun crews to deploy forward. The M3s with Sergeant Tabron's and Corporal Hockaday's ten-man gun crews hit their accelerators. They sped 25 yards beyond the smoldering scout car and began to deploy their guns as enemy artillery, tank, and mortar fire rained down all around them.

Thomas, ignoring his pain and the bleeding, crawled up on the M20 to cover his men's deployment of the two guns. He kept his finger on the trigger of the Browning and raked the enemy positions. His only thought was, *deploy the artillery, start firing, or we're dead.*[19]

Sgt. Tabron on the forwardmost .50cal machine gun on his M3 blazed away at the German positions, but his gun crew was whittled down from enemy small arms and rifle fire within minutes. Other men stepped in to perform their duties.

Unbeknownst to the 614th, the 21st Panzer Division had concealed an infantry company in the woods northeast of the road in anticipation of ambushing any frontal assaults. As Thomas directed his gun crews, he sensed movement in the woods in his peripheral vision and turned.

Momentary shock swept over his face as he shouted, "They're comin' from the woods!"

Thomas instantly ordered the half-track machine gunners to target the advancing enemy. The men had already swung their guns in that direction. Thomas further ordered every available man to target the foot soldiers and leave one gunner on each of the two artillery pieces. Thus, the 614th armed with M1s, carbines, .45cal pistols, and submachine guns and the two half-track machine guns poured a devastating fire into the advancing company of panzergrenadiers.

At the edge of the valley, with a clear view of the deteriorating situation, Lt. Col. Blackshear ordered his infantry forward and to the right for a flanking attack, shouting, "Move! Move!" Then he directed a half-ton truck driven by William Phipps of the 614th from North Carolina to take some of the infantry forward and also evacuate the wounded. By this point in the battle it was just past 1500 hours in the afternoon. While the 411th infantry was on the move, the 614th repulsed the German panzergrenadiers, killing most of the assaulting force.

At Sgt. Tabron's artillery position, gunner Cpl. Pete Simmons, running out of ammunition, fell mortally wounded from a bullet in the neck just as an 88mm Mark IV shell blew his gun position apart.

Cpl. Hockaday's gun crew was faring little better. T/5 (Technician 5th Grade) "Art" Perry, Hockaday's driver, kept up machine gun fire atop his half-track even though he was bleeding from shrapnel in his left leg. Hockaday's gunner, Corporal Shelton Murph from St. Matthews, South Carolina, had been coolly performing his duties under a hailstorm of fire until an 88mm shell landed just behind him, blowing his left leg off. Thomas ordered his medic, who'd been attending his wounds, to assist Shelton. Thomas tried to comfort Cpl. Murph, telling him he would be alright as the man screamed in agony, clutching his tattered thigh. Unfortunately, the 25-year-old would die in the hospital 12 days later.

Thomas was mindful that his calm deportment, even though he was severely wounded, would steady his men. They were all highly trained and operating for the most part on automatic. Thomas figured, however, that if they could look at him covered in blood, remaining poised, they would continue to do their jobs without faltering.

Truck driver Phipps returned from taking some of the wounded back and parked, waiting for the medic to finish up with Cpl. Murph. The medic finished attending to Murph and, while assisting him on to Phipps' truck, noted that the man was bleeding from shrapnel wounds. He asked Phipps to let him bandage his wounds. Phipps brushed the medic off, saying he didn't have the time.

The medic turned to Thomas, who'd grown paler, and told him he'd better evacuate as well. Thomas refused. He said he needed an officer who had commanded a company to come up to relieve him, and this was not the place to learn on the job. Thomas had few options though his subordinate, Lt. George Mitchell, was back with the two reserve gun crews. He considered the matter momentarily, then pulled Private McDaniel off his machine gun post on the second half-track. Thomas ordered the Private to head back on foot to get Lt. Mitchell and his two guns and bring them forward.

Pvt. McDaniel set out at a sprint across more than 100 yards of exposed ground. He endured mortar, machine gun, and small arms fire the entire time. Finally, he reached Lt. Mitchell with Sergeant Roosevelt Robertson's and Sergeant Dillard Booker's gun crews who were already rumbling up the hill on their own initiative. Pvt. McDaniel stopped and jumped on the first half-track with Robertson's gun crew. Booker, from the Bronx, shouted over to him, "'bout damn time!"

Robertson's half-track sped ahead to a position 50 yards forward, and his men began quickly deploying their gun. PFC Lucius Riley of Hillsboro, North Carolina, atop the vehicle, covered his comrades, raking the surrounding woods with his .50cal machine gun. Artillery fell all around him as he continued to fire until a direct artillery strike on his position killed him instantly. The explosion set the vehicle ablaze. Men, recognizing the danger, shouted to grab the live ammunition off the half-track. Several soldiers then jumped on the burning wreck and safely removed the artillery shells.

Lt. Col. Blackshear, back in the line, almost overcome with emotion, pulled down the field glasses from his face and whispered aloud, "This is the most magnificent display of heroism I have ever witnessed."[20] He cleared his throat and returned the field glasses to his eyes.

The situation at Thomas's position was critical. Three guns were out of action, and Booker's gun, which had found a protected area in a hollow, was dangerously low on ammunition but laying down very effective fire. Booker's crew sighted a muzzle blast from a camouflaged house, and threw in three rounds of high explosive until the German gun stopped firing. Booker's crew also accounted for a few 88s and several German MG and mortar positions.[21]

Thomas, fading in and out, was still conscious as he oriented Lt. Mitchell, now on the scene, about enemy gun dispositions and the general battle situation.

Mitchell, taking command and seeing driver Phipps return from evacuating more wounded, ordered the soldier to bring him forward to collect more of the injured. Thomas intended to evacuate on this half-ton truck as well.

Phipps, still bleeding and severely weakened from shrapnel wounds and injuries sustained driving through constant small arms fire, complied. He shuttled his platoon leader forward, and when they arrived at the medic's location, Phipps slumped over the steering wheel dead.

It was just past 1700 hours, and the 614th had been engaged in intense combat for nearly four hours. Three of the four guns were out of commission, and the last one, Booker's gun, was out of ammunition. He and his crew felt "stark, stripped naked, and figured that was it."[22]

Booker and his men were reduced to lying flat on the ground, returning fire with their M1s and carbines. With Thomas's platoon suffering over 50 percent casualties at this critical stage, soldiers of Blackshear's task force who hadn't engaged in the battle took matters into their own hands.

Three BAR (Browning Automatic Rifle) men from the 411th voluntarily headed out with their automatic weapons to provide flank security for Booker's gun. Within minutes, two of these men were casualties.

Truck driver T/5 Robert Harris from Missouri, seeing that Booker's gun crew were now resorting to small arms and rifle fire, knew they were out of ammunition. So he and several other men loaded up his half-ton truck with artillery shells, and Harris sped toward the battle line.

Blackshear stopped Harris midway and said he couldn't go forward; the enemy fire was too intense. Harris, undeterred, told Blackshear to get the hell out of his way and nearly ran the Colonel down, throwing a few expletives his way. Subsequently, Harris got within 25 yards of Booker's gun, the only remaining operative piece of artillery, and delivered the desperately needed ammunition.

T/4 Paul Warner of Charlie Company Headquarters, back at the task force location, seeing that Thomas had slumped to the ground, realized that immediate evacuation was necessary. Warner jumped in his jeep and prepared to speed across 75 yards of fire-swept terrain to rescue his company commander.

At this same time, 1st Lt. Floyd Stallings, who had heard of the dire situation, came forward to the battle area from the CP. He also saw Thomas slumped on the ground and did not hesitate. With complete disregard for his own life, Stallings began a 100-yard sprint uphill over exposed terrain. He endured severe enemy machine gun, mortar, and artillery fire during his entire dash to reach Thomas.

As Stallings arrived at the severely wounded Thomas, T/4 Warner drove his jeep into the firestorm. He weaved in and out of the enemy's small arms and artillery fire that blasted his path the entire route. Warner continued undaunted and miraculously also reached Thomas's position. He remained there for over 15 minutes, helping other men place Thomas into the jeep. Warner then made the same weaving return trip with Thomas, semi-conscious under a curtain of intense enemy fire. Finally, they safely made it back behind the line and to the closest aid station.

The artillery shells brought forward by Harris and the subsequent harassing fire were able to keep the Germans occupied as a company of the 411th Infantry and the 47th Armored entered the town of Climbach from the east.

At 1546 hours, the 411th unit journal recorded that the tank force and 1st Battalion had entered the town. The same entry records that the "TD (tank destroyer) CO had been lost." Many of Thomas's own men, seeing how severe his wounds were, also believed he had died.

By 1844 hours, the same unit journal recorded that "Taskforce Blackshear and 1st Battalion captured Climbach at approximately 1720." The Germans mounted a weak counterattack in the town, but it was repulsed by 1900 hours, and the ferocious battle of Climbach was over.

Thomas, who most still believed was dead, spent the next several weeks in a hospital in England before transferring to Percy Jones

Hospital in Michigan for rehabilitation. His actions so deeply impressed Lt. Col. Blackshear that he submitted the Lieutenant's name for the Distinguished Service Cross in late December 1944. The award was announced in January 1945, and Thomas was promoted to Captain. He received the award in a ceremony on March 27, 1945 at Percy Jones Hospital, surrounded by hundreds of cheering patients.

On April 7, 1945, the *Michigan Chronicle* published a full-page pictorial spread of a gala hero's banquet they had hosted in Thomas's honor the prior week at Detroit's legendary Hotel Gotham. The upscale affair was attended by Olympian Jesse Owens, distinguished citizens, and prominent city officials.

Blackshear also decorated other soldiers in the 3rd Platoon. He recommended the Silver Star for 1st Lt. George Mitchell and posthumous Silver Stars for Cpl. Peter Simmons and PFC William Phipps. Robert Harris received the Bronze Star for his courageous actions, as did Pvt. Thomas McDaniel, Sgt. Dillard Booker, 1st Lt. Stallings, T/4 Paul Warner, Sgt. Tabron, Cpl. Hockaday, and T/5 James "Art" Perry.

In total, during the war, the 614th Tank Destroyer Battalion received eight silver stars, 29 bronze stars, including one for their commander Lt. Col. Frank Pritchard, and 79 Purple Hearts.

Thomas always refused to take credit for his heroics, believing his soldiers deserved the accolades, especially those who did not return home. "He knew his job was to draw fire, but he didn't think he'd draw *that* much fire."

The battle was a turning point that facilitated the Allies' crossing the Siegfried Line into Germany. It was an extraordinary accomplishment, which was recognized with the highest honor a fighting unit can receive, the Presidential Unit Citation. Third Platoon, Charlie Company of the 614th Tank Destroyer Battalion was the first black unit to be honored with the prestigious military award.

Presidential Unit Citation:

By direction of the President, under the provisions of Section IV, Circular No. 333, War Department, 1943, the following named organization is cited for outstanding performance of duty in action:

THE 3D PLATOON, COMPANY "C", 614th TANK DESTROYER BATTALION is cited for outstanding performance of duty in action against the enemy on 14 December 1944, in the vicinity of Climbach, France. The 3d Platoon was an element of a task force whose mission was to storm and capture the strategically important town of Climbach, France, on the approaches of the Siegfried Line. Upon reaching the outskirts of the town, the task force was halted by a terrific hail of fire from an enemy force firmly entrenched in the surrounding woods and hills overlooking the route of approach. The only position available for direct fire upon the enemy was an open field. As the 3d Platoon moved into position, its commander and several men were wounded. Undeterred by heavy enemy small arms, mortar and artillery fire, which was now being directed against their position, the men of the 3d Platoon valiantly set up their three inch guns and delivered accurate and deadly fire into the enemy positions. Casualties were mounting; two of their four guns were knocked out; nevertheless the remaining crew members heroically assisted in the loading and firing of the other guns. At the height of the battle, enemy infantry converged on the position from the surrounding woods, threatening to wipe out the platoon's position. While a few members of the gun crews remained firing the three inch guns, others manned machine guns and individual weapons laying down a devastating curtain of fire which inflicted numerous casualties on the enemy and successfully repulsed the attack. During the firefight an ammunition shortage developed, and gun crews were reduced to skeleton size, one man loading, aiming and firing, while the other men repeatedly traveled a distance of fifty yards through a hail of mortar and small arms fire, to obtain shells from a half-track which had been set on fire by a direct hit from an enemy mortar shell. Heedless of possible injury, men continuously exposing themselves to enemy fire to render first aid to the wounded. In this engagement, although the Platoon suffered over fifty percent casualties and lost considerable material, its valorous conduct in the face of overwhelming odds, enabled the task force to capture its objective. The grim determination, the indomitable fighting spirit and esprit de corps displayed by all members of the 3d Platoon reflect the highest traditions of the Armed Forces of the United States.

CHARLES L. THOMAS, MEDAL OF HONOR CITATION

For extraordinary heroism in action on 14 December 1944, near Climbach, France. While riding in the lead vehicle of a task force organized to storm and capture the village of Climbach, France, then First Lieutenant Thomas's armored scout car was subjected to intense enemy artillery, self-propelled gun, and small arms fire. Although wounded by the initial burst of hostile fire, Lieutenant Thomas signaled the remainder of the column to halt and, despite the severity of his wounds, assisted the crew of the wrecked car in dismounting. Upon leaving the scant protection which the vehicle afforded, Lieutenant Thomas was again subjected to a hail of enemy fire which inflicted multiple gunshot wounds in his chest, legs, and left arm. Despite the intense pain caused by these wounds, Lieutenant Thomas ordered and directed the dispersion and emplacement of two anti-tank guns which in a few moments were promptly and effectively returning the enemy fire. Realizing that he could no longer remain in command of the platoon, he signaled to the platoon commander to join him. Lieutenant Thomas then thoroughly oriented him on enemy gun dispositions and the general situation. Only after he was certain that his junior officer was in full control of the situation did he permit himself to be evacuated. First Lieutenant Thomas' outstanding heroism was an inspiration to his men and exemplified the highest traditions of the Armed Forces.

PART TWO

Vernon J. Baker

Chapter 4

The Boy from Cheyenne

MINERAL WELLS, TEXAS
MAY 9, 1941

A fresh-faced African American young man with a white canvas duffle slung over his right shoulder stepped three steps down from the train onto the windswept platform of a bleak central Texas town. Although the 22-year-old was under six feet, he had lettered in basketball, track, and football and graduated with honors from high school.

Taking in the drab Texas town, which wasn't his final destination, the young man shielded his eyes and squinted across the steaming parking lot, searching in vain for the local bus that would take him to camp. His transportation was nowhere in sight. The young man sighed then noticed stares from passing citizens; there were no other black men at the train station.

He found a bench to wait on as he considered his journey so far, enlisting at Cheyenne, Wyoming, telling the recruiter he wanted the quartermaster section. Still, the Sergeant instead penciled in the infantry, perhaps as a joke, but at least the eager recruit was now part of the coming war effort. The first recruiter he applied with had turned him down flat a month earlier, telling him that the Army didn't have quotas for *you people* yet.

After a few minutes waiting at the near desolate train depot, a green Midland Lines bus pulled into the lot, halting with a screech of its air brakes 20 yards in front of him. The recruit grabbed his duffle and noted two white men his age also with duffles heading for the bus as well. They made a point of cutting in front of him, and he let them pass.

Climbing last onto the hot, stuffy bus, the young black man spied a vacant seat behind the obese middle-aged driver and threw his duffle down on it. The nearly empty bus turned silent as the driver pivoted and said, "Hey nigger, get your bag and get to the back of the bus; that's where you belong."[1]

Fury gripped the young man. On the train to Texas passing through Junction City, Kansas, a porter had corralled him from his seat and escorted him to the "blacks'" car. It was up in front next to the engine, soot-filled and sweltering. The treatment by the bus driver was his breaking point. He reared back, ready to knock the driver senseless, but an older black gentleman who had watched the scene from the back of the bus was by his side. The older man grabbed his arm, calming him. He motioned the young man to the back of the bus where he'd been sitting. Once settled in the back, the older man, wise and kind, asked the boy his name.

"Vernon, Vernon Baker."

"Well Vernon, look boy, you're coming down here, and the first thing you are gonna do is you're gonna get yourself killed."[2]

The older man went on to tell Baker he'd better keep those fists in his pockets cause clenching his fists in the presence of a white man was liable to get him brought up on charges. He said, "Black man's justice in these here parts is done with a tree and a rope."[3]

Baker's mind filled with his grandfather Joseph's similar parting advice when he headed south to Camp Wolters, Texas; *if you want to live, boy, learn how to conform.* Baker's grandfather, Joseph Baker, had been a guiding influence in shaping Baker's character and taught him to hunt and handle a rifle, one Christmas presenting him with a .22cal Remington. His grandfather, the chief brakeman for the Union Pacific railroad, was a man of few words, but as Baker later described him, his grandfather counted out every word with authority. Wisdom handed down now flooded back to Baker on the dusty ride to Camp Wolters; *think with your brain, boy, not with your fists.* And, *don't hate no matter what; hate will destroy you.*[4]

In the heat of the moment, Baker had forgotten his grandfather's advice but, reflecting on the wise black man beside him, Baker felt as if the spirit of his grandfather had materialized just when he needed him the most.

FORT HUACHUCA, ARIZONA
OCTOBER 1941

Standing in formation under the penetrating Arizona sun at Fort Huachuca, Arizona, Vernon Baker, fresh from basic training at Camp Wolters, listened as his company commander, Captain Green of the 25th Infantry,* outlined the "rules." Huachuca, Baker's new home, was where the Army had routed many of the incoming black recruits. Most of the enlisted men in the 370th were older than Baker and illiterate, many never having finished high school.

At the end of the recitation of the rules, Green asked if anyone knew how to use a typewriter. Almost no hands went up but Baker, forgetting another piece of sage advice from his grandfather *never to volunteer*, raised his hand. The commander nodded to Baker, and the former high school honors graduate stepped forward. Baker confirmed that he knew how to type and well. The CO immediately pressed him into service as the new company clerk for Dog Company.

Baker performed well in the clerical role and soon was promoted to Supply Sergeant. With the United States declaration of war against Japan after the attack on Pearl Harbor in December 1941, Baker and all the noncommissioned officers were promoted one rank, and he became a Staff Sergeant. As a Supply Staff Sergeant, Baker settled into what he considered a very comfortable and successful position in the military.

The low-stress job, however, was not destined to last. One particular fall day in 1942, Baker, clutching a clipboard in an oppressive, hot cavernous army warehouse, checked off the last 4 x 12ft munitions

---

* In 1933, the 25th Infantry Regiment replaced the 10th Cavalry as the main combat unit at Fort Huachuca. The 25th in turn was absorbed by the 93rd Infantry Division during World War II. (https://swabuffalosoldiers.org/history/fort-huachuca-history-1877-to-1945/)

crate as three fellow African American soldiers lifted it onto a rolling pallet. With a smile of satisfaction, Baker told the men they'd gotten the last one, and the soldiers began wheeling it in the direction of the open double doors toward the supply depot. One of the men called back to Baker to meet later at the on-base watering hole. Baker assured the man he would see him there and joked that he'd be happy to collect his money in a few hands of poker.

As the men left, Baker paused to reflect on his good fortune. As a Staff Sergeant in the 25th Infantry, he felt he'd made it, and his grandparents might not recognize the troubled, hurting, orphaned boy they raised whom they'd sent off to reform school. Baker's parents had been killed in an automobile accident when Vernon was only four years old, and Joseph and Dora had raised him and his sisters Cass and Irma.

Grandma Dora, whom Baker characterized as giving new meaning to the title "meanest woman alive," was confined to a wicker-back wheelchair from rheumatoid arthritis. When Baker cried as a young child, she would chase him in her wheelchair and crack him with her black ironwood cane, screaming, "Shut up, you little son of a bitch." Her foul demeanor, Baker realized later in life, was due to living daily with great pain.

Baker's rise in the military had been swift, and fellow soldiers took notice. Baker, who was soft-spoken and kept to himself, never sought trouble. However, when Baker returned alone to the barracks from a movie one night, waiting for him in the darkness were three older black Corporals. Targeting him, they emerged from the shadows pushing and shoving him, in a seeming retaliation for him gaining his Sergeant stripes so quickly.

Then one of the men landed a sucker punch to his gut, and they all jumped him. Baker later reflected that they beat the hell out of him that night. The men left him on the ground bleeding and bruised.

When Baker stumbled back to the barracks after the incident, everyone seemed to know what had happened. He put the fight aside and tried to forget about it. Reporting it, he believed, would be an open invitation for another assault. Baker chalked it up to ignorant, envious people trying to pull you down when you're determined to make something of yourself.

Like many black men who enlisted, Vernon wanted to better himself and his situation in life. He was jobless before entering the military and saw the service as a way to learn valuable skills. He also believed he was serving for more than freedom abroad; he saw the war as a chance for liberation at home. Everyone by this time had heard about the popular Double V Campaign spearheading racial equality for black soldiers for their service in the war. And many men, including Baker, kept that in the back of their minds.

After reflecting on his good fortune in the supply warehouse, Baker's thoughts returned to the work at hand as he signed the supply manifest and hung the clipboard back on a hook. As he pictured joining his friends later for poker, he heard his name called. He turned, and approaching him was D Company commander, Captain Green.

Baker's first thought was that he was in deep trouble because of the fight with the three Corporals several weeks earlier. He prayed that wasn't the case, but he didn't know what to make of the appearance of Green as he responded, "Yes, sir?"

Green ordered Baker to report to Regimental Headquarters on the double. Baker asked what the matter was about but received a terse response to comply and not ask questions. Baker knew the protocol, of course, but an order to report to Regimental Headquarters was never good.

25TH INFANTRY REGIMENTAL HEADQUARTERS

Baker stood quietly at attention as regimental commander Colonel Everett Yon of the 25th Infantry Regiment flipped through a stack of files, pausing time and again to cross-check items. When he finally gave Baker his attention, he said, "Sergeant Baker? Sign these," as he handed him a stapled form with an "X" marked for where to sign.

Baker didn't read the papers or know what they concerned; he simply followed orders and signed. He assumed the paperwork was some kind of punishment for the fight such as a cancellation of leave and other even worse measures he did not want to contemplate.

When Baker, glum, finished signing, he handed the papers to Col. Yon, who matter-of-factly informed him he had just "volunteered" for Officer Candidate School (OCS).

In this matter, however, Baker had no choice; Col. Yon, a Fort Benning Officer Candidate School graduate himself, had the papers all prepared. In fact, Baker had no desire to attend OCS; he had a cushy job as a supply Staff Sergeant. He desperately prayed that the officer candidacy paperwork would get lost or hopefully forgotten. The submission meant if Baker successfully completed the 13-week course at Fort Benning, Georgia, he'd be commissioned as a 2nd Lieutenant in the United States Army.

Baker was surprised, to say the least, at the turn of events. He had been comfortable in his role on base, and he performed his duties very well. Perhaps that is what attracted the attention of command. Becoming a commissioned officer, Baker knew, meant greater responsibility, a more challenging workload, and a whole lot of headaches.

Although he didn't know it, Baker was the beneficiary of a recent change in Army policy. In 1942 Officer Candidate School was the Army's first formal attempt at racial integration. The new training policy stated that black and white candidates would share officers' quarters, with bunkmates assigned alphabetically, regardless of race, and all candidates would train together. Baker would be joining an elite group. According to a 2001 Defense Study by Morris MacGregor at the Army's Center for Military History, less than 1 percent of black soldiers in the Army became officers in 1942.

Officer Corps integration had a powerful advocate in Army Chief of Staff General George Marshall. He was insistent on providing equal opportunity for all qualified candidates, both black and white.

Word spread like wildfire across Fort Huachuca of Baker's elevation to officer candidate. He had come to accept it as a golden opportunity for which he should be grateful. Baker had earned it, and the men he worked with at the Supply Depot were all congratulatory.

***

Baker found OCS in Georgia to be both challenging and eye-opening in the Jim Crow south, and he was ill-prepared for the elevated level of racial prejudice he encountered in the state.

He felt less than a second-class citizen when he stepped off the bus, officer candidate or not. When Baker and other black officer candidates went into town from Fort Benning, they noticed black civilians staring at the ground when talking to white people. Looking a white man in the eye was considered "uppity." Black officers expecting respect got none. White enlisted men refused to salute black officers. If a black officer complained, an MP would harass him for making an "issue" out of it.

Toward the end of his 13 weeks, Baker's TAC (Training, Advising and Consulting) Officer gathered graduating OCS Class 148 together and asked if anyone had any final questions. One candidate near Baker tentatively asked why the Army was commissioning so many 2nd Lieutenants. The TAC Officer replied with a smirk that 2nd Lieutenants were expendable. The statement eliminated any further questions. Baker successfully completed the course and graduated as a 2nd Lieutenant on January 11, 1943. He was assigned for a short time to Camp Rucker, Alabama, before returning to Fort Huachuca as a weapons platoon leader in the 92nd Division.

By the late spring of 1944, the war was in full swing; the planning for ultra-secret Operation *Overlord*, the invasion of German-occupied France, was down to its final details. In the Pacific, an armada of American warships invaded Japanese-held islands of the central Pacific on a path leading toward Japan. Five hundred and thirty-five US ships with 127,000 troops, including nearly 80,000 Marines, sought to capture the Mariana Islands. This strategic location formed the ocean-based front lines where Japan would consolidate to defend its empire.

The liberation of Italy, which began in September of 1943, was grinding forward. On May 11, 1944, the Allies launched Operation *Diadem*, designed to break through the Gustav Line defenses and open up a path to Rome.[5] The capture of Rome was critically significant to the Allies. High command believed that the capture of the Italian capital might draw German troops away from France in time for the planned D-Day landings in early June.

Rome's capture would also have immense propaganda value for President Roosevelt. He had expressed a desire behind the scenes to see that American troops secured Rome. Perhaps this was why the commander of Fifth Army, Lieutenant General Mark Clark, chose to target Rome from the Anzio beachhead after the fall of Monte Cassino. This decision was in direct disobedience of the orders of the British officer in overall command, General Sir Harold Alexander. Alexander had directed Clark to flank the German 10th Army and sever its northbound line of retreat from Cassino. This maneuver never occurred, and the Germans had time to dig in and build even more formidable entrenchments across the rugged terrain of northern Italy.

Back in the States on April 4, 1944, at the completion of field maneuvers at Camp Polk in the vicinity of Merryville and De Ridder, Louisiana, division commander Major General Edward M. Almond announced that the almost exclusively African American 92nd Division would join the Fifth US Army in the Mediterranean Theater of Operations.

A graduate of the Virginia Military Institute and a veteran of World War I, Almond was nonetheless a controversial figure within the military. He had been promoted ahead of most of his peers to command the 92nd due primarily to his friendship with General Marshall. Almond was an odd choice for this role due to his outspoken racist views that black men made poor soldiers. He is reported to have said, "No white man wants to be accused of leaving the battle line. The Negro doesn't care. Being from the South, we understand the Negro's capabilities. And we don't want to sit at the table with them."[6]

After maneuvers in Louisiana, Baker and all the other black 2nd Lieutenants at Fort Huachuca were summoned to General Almond's headquarters. The black officers were told to wait in the blazing Arizona sun in the back of the headquarters building. The Chief of Staff of the 92nd Division, Colonel Frank E. Barber, was to come and address them.

As Baker and the other officers sweltered waiting for Col. Barber, Baker imagined it might be some type of pep talk for the group and confirmation of the rumors which had been circulating about heading overseas. The speech that Baker and the other men received, however, would not be a pep talk and would not be forgotten. It would fester in Baker and continue to anger him later in life.

After nearly 20 minutes, Col. Barber appeared and strode out to the gathered black officers. His attitude toward them was no secret; like his commanding officer Almond, he believed they didn't belong in the Army. Frowning a moment to survey the group, Barber got right to the point. The Chief of Staff announced that the 92nd had received its orders and would be going overseas within a month. A regimental combat team was forming, the 370th RCT, and would include the best officers and enlisted men from several infantry companies.[7] The black officers welcomed the news with smiles and understated enthusiasm, but then the Chief of Staff concluded with, "All these years our white boys have been going overseas to get killed. Well now it's time for you black boys to go over and get killed."[8]

After Barber left, several disgruntled black officers repeated the Chief of Staff's parting line sarcastically and expressed the view that if that's how the brass felt about black officers, then hell with them.

Many decided to transfer out to the 365th and 371st Regiments. Baker, however, felt a thrilling sense of anticipation for combat and had made up his mind at that moment: *yes he was going to go overseas, but no, he wasn't going to get killed.* He would serve with honor and he would prove Colonel Barber wrong in the process.

In readying itself for service in Italy, the newly formed 370th Regimental Combat Team, commanded by Colonel Raymond G. Sherman, went through a top-down evaluation before serving as the advance unit of the 92nd Infantry Division in Italy. A period of intensive training commenced in preparation for heading overseas. Non-qualifying 370th men failing field tests were reassigned to other units and replaced with higher qualifying men with the necessary capabilities. Many of these soldiers were volunteers. The entire combat team consisted of the 370th Infantry, the 598th Field Artillery Battalion, and detachments from each of the special units of the 92nd Division, including combat engineers, medical, ordnance, military police, and headquarters company.[9]

Chapter 5

The Italian Front

Baker had never been to a United States Naval facility before, but as he stood in wonder on the docks of the US Atlantic Fleet's home at Newport News, the tremendous power of the US military was brought home. Stretching nearly the length of the pier was the 632ft former luxury liner, the SS *Mariposa*. Built at Fore River Shipyard in Quincy Point, Massachusetts, and launched in 1931, the liner served as a troop transport ship for the Army. Operating under the War Shipping Administration (WSA), the SS *Mariposa* was one of the largest and fastest class of troop carriers nicknamed "Monsters." Baker watched in awe as the "Monster" was loaded down with more than 7,000 troops of the 370th Regimental Combat Team and all their equipment.

Once aboard and underway, Baker became a father figure to his platoon as the men got to know each other better. Most couldn't read or write, so Baker would read their letters from home to them and help the men write letters back. Through the process, he and the platoon grew close. He hoped this bond would breed trust so that they could come to rely on each other and band together in battle when the going got rough.

The majority of his platoon was younger than he was and towered over his 5ft 5in. stature and 145lb frame. Baker thought of them as quite dashing warriors with their pencil-thin mustaches and confident smiles. They carried an air of self-assured expectancy in defeating any unfortunate German soldier who dared tangle with them, immortal as any eager young soldier who hadn't yet experienced the cataclysm of combat.

Their journey across the Atlantic toward the Mediterranean was to take two weeks with a brief stopover in North Africa. One of the first things the men noticed, which alarmed them after they embarked, was that they were completely alone without a single escort ship. They knew this was unusual and made them utterly vulnerable to German U-boat attacks.

Rumors began circulating about a British troop carrier sunk six months earlier in the Mediterranean by the Germans, taking more than 1,000 American soldiers' lives. That ship, a former cargo vessel converted to a troop carrier, was the HMS *Rohna*, sunk on November 26, 1943. It was the most significant loss of life at sea by enemy action in US history, and the US desperately wanted to keep the matter quiet.

Political pressure kept the successful sinking of the *Rohna* under wraps to prevent morale from plummeting at home.* The maritime disaster was subsequently classified "secret" by both the US and British governments, and that's why its sinking remained a whispered rumor.

Soldiers of the 370th were on edge throughout the transatlantic crossing and voiced their concern with command. The men were told the ship was fast enough to outrun any German torpedoes; as the *Mariposa* was an unprotected troop carrier filled mostly with African Americans, nobody believed it, including Baker.

Arriving in Italy on July 28, 1944, after a nervous voyage across the Atlantic, the SS *Mariposa* dropped anchor outside of Naples harbor. The ship couldn't enter the port because the Germans had left it clogged with wreckage.

Baker looked out from the bow of the *Mariposa* to a maze of half-sunken ships blocking the harbor. Cargo boats jammed against listing overturned fishing vessels; others ships had a hint

---

* In fact the *Rohna* had been sunk by a German glider bomb launched from a Luftwaffe aircraft and not a U-boat but this was not known at the time.

of a bridge or bow sticking straight out of the maritime graveyard. Army engineers had erected a haphazard network of gangplanks and catwalks between the smashed vessels, and this was the path all 7,000 men had to traverse to reach dry land.

As Baker and his platoon and the thousands of troops of the 370th disembarked from the SS *Mariposa* in single file, in full battle dress, over the catwalks and gangplanks toward the shore, they were greeted with sights and sounds they didn't expect. Historian Hondon Hargrove paints a vivid picture of jubilation: "a low rumbling sound rose from hundreds of black service troops on the docks swelling to a crescendo of thunderous cheering until the last Buffalo unit* disappeared."[10]

The black service troops hailed the 370th RCT as conquering heroes before they had even fired a shot, simply for what they represented. The combat assignment of the primarily African American 92nd Division was the climax of a long, difficult struggle for recognition and equality in treatment for black Americans and the opportunity to fight for their country as soldiers.

After such an emotional welcome, Baker and the 370th had a chance to catch their breath and survey their new surroundings in Naples, and it was a pitiful sight to behold. The Germans had left this ancient city, founded in the 6th century BC, virtually in ruins. Not only were the docks torn apart; the Germans had destroyed the city water and sewage systems, and the stench was overwhelming. All electrical lines were also severed. Adding insult to injury, the fleeing Germans demolished most museums and libraries, torching more than 200,000 priceless books and manuscripts in the city square. Booby-trapped explosives were left on timers, and later Lt. Gen. Mark Clark of Fifth Army narrowly escaped being blown to bits by a 1,500lb bomb hidden in the hotel he used for his headquarters.

Baker and the 370th didn't have time to consider the destruction surrounding them; they had to begin the laborious process of removing their gear from the *Mariposa* and continue combat preparations from a staging area at Civitavecchia, a small port city 40 miles northwest of Rome.

---

* "Buffalo soldiers" was a term first used in 1866 to indicate black troops or units.

In readying for combat, Baker studied past missions and every field manual he could find to be mentally prepared. After more than a week in the staging area, new orders came through that soldiers should reduce their belongings to the bare essentials needed for battle, and Baker would pack the rest for storage.

Baker, in his tent, opened an old battered suitcase he had lugged overseas and surveyed what he would leave behind. First, he packed his civilian clothes away, then his "pinks and greens," which were his dress trousers and winter olive drab uniform. Baker then packed into his musette bag, which he'd take with him to the front, a spare Class A uniform, long johns, field manuals, and an Eisenhower jacket. He had lightened his physical load considerably, but the coming months' emotional load would weigh heavily on him. In late August, the 2½-ton, 6 x 6 transports arrived, and a convoy of the 370th RCT began a several-day journey toward the battlefront.

At this time in late summer 1944, the Allied push had bogged down. The Germans had burrowed into northern Italy and, for nearly a year, Allied forces had been unable to dislodge them. The enemy had erected a formidable line of defense, the Gothic Line, which ran 170 miles across northern Italy through rugged mountain terrain. The herculean task before the 370th was to clear the Germans from the mountains and otherwise tie up a maximum number of enemy troops so they couldn't be withdrawn and sent to other major battlefronts.

Baker and the men arrived at the front just south of the Arno River in the Pontedera region east of Pisa, where they were attached to the 1st Armored Division, IV Corps. Major General Willis Crittenberger was in overall command. "Critt," a Westpointer, was one of Eisenhower's trusted commanders.

The newly arrived 370th lacked the knowledge or experience of what Allied troops had faced at Salerno, Anzio, and Monte Cassino and, for that matter, the grasp the Germans had of the terrain. However, they would soon experience the tenacity and seasoned combat tactics of the enemy forces opposite them. Baker and the lead elements of the Combat Team, in the early going, falsely believed they were making headway in four- and five-mile progressions a day up the slopes of Mount Pisano. The *New York Times* even heralded their actions in an article on September 2, 1944:

> The American 5th Army lashed out a new offensive today, bursting across Arno on a wide front. Negro troops of the 92nd Infantry Division, making their first appearance in the battle line stormed up the southeast slopes of Mount Pisano from whose frowning heights the enemy had lobbed shells into the American lines during the prolonged stalemate.

The article didn't mention the Germans were watching and aware of the 92nd's every move as they lured the Americans up and over Mount Pisano into the valley. They fell back, encircling the Americans, then pounded the hell out of the lead elements of the 370th. Baker and his platoon, now part of a reconfigured Charlie Company, escaped virtually unscathed in the first several weeks. They also gained a new company commander, African American 1st Lieutenant Montie Montjoy. A New Jersey native, Montie had earned his officer's commission through Reserve Officers' Training Corps (ROTC), attending a traditionally black college. Montie shared his command wisdom with Baker, which the platoon leader would carry forward with him. Montie told Baker that a commander must understand exactly what he was ordering his men to do. In that way, a commander would make smarter decisions and gain his men's trust.

Baker was keenly aware of securing and keeping his men's respect. They came to him with their confidences as well as concerns. A solitary man by nature, Baker found this growing closeness complicated the job of war, and he tried to keep a distance to protect himself. He believed he couldn't be someone's buddy then send them out to get killed. He avoided directly picking the men who went on patrols. Instead, Baker shifted that task to squad leaders. Baker only dictated the numbers of men needed, then the squad leaders made the selections.

It wasn't that he was cold or impersonal but rather that he felt deeply responsible when any of his men were wounded or killed. He believed his attention had to be completely focused on the mission and task at hand. He already knew of friends who were killed, but his effort to make his men anonymous never really worked by his own admission after the war. Living and being around soldiers 24 hours a day, he found their faces and personalities became acutely etched in his memory.

In those first several months in Italy, Baker was ordered to take his men on seemingly endless patrols. Battalion and division commanders would zero in on an area in enemy hands they wanted more intelligence about. His superiors would supply vague maps and intelligence reports which Baker deemed virtually worthless. Instinct became his survival mechanism. The majority of patrols occurred at night, which Baker preferred as he had excellent night vision, and his body operated on what he termed "nine parts adrenaline to one part blood."

Once his patrol reached their objective, they would sit down in a circle back-to-back, rifles at the ready, and wait for signs of the enemy. The communal warmth was a blessing for men living out of cold, muddy, rain-filled foxholes. Invariably, however, his tired men would begin to nod off. They had to be prodded back awake by the butt of a rifle when their snores alerted the rest of the patrol. One man, Casey Emmet, earned the unenviable platoon honor of "famed snorer." Apparently it was indeed something to behold, and it would have been quite comical if it didn't put all their lives in danger. Baker lost count of how many times he heard the whisper, "somebody shut that sonofabitch up!"

As Baker and the lead elements of the 370th progressed north along the coast through the rubble of once quaint and picturesque villages and towns, he met more of the locals, mainly children and the elderly. Baker came to love the Italians who were grateful to welcome their liberators, but he soon realized most of the residents he encountered had never seen a black man. They stared at him and his men in wonder.

The Germans had told the local residents that blacks were less than human. White American soldiers who preceded his regiment, according to Baker, had even informed the local population that "black people had tails and ate humans." However, the locals' fears gave way to kindness, and the black GIs provided cigarettes and chocolate to help the situation. The Italians reciprocated the GIs' goodwill by delivering what helpful information they could on the whereabouts of enemy troops and opening their doors to the Americans when the frequent German shells rained down.

After one particularly tragic engagement, Baker would witness how deeply the Italians cared. Regimental command directed Baker's weapons platoon to push any Germans or stragglers out of a town in the foothills north of Lucca. The village sat between two dry canals that converged at the opposite end of the community. The area seemed quiet, too quiet as Baker and Montie scanned the empty stone buildings and a vineyard across the canal through their field glasses. Their objective was to cross the dry canal and move north where the channels converged. The Germans had left a half-demolished bridge standing, just stable enough for soldiers to traverse, not motorized vehicles. Montie ordered Baker's platoon to cross the bridge then split into two groups to probe the area.

Baker's patrol successfully crossed the bridge then moved to split up. Before they had gone 10 yards, a German light machine gun erupted 20 yards to their front from a vineyard. Baker swung around to check the other half of his platoon just in time to see two of his men crumple to the ground. Baker only knew their ranks, not their names. He directed his section to seek cover as his BAR (Browning Automatic Rifle) man Eldridge Banks stepped forward and unloaded two bursts in the direction of the enemy machine gun nest. The Germans zeroed in on him, and Banks dropped to his knees, his eyes rolling back in his head, his body riddled with 57mm shells.

Baker and the remainder of his men hugged the ground, but they couldn't stay there long. After a significant pause in enemy fire, Baker decided to wave his men back; they all took off sprinting in a zig-zag pattern toward the half-demolished bridge. Baker came upon men from the other half of his patrol hovering over two dead Germans they had just taken out. One of the deceased had an ammo belt slung over his left shoulder. A quick determination identified them as the ones who had ambushed the patrol from the vineyard. The machine gunners had attempted to escape to rejoin their unit after firing on Baker's men.

Baker located his medic and had him examine his two men, whom the machine gunners had hit first near the canal. Baker already knew his BAR man Banks was dead. The medic returned quickly, and his grim expression conveyed all Baker needed to know.

The ambush shook Baker as he replayed the images of his men's deaths in his mind and fought back nausea. His dry heaves came and went as the emotions swelled and then subsided. Baker blamed himself for his poor judgment in patrolling in such an exposed manner, and now three of his men would never be returning home. Guilt, anger, and frustration took turns tormenting his mind.

After a day and a half of quiet, it was deemed safe to retrieve the bodies. Jeeps brought volunteer stretcher-bearers forward, and they wrapped the men in blankets. The jeeps emerged out of the dry canal onto the town's cobblestone street. The covered bodies on the stretchers were laid crossways and tied down on the back of the two vehicles. Men saluted, and Baker took a seat next to the driver of the lead jeep.

As the laden vehicles began slowly navigating the town's narrow stone streets, residents' doors creaked open and solemn women and children came forth with armloads of flowers. The locals approached the jeeps, which came to a halt, and gently laid the bouquets on the blanketed bodies without saying a word, all making the sign of the cross before they turned. Baker felt emotions well up that he couldn't push back down. As he wiped a tear from his cheek, he looked around and saw that in his expression of grief he was not alone.

As September 1944 faded into memory, the new month brought the arrival of the rest of the 92nd Division and General Almond and his command staff on October 1. The 370th now transferred from 1st Armored to the 92nd and experienced a marked increase in casualties. The arrival of continuous torrential rains perfectly matched the darkening gloom. The glory of war, if there ever was such a thing, faded to a miserable wet slog up steep mountain sides with overgrown brush that tore men's boots off and was as tiring to maneuver as walking through glue.

Baker, muddy and exhausted from one particular day's advance, returned to deliver his field report on the afternoon of October 3 and paused to speak with several men near the Command Post (CP). The day's pounding rains had subsided. Sharing a joke, Baker smiled then turned to see a clearly upset Deputy Chief of Staff of the 92nd exit the Headquarters tent in a flurry searching for someone. He saw Baker and shouted over to him, "Baker!" waving him over.

Arriving, Baker saluted. "Yes, sir?" The Deputy Chief needed someone to immediately lead a patrol to recover the bodies of two men. The intensity of the request felt unusual, and Baker could see the man was upset, so he asked who they were recovering. The Headquarters Officer replied grimly, "Colonel Barber."

Baker stepped back in shock as the Deputy Chief informed him that the Chief of Staff had taken a jeep with a driver out to inspect a blown bridge across the Cinquale Canal. The area was still crawling with Germans, and Barber and his unsuspecting driver became easy targets. The enemy cut them to pieces with machine guns from across the canal.

Baker directed his squad leader, Sergeant Napoleon Belk, to select a team, and Baker led the men out to the site near the blown bridge. Baker couldn't help reflecting as he stood expressionless, overseeing his men cover the dead body of the Chief of Staff, and his hatred for the man dissolved, only the cruel words *that it was time for the black boys to die* remaining.

✳✳✳

As October progressed, Baker and his patrol started to meet stiffer resistance within the towns. Picking his way through the streets of one particular village toward another blown bridge, Baker sent his squad leader Sgt. Belk and Casey Emmet, their "famed snorer," forward the next 100 yards to a section of the town nearest the river crossing. The remainder of the platoon stayed back within the shadows. Within minutes Belk returned alone, shaken and pale as a sheet. Baker asked where his partner Emmet was.

Belk silently motioned Baker to follow him and keep low. As they weaved their way through and around broken buildings, they came up behind Emmet's wiry frame. He was kneeling by a fence gate with his rifle poised on a rail eyeing the general area. Baker, perplexed at what the problem was, threw up his hands, whispering, "What?"

Belk responded softly, "He's dead."

Baker leaned in to get a closer look and see Emmet's front. The man appeared utterly natural and alive except for the bullet hole between his still open eyes. Baker felt a tug on his sleeve from Belk, and realized immediately that he was also in the sights of the unseen German sniper.

Baker spun around, and he and Belk sped away from the area back to the platoon as fast as their legs could carry them, feeling the hidden sniper's sights on them the entire way. Pressure from command or not, to Baker daytime patrols seemed the height of foolishness, and he had another dead man in his platoon to attest to that. He sent a message back to the CP asking to patrol at night whenever possible.

SERAVEZZA, ITALY

The first officer killed in Charlie Company, 2nd Lieutenant Al Frazier, dissected by a hidden machine gun nest at what was believed an abandoned farmhouse on October 6, 1944, sent shock waves through ranks. Baker and the men were emotionally shaken and angry as the odds seemed ever to be stacked against them, and forward progress was measured in city blocks, not miles. Still, battalion commanders kept the pressure on to keep pressing forward into unexplored and unscouted enemy territory.

A day or two later, in the early morning 2 a.m. darkness, Baker was ordered to take a squad and assault the same two-story farmhouse where Frazier had been killed. It was on a slope next to an olive grove. Under the blessed cover of darkness, he and his assault squad stealthily crept toward the enemy location. In the quiet, he was reminded of his grandfather's words when they were out stalking elk: *surprise was more valuable than speed.*

Baker prayed that the element of surprise was on his side when they were 20 yards from the house. He grabbed his Platoon Sergeant, Jacy Cunigan, and circled to the right of the farmhouse, communicating by hand signals. Baker directed his other men to cover the front and the left side to prevent any escape. Hoping to blend into the darkness as much as possible proved unsuccessful;

their movements alerted a guard standing watch on the right side of the farmhouse who shouted and fired his Mauser in their direction.

Baker and Cunigan, in the inky morning blackness, dropped prostrate to the ground in a shooting position and returned fire. Baker felt a tiny nick on the bottom of his wrist, which he ignored as he asked Cunigan if he was okay. The response came back affirmative, as fire from the now assumed dead sentry went silent. They heard a machine gun open up on the opposite side of the house as Baker shouted to Cunigan to head for the back.

Reaching the back door, they kicked it in guns blazing and struck down five still-groggy Germans. Baker and Cunigan considered themselves highly fortunate; the dead Germans had been such heavy sleepers they hadn't heard the sentry's initial fire or shouts.

On the other side of the farmhouse, the machine gun fire went silent after a few minutes as Baker's men eliminated the two Germans operating it, the same men who had killed 2nd Lt. Frazier. However, the cost was high as two more of Baker's men were felled by the MG-42. A messenger was sent back to Montie at Company Headquarters with word of the patrol's success. Baker left several seasoned men behind to protect the location from falling back into the Germans' hands.

Arriving back at Charlie Company HQ, Montie directed them to gather at the CP for a briefing. As Baker settled his weary body back against a wall in the CP, closing his eyes and letting his arms rest in his lap, Cunigan shouted over to him, "Hey, you're wounded."

Baker was surprised and protested that it was impossible, but he looked down and saw his legs covered with blood as well as the underside of his forearm. Montie arrived and rushed over to Baker and shouted at him, showing surprisingly more concern than expected. He told him to get out and get over to the aid station before he bled to death.

Not realizing he'd become weak and dizzy with blood loss, Baker needed help to walk the two blocks to the dispensary. Upon his arrival, the medical officer, Dr. Gill, invited him to sit for an examination. Baker did, and he immediately passed out.

Waking up in 64th General Hospital outside of Pisa in a segregated ward, Baker spent the next two months with his arm elevated in a sling. Far from an enjoyable recovery, except for the pretty Italian nurse's aides, Baker felt sick to his stomach most of the time. His discomfort was due to the air reeking like a "hot summer day in an unventilated mortuary" because of the numerous draining wounds. He was eventually discharged and returned to the front and his old platoon the day after Christmas 1944 near Sommocolonia, Italy.

By chance or perhaps providence, coming back to the front, Baker would witness one of the most heroic acts by a black officer during World War II. The bravery the officer demonstrated would earn him the Distinguished Service Cross more than 40 years later and the Medal of Honor in 1997.

At a height overlooking the hamlet of Sommocolonia, as Baker was helping to prepare a defensive line, he looked down and saw fellow American soldiers battling back the Germans in an intense fighting retreat from the town as American artillery pounded the overwhelming German onslaught. The German attack was a coordinated assault, Operation *Wintergewitter* (Winter Thunderstorm),* targeting the relatively inexperienced 92nd.

Directing the 598th Field Artillery Battalion's fire from a stone tower within the village was 1st Lieutenant John Fox. He served as a Forward Observer and had been calling in deadly accurate offensive fire since 0430 that morning.

He had been ordered to stay behind and defend the town with two platoons and about 25 Italian partisans directing the 598th's fire closer and closer to his location. Near noon that day, he radioed in coordinates to bring the American shells right down on his position.

The fire control officer back at the 155mm howitzer battery shouted that Fox had just transmitted coordinates that would bring the shells right on top of him. Fox insisted that that was where he wanted them, but fire control protested again. Fox shouted, "Fire it, there's more of them than there are of us!" The

* This was also the name of an operation on the Eastern Front in 1942.

598th subsequently complied after headquarters approved the request, and Fox's radio transmissions went silent.

In less than 24 hours Baker and most of the 370th had heard about Fox's soul-stirring heroics. When American troops captured the town a day later, they found Lieutenant Fox's body amidst the rubble.

Winter settled in, and for the men in the foxholes in northern Italy it was a cold, damp hell, so Baker tried to pack as many of his platoon as he could into the civilian homes he had the good fortune to bunk in as an officer. There were only a few familiar faces left in the company when he had returned from the hospital; the majority were inexperienced replacements, a challenging situation in any war.

As 1944 slipped into the final year of the war, Baker became the de facto senior ranking officer of Charlie Company in the 3rd Battalion. Montie had been replaced while Baker was in the hospital by Captain Booker T. Matthews, a mountain of a man as well as a preacher. But Capt. Matthews, one of the few black Captains Baker met while in Europe, only stayed long enough to appoint Baker Executive Officer.

Late one afternoon, Baker returned from a patrol to the villa he shared with Matthews. He met him in the driveway, being carried out on a stretcher, pale and going into shock. Matthews had been scanning the hills from a second-floor window when a pinpoint-accurate German mortar shell slammed into the second-floor windowsill tearing Matthews' arm off at the shoulder.

Baker stood in stunned silence as the stretcher-bearers carted his commanding officer past him. The Captain, with his last bit of consciousness catching Baker's eye, mouthed, "Sorry, Lieutenant." Baker shut his eyes a moment then shook his head, saying, "No sorries, Captain. This is war."[11]

By February 1945, Hitler had firmly established his virtually unassailable Gothic Line across the rugged mountain terrain of northern Italy. German Field Marshal Albert Kesselring personally designed the defensive line. He subjugated 15,000 Italians into back-breaking labor for nine months to construct the fortification. They worked round the clock until the Germans perfected the line. The Gothic Line boasted cleverly camouflaged concrete dugouts, hundreds of 88mm howitzers, antiaircraft batteries, and almost 2,400 machine gun emplacements. Everything about it was designed for killing and in massive numbers.

In the second week of February 1945, the 92nd's first major offensive was launched, Operation *Fourth Term* against the Gothic Line, which included the 1st and 2nd Battalions of the 370th. Baker in the 3rd Battalion was in reserve but watched the assault from an observation post. The objective was to secure a series of terraced hills named X, Y, and Z leading up to an ancient fortified stronghold, Castle Aghinolfi, built in the 8th century. The Italians called the area and the adjacent mountains the Triangle of Death.

The assault by 1st and 2nd Battalions became a monumental disaster and would be called off reluctantly by General Almond three days into the bloodletting. The commander of Fifth Army, General Lucian Truscott, witnessing the carnage, had strongly recommended it be called off immediately.

Baker watched it all unfold while in reserve and was sickened. He wept openly and pounded his fists against the wall of the observation post until they were raw. His fellow soldiers had absolutely no chance as they advanced up Hill X toward Hills Y and Z into a torrent of deadly accurate German mortars, artillery, and machine gun fire.

Spectacularly poor planning, overconfidence, and an absence of strategy were to blame for the inability of the 92nd to press the attack. Almond praised his white battalion and regimental commanders for their courage while placing the blame squarely on the shoulders of the black enlisted men saying, "Little if any determined offensive spirit to meet the enemy at close quarters existed in most of the infantry units."[12]

Word of Operation *Fourth Term*'s failure spread quickly and led to a visit days later by General George C. Marshall. High command recommended a complete top-down reorganization of the division immediately so the fighting group would be ready for a new spring offensive in early April. What never came to light or was even discussed by senior command was General Almond's complete failure in strategy and leadership, which the men on the ground saw only too clearly.

Morale plummeted in the 370th, and Baker found it increasingly challenging to keep his men motivated. One night after supper, a soldier in his platoon, Will Boswell, spoke his mind saying that he wondered if there was enough sense in the white commanders to do anything but throw them straight at the same damn line in the same damn place every time. Boswell concluded by recommending to all that they might as well write those last letters home now.

Although Baker had served as unofficial Charlie Company commander for months, performing all the necessary duties, he was doubtful that General Almond and regimental commander of the 370th Colonel Sherman would officially elevate him into the position. Promoting black soldiers to higher-ranking officers would do nothing to further their own careers.

Baker's doubts were confirmed with the arrival in late March of three new white officers: a 2nd and 1st Lieutenant and a Captain who would serve as Charlie Company commander. Prewar, Captain John F. Runyon had been an efficiency expert with Continental Baking and had impressed senior command of the 92nd by overhauling their maintenance program. He had never experienced a minute of combat. His promotion to Captain occurred stateside during the Louisiana Maneuvers when his senior officer was accidentally shot. Runyon looked as soft as they come to Baker and the men, but the Captain carried himself with more than a fair share of arrogance.

Runyon's first action was to bump Baker from Executive Officer back to platoon leader, but Baker wasn't allowed to return to his old rifle platoon. Instead, Baker was assigned to a weapons platoon consisting of two mortar squads and two light machine gun squads. Baker was less than pleased as he was taken from the men he had fought with and trusted, soldiers he knew would have his back.

The arrival of the three new white officers only aroused suspicion and mistrust among the black enlisted men who had no rapport with their white commanders to begin with. Additionally, fully 70 percent of their ranks were filled with replacements whom they didn't even know. Baker and the handful of seasoned combat veterans who remained knew they would have to rely only on themselves.

Chapter 6

Storming the Castle

"I am haunted by the memory of nineteen men, men I left on a ridge in northern Italy five decades ago. I still hear a German commander scream, Feuer, howitzer shells whistling in, followed by the rush of mortars, the trees around us shredding, wounded and dying men screaming. My only medic, killed by a sniper as we tried to withdraw."

LT. VERNON BAKER

CASTLE AGHINOLFI, ITALY
APRIL 5, 1944

In early April, the 92nd Division ordered Charlie Company to lead 3rd Battalion of the 370th in a new attack on Castle Aghinolfi before dawn on April 5. It was repeating the pattern that Will Boswell had predicted. The assault was "the same damn line in the same damn place."

After a sleepless night, Baker rose at 3 a.m. in the farmhouse that served as the home of his platoon. He had already decided on his uniform of choice as he snapped open his battered brown suitcase, which he'd asked the Supply Sergeant to fetch for him a week earlier, without knowing why, and carefully lifted his dress green uniform and Eisenhower jacket out. He set aside his steel helmet and donned his wool helmet liner. The steel helmet inhibited his hearing, which had already been damaged in mortar training. Baker knew he would need all his senses to be operating at their peak. The day and zero-hour augured death, and Baker *wanted to go up sharp if he was going to die.*[13] He strapped four grenades to his Eisenhower jacket and two bandoliers of ammunition around his waist, and he was ready.

Baker joined his subdued men for a coffee downstairs in the tiny farmhouse kitchen. They brightened when he arrived looking so sharp, not knowing the reason their commander had chosen his battle attire. All exited the farmhouse at 0330 hours in their understrength weapons platoon. Usually, at full strength, they would have 36 men. This morning they were ten short of that number. Baker met up with Capt. Runyon emerging from another home who gathered Charlie Company together on the road then gave the order to move out.

Two hundred and fifty yards from the jump-off point near a clump of bombed-out trees, Baker halted his platoon and gave final instructions that there was to be no talking during the advance, only hand signals. Then Baker added an unexpected confidence boost, telling the men that "today they were going to do it" to which his men returned an all-business nod.[14]

American artillery began the barrage at the appointed hour of 0445, as it had for the past week, so that nothing would seem unusual to the Germans. At that moment, tanks, 155mm howitzers, and British battleships combined into a bombardment symphony, lighting up Hills X, Y, and Z.

As the last volley echoed away at the appointed pause time of 0500 hours, that was the company's signal to make the dash across Highway One toward the base of 450ft-high Hill X half a mile distant.

When Baker and his platoon rendezvoused with Capt. Runyon at the foot of the trail leading up the hill, Runyon was sidestepping along its rocky edge. He was probing forward with a stick for mines, and such excellent tactical thinking initially impressed Baker. Runyon knew of the German propensity for paving paths with mines. Baker whispered an order back to his men to walk only along the trail's edge rock-to-rock. All the men carried their M1s in front of them, not slung over their backs; they knew they'd never have time to unsling them when the enemy bullets started flying. Capt. Runyon then disappeared into the flanks checking on other platoons.

As Baker reached the crest of Hill X, he signaled for a short break. He knew the American artillery would resume to his front at any moment as he caught his breath. Suddenly the artillery fire began, but it was behind them. Baker's platoon had advanced beyond their own guns, and now the deadly salvo was crawling up Hill X to meet them. Baker ordered his men rapidly forward with a windmill motion of his arm to outrun their own artillery.

As the artillery fire settled, Baker realized that he had also out-advanced Able and Baker companies on his left and right flanks as well. He decided to establish a mortar position to cover their advance, but his two mortar squads were nowhere in sight. They had been caught up in the resumed Allied artillery fire. At that moment, several men from Baker's old rifle platoon who'd gotten lost wandered into his weapons platoon, and Baker ordered them to join him. The wayward men's arrival brought the platoon's strength up to 26.

Ascending Hill Y, Baker and his men noted the increasing destruction to the olive groves. They had been blessed in the darkness by the leafy cover of trees on Hill X. Here, there wasn't a leaf or an existing branch on the remaining broken tree spires. Soon they came across an odd sight stepping through the groves in a spread-out formation. Taut yellow plastic wires crisscrossed the olive grove everywhere, three inches off the ground. Baker had never seen plastic, but he knelt, grabbing wire cutters from his pocket, and snipped. It was the Germans' solid copper-core communications lines. The platoon then cut every wire they encountered.

American artillery resumed pounding the hillside ahead of them as daylight broke. The salvo this morning was scheduled to conclude at 0900 hours instead of the usual 0645. The more protracted bombardment was intended to saturate the area for the attack. Advancing further up Hill Y, the platoon encountered its first Germans. Baker sighted movement ahead then the tell-tale

German helmet profile near some brush. He sidestepped from his men, raised his rifle, took aim, and fired. The two Germans dropped instantly. The platoon reached the now-dead enemy machine gunners and replaced their MG-42 with their own .50cal Browning, and two of Baker's platoon gunners settled into that position. One hundred yards further, the platoon encountered another German machine gun nest which they quickly eliminated. Baker and the men were fortunate as the sustained Allied artillery fire concealed the sound of their M1 Garands.

As the platoon progressed further with Baker in the lead, they eliminated two more Germans in a hidden observation post then stumbled right into another German machine gun nest that was thankfully unmanned. The German gunner and assistant gunner were in the back of the nest peacefully having breakfast. Baker in the lead took them out as they leaped up, dropping their breakfast, and tried to scramble toward their gun.

By 0630 hours, Capt. Runyon met back up with Baker's platoon that had now advanced nearly three miles up Hills X, Y, and Z. Only 300 yards remained between them and the German stronghold, Castle Aghinolfi. The last bit of terrain, however, was treacherous. The ground dropped into a 50ft-steep brush-covered ravine then rose to a knob where the castle sat.

Baker and Runyon stood on the edge of the draw overlooking the ravine and debated the best way to proceed. They didn't have many options, only a narrow path just below them that they expected to be very well defended. As the two talked, a German soldier emerged below them 25 yards to their left on the trail heading toward the castle.

Both Runyon and Baker stopped their conversation short in surprise. The German soldier turned instinctively, pulled a potato masher grenade from his belt, and reared back to heave the explosive in their direction. As Baker raised his rifle to fire, Runyon shrieked in fright and jumped back, nearly knocking Baker's rifle out of his hands as the German's grenade landed five feet from them.

Baker recovered his M1 nearly in midair, took aim, and struck down the fleeing German with two shots in the back. He was unaccustomed to shooting soldiers in the back, but his anger and adrenaline got the better of him.

The German grenade had bounced on the ground but did not explode. Thankfully it was a dud. Runyon, however, was now nowhere in sight, disappearing back into the brush. Baker's Staff Sergeant, Willie Dickens, asked if Baker was okay then offered to put together a patrol, but Baker waved him off. He told Dickens to keep the platoon up top to cover him as he intended to explore forward alone.

Before Baker set out, they exchanged guns, Dickens handing him his Thompson submachine gun and Baker tossing him his M1. As Baker stepped forward, Dickens yelled for him to wait, Baker turned, and Dickens tossed him an extra 30-round clip. Baker nodded his thanks and set out alone down onto the path in the unexplored ravine.

He headed toward the prostate soldier he'd shot; the soldier lay dead just outside an earthen dugout. Baker slid up to the side of the dugout cave then pivoted, firing a dozen rounds into the hillside cavern. He slid back, hugging the side of the entrance expecting return fire; none came. Baker slowly entered the cave dugout, empty except for a few hand grenades strewn on the floor, which he scooped up.

Continuing forward again on the path, Baker came upon an odd sight, a gray Volkswagen car door covering the entrance of another enemy dugout. He grabbed onto it but couldn't dislodge the door, so he stuffed a grenade under it, and blew it off its hinges.

A groggy German poked his head out of the now open entrance, and Baker split his skull with a single burst of his Thompson then charged the opening, pulling the pin on one of his German grenades and tossing it in. After the dust and debris of the explosion cleared, Baker sprayed several submachine gun blasts into the dugout. He waited a minute, but only silence remained. Baker entered the 8 x 8ft hideaway and saw three Germans piled up against the far wall from the impact of the grenade blast. They had also been having breakfast, and it covered their faces and the walls.

Baker explored further on the trail, and there was a final brush-covered hideaway, and without checking it out, he tossed another grenade into the top hole in the dugout and took out three more enemy soldiers.

After infiltrating the third dugout, Baker felt it best to circle back, and he returned to the spot on the draw where he'd stood with Runyon. By this time, however, the Germans had discovered his men. Mortars and machine gun fire blanketed the area from the castle. Baker and his men were caught in the open, totally exposed. Mortar shells continued to rain down in sheets, tearing the unprotected men apart. They were so close to the Germans Baker could hear their commands, *Feuer!*

Baker's Forward Observer, 2nd Lieutenant Walker, was screaming fire coordinates into a handset for counter-battery fire. Baker ran over to him, and Walker paused long enough to curse and shout that fire control didn't believe him. They didn't think that the platoon had gotten this far behind enemy lines. The men were trapped, and Baker's medic couldn't even reach any of the wounded. The situation was deteriorating to beyond desperate. Baker moved away from Walker and saw Sgt. Belk. He shouted the burning question on his mind, "Where the hell's Runyon?"

Sgt. Belk pointed to a small stone shed-like structure 30 yards to the rear. Baker sprinted toward it and found Runyon on the floor with his arms pulled up around his knees, his face as pale as a ghost.

Runyon said, "Baker, can't you get those men together out there?" Baker replied to the Captain that "he was trying his Goddamn best."[15]

Then the Captain asked if everything was alright out there, and Baker replied coldly, "Everything's fine, sir."

Runyon finally asked his subordinate if they were going to stay there, his voice beginning to falter. Baker, not in a position to make such a decision, replied that, of course, they should stay. They'd gotten this far when four previous attempts had failed, and the castle was within striking distance.

Runyon swallowed hard then stunned Baker by telling him that he would head back and get reinforcements.

Baker boiled in rage and wanted to kill the man but calmed himself and with a hard stare replied in a tone matching his fury, "Okay, Captain, you go on, we'll be right here when you get back." Baker knew Runyon would never be coming back as he watched him retreat down the hill in the late morning haze.

Baker's platoon had accomplished something the entire regiment hadn't been able to do in three months: reach the castle stronghold. Yes, they were battered and bruised, and many men lay dead all around them, but Baker believed they still had a chance if they could simply hold on.

Baker exited Runyon's hideaway to a pause in the German mortar fire. He took the opportunity to collect the dog tags on his fallen men, six in all. Then Baker headed forward to find Walker, his Forward Observer. Baker came upon him bleeding from a shrapnel wound but alive. Walker's radioman was dead, and the field radio lay in a thousand pieces.

Walker stammered out that fire control finally believed him, counter-battery fire was on the way, and he added that they were sending reinforcements. Baker shouted, "When?!"

Walker replied, "They said immediately."

Suddenly a screeching whistle rose behind them from the far side of Hill X; low-trajectory 90mm antiaircraft shells were coming in hot. Everyone hugged the ground as the American artillery hurtled over their heads at tree-top level and slammed into the 8-inch-thick castle walls. Several more salvos followed.

The American artillery kept the German mortar fire silent temporarily. It was time enough for Baker to order his remaining men to establish a perimeter. His platoon wasn't happy; everyone had the same thought: *when would they get the hell outta there?* The platoon knew the Germans would send infantry out to try to capture them.

Baker's men formed their circular perimeter; he ordered them to stay in position and shoot at anything that moved. None of them were to move, and that's how they would survive. Within minutes, the Germans unleashed three more rounds of mortar fire and indirect artillery fire, killing six more of Baker's men, leaving just eight alive, including the medic.

The eight men kept an eye on Baker, and he read their minds – *Lieutenant, are we gonna stay here and die?* As Baker was deciding whether to go, a platoon-sized group of Germans disguised as medics and litter bearers wearing red cross armbands appeared 50 yards from their position. The men stared questioningly at Baker; they knew how far behind enemy lines they were. Baker waved them off with a shake of his head and raised the rifle he'd gotten back from Dickens. Baker's suspicions were confirmed when the Germans suddenly pulled the blankets from the litters revealing their concealed machine guns.

Baker didn't need to order his men to fire; they were already pulling their triggers, and the disguised German platoon crumpled to the ground. None of Baker's eight remaining men was struck, but the incident was the final catalyst to fall back. Each man had only a few clips remaining. Reinforcements were never coming. It was time to head back down the mountain.

Working their way down, they encountered a German light mortar crew who fired upon them, seriously wounding one of the men and bringing their effective strength down to seven. Just 300 yards further, after taking out the enemy mortar crew, their only medic was killed by a sniper atop a nearby hill. Baker's BAR man, the enormous Pvt. James Thomas, went crazy with anger. He stepped behind the shelter of a tree and blasted the sniper position to bits. Soon a German sniper rifle came clattering down the hill.

With only six of his men remaining, Baker continued forward but was far from out of danger. His platoon came upon a German machine gun nest they'd missed on the way up. Baker, taking the task to eliminate it into his own hands, turned to Pvt. Thomas and asked the soldier simply to cover him. Thomas, with a toothy grin, told Baker to go get 'em. Thomas began firing his Browning Automatic Rifle inches above Baker's head as he crawled toward the German machine gun nest. Baker got as close as he could, pulled the pin on his "Willy Pete" M15 White Phosphorus Grenade, and incinerated the two Germans.*

* The M15 burns at 2,700°C.

79

Baker sprinted back to his platoon and continued the push down the hill. They soon came up behind another German machine gun nest that was firing down Hill X. Baker turned to his BAR man Thomas with a nod. Thomas smiled, responding that it had worked the first time. They repeated the same action and eliminated the second German machine gun nest.

After an arduous trek down, Baker and his men finally reached the bottom of Hill X safely; his adrenaline stopped pumping, and his body convulsed.

Baker dropped to the road, bent over, put his head between his knees, and vomited his guts out. He and his men had endured intense combat for over 12 hours, and it was a miracle they had made it out alive.

Baker and his platoon had accomplished a feat the entire regiment couldn't manage; they had broken through. Everything was now on the move: tanks, trucks, and jeeps on Highway 1, the main north-south coastal highway. Yet scores of wounded men hobbled everywhere. The decisive breakthrough had come at a great cost.

Baker pulled himself together then received word that Colonel Murphy, his battalion commander, wanted to see him at his headquarters. When Baker arrived at the house, an aide let him in and pointed up to a closed door at the top of the stairs. The aide told Baker that Murphy was expecting him to knock on the door and announce himself.

After Baker knocked, a shout came forth, "Lieutenant Baker?" Baker confirmed that it was, and was told to let himself in. Baker entered a small bathroom, saluted, and saw Murphy covered in soap bubbles, enjoying a hot bath in a tin wash tub.

The Colonel told Baker to sit down and forget formalities, and called him by his nickname, "Bake." He knew his platoon had had a rough day. Then he informed Baker in a probing monotone that Runyon had stopped by to see him earlier.

Baker shut his eyes in anger as Murphy asked him to tell the *whole story* of what had happened up on that hill. Baker told him the entire story, absent his feelings toward Runyon. When Baker concluded, Col. Murphy was very appreciative, telling Baker to inform his men that they had done a good job. Col. Murphy was the only commander who complimented Baker on his platoon's heroic actions. Baker learned much later that when Capt. Runyon arrived at Col. Murphy's headquarters, the Captain told the commander not to worry about Baker's men; they had all been wiped out. This was the reason Baker's platoon never received any reinforcements.

After his meeting with Murphy, exhaustion began to overtake Baker, but he still carried his fallen men's dog tags, the metal jangling in the front pocket of his Eisenhower jacket. Sleep could wait until he delivered them to the Regimental Intelligence Officer, Lieutenant Spenser, as was the protocol.

Baker found a jeep and a driver to take him to the three-story villa that served as Regimental HQ. He felt himself nodding off en route, and his driver had to nudge him awake when they arrived. Baker stepped out of the jeep and made his way up the gravel driveway considering the solemn task he was performing. He had refused to look at the names on the tags. He felt putting faces together with names would be more than he could bear at that moment.

As he stepped into Headquarters seeking Spenser, he encountered regimental commander Colonel Raymond Sherman in conference with Lt. Spenser. Baker's hand sprung to a salute. Sherman asked him if he'd just been out in the field. Baker replied that he had. Then Sherman proceeded to give him one of the more colorful ass-chewings he'd ever received in the Army, calling him a disgrace to his unit, the regiment, and the entire country if not the universe for not wearing his steel helmet.

Not wearing a helmet into battle was an abomination of stupidity, the commander continued, while Baker stood dumbfounded, not knowing how to respond. The Colonel paced in front of him, telling Baker that this would not stand. Then the Colonel motioned for Spenser to transfer his helmet to Baker. Lt. Spenser handed it over, and Baker jammed it on his head.

Col. Sherman said, "Now Goddammit Lieutenant, since you're in uniform, I've got a job for you to do. Tomorrow morning, you're volunteering to take the 473rd infantry back up to the castle."[16]

Sherman immediately dismissed Baker, and Baker reported to the 473rd's Command Post and met with a company commander there. The 473rd was one of the few all-white units in the 92nd, and it had come into being during the recent reorganization. The commander assigned Baker to one of his companies with about three dozen men. Baker added his Platoon Sergeant and another sergeant to the assault.

At 0430 hours the following day, Baker led the 473rd up the hill, and they encountered Baker's own dead men barefoot. The Germans had taken their boots and socks. No enemy shots were fired, the Germans had bugged out, and the castle was deserted. The battle for Castle Aghinolfi was over.

The Germans surrendered Italy in its entirety in early May, and a few weeks later, the 92nd pulled Baker's unit back to near Viareggio. While there, Baker's battalion commander Lt. Col. Murphy elevated him to 1st Lieutenant, arriving at Baker's Command Post himself with the set of single silver bars to announce the promotion.

As May slipped into June 1945, Baker could finally enjoy a well-deserved rest. However, that rest was interrupted when he was unexpectedly summoned to Division Headquarters in Genoa on June 15. Baker couldn't fathom why he was being called into Division except possibly for a violation he wasn't unaware of. Perhaps someone had seen him without his helmet on because he still didn't wear it.

The next day Baker loaded into a jeep beside a driver for the 80-mile drive up the coast. He brought his helmet with him just in case. Baker didn't look forward to meeting General Almond for the first time under these circumstances. Baker knew the commander's opinion toward Buffalo soldiers, and mentally prepared himself for a thorough dressing down.

Arriving at 92nd Division Headquarters, a sprawling ornate villa perched atop an overlook with a sweeping view of the Mediterranean, Baker approached the building feeling minuscule. He made sure to put on his helmet before he entered.

General Almond's aides were expecting him, but Baker had to wait nearly 20 minutes before being led up a sweeping marble staircase to General Almond's office. He was announced by an aide and entered the large suite and saw Almond peering out his second-floor window toward the sea. Baker, breathless, held a salute waiting for Almond to turn as the heavy wooden door closed behind him, sealing Baker in.

The General turned and begrudgingly returned Baker's salute as if he was swatting away a fly. He offered no salutations or small talk as he walked over to his massive mahogany desk.

He told Baker he wanted him to write a report of what went on up on that hill and have it on his desk the day after tomorrow, pounding the desk with his index finger for emphasis. Then Almond asked if Baker had any questions. Before Baker could finish replying, "No sir," he was dismissed with an unsettling glare.

Baker returned the 80 miles to Viareggio, found a typewriter, wrote up a three-page report on precisely what transpired on April 5, and submitted it. It was simply the facts and contained nothing about Runyon or his leaving them to die.

Baker heard nothing back until he was summoned to Genoa on July 4 to receive the Distinguished Service Cross in a ceremony presided over by General Lucian Truscott. Alongside him were General Almond and Capt. Runyon, whom Baker hadn't seen since he left them behind at Castle Aghinolfi. The officers also were receiving decorations, Almond, oak leaf clusters on his Silver Star and Runyon, the Silver Star.

When General Truscott pinned on Baker's DSC, he became the most highly decorated black soldier in the Mediterranean theater. It would be the last time Baker ever saw the two men who received medals beside him.

✳✳✳

Although it is believed that Captain Runyon was the commander who recommended Baker for the second-highest medal for valor, the lineage is not clear. Baker himself never discovered who submitted the recommendation.[17]

However, what is evident in the record is an eyebrow-raising footnote to this extraordinary story of bravery on April 5, 1945. Seven months after Baker received his Distinguished Service Cross, on February 8, 1946 in War Department General Orders No. 16, Captain John F. Runyon also received the Distinguished Service Cross. The citation stated it was for his actions on April 5, 1945, taking specific credit for the actions performed on that day by Vernon Baker.

The full text of Captain Runyon's Distinguished Service Cross follows below:

GENERAL ORDERS:
War Department, General Orders No. 16 (February 8, 1946)

CITATION:
The President of the United States of America, authorized by Act of Congress, July 9, 1918, takes pleasure in presenting the Distinguished Service Cross to Captain (Infantry) John F. Runyon (ASN: 0-1324872), United States Army, for extraordinary heroism in connection with military operations against an armed enemy while serving with Company C, 370th Infantry Regiment, in action against enemy forces on 5 April 1945. On that date, Captain Runyon heroically led his Company in an assault on the Germans' Gothic Line near Montiganosa, Italy. While other elements of the attacking force were able to make only limited gains, he accomplished an advance of nearly two miles against strong enemy forces advantageously placed on high ground. Forced to withdraw when support of the deep penetration failed, he returned with the remnants of his company, leaving behind 26 enemy dead, uncounted wounded, and a trail of havoc, which included the destruction of six machine guns, four dugouts, and two observation posts. Captain Runyon's fearless conduct, soldierly skill, and great determination inspired his company in an exploit which opened the way for a successful onslaught by a fresh regiment. Captain Runyon's outstanding leadership,

personal bravery and zealous devotion to duty exemplify the highest traditions of the military forces of the United States and reflect great credit upon himself, his unit, and the United States Army.

VERNON BAKER, MEDAL OF HONOR CITATION

For conspicuous gallantry and intrepidity at the risk of his life above and beyond the call of duty: First Lieutenant Vernon J. Baker distinguished himself by extraordinary heroism in action on 5 and 6 April 1945. At 0500 hours on 5 April 1945, Lieutenant Baker advanced at the head of his weapons platoon, along with Company C's three rifle platoons, towards their objective; Castle Aghinolfi – a German mountain strong point on the high ground just east of the coastal highway and about two miles from the 370th infantry Regiment's line of departure. Moving more rapidly than the rest of the company, Lieutenant Baker and about 25 men reached the south side of a draw some 250 yards from the castle within two hours. In reconnoitering for a suitable position to set up a machine gun, Lieutenant Baker observed two cylindrical objects pointing out of a slit in a mount at the edge of a hill. Crawling up and under the opening, he stuck his M-1 into the slit and emptied the clip, killing the observation post's two occupants. Moving to another position in the same area, Lieutenant Baker stumbled upon a well-camouflaged machine gun nest, the crew of which was eating breakfast. He shot and killed both enemy soldiers. After Captain John F. Runyon, Company C's Commander, joined the group, a German soldier appeared from the draw and hurled a grenade which failed to explode. Lieutenant Baker shot the enemy soldier twice as he tried to flee. Lieutenant Baker then went down into the draw alone. There he blasted open the concealed entrance of another dugout with a hand grenade, shot one German soldier who emerged after the explosion, tossed another grenade into the dugout and entered firing his submachine gun, killing two more Germans. As Lieutenant

Baker climbed back out of the draw, enemy machine gun and mortar fire began to inflict heavy casualties among the group of 25 soldiers, killing or wounding about two-thirds of them. When expected reinforcements did not arrive, Captain Runyon ordered a withdrawal in two groups. Lieutenant Baker volunteered to cover the withdrawal of the first group, which consisted mostly of walking wounded, and to remain to assist in the evacuation of the more seriously wounded. During the second group's withdrawal, Lieutenant Baker, supported by covering fire from one of his platoon members, destroyed two machine gun positions (previously bypassed during the assault) with hand grenades. In all, Lieutenant Baker accounted for nine enemy dead soldiers, elimination of three machine gun positions, an observation post, and a dugout. On the following night, Lieutenant Baker voluntarily led a battalion advance through enemy mine fields and heavy fire toward the division objective. Lieutenant Baker's fighting spirit and daring leadership were an inspiration to his men and exemplify the highest traditions of the military service.

PART THREE

Willy James Jr.

Chapter 7

A Fifth Platoon

In early December 1944, Lieutenant General John C.H. Lee, Deputy Commander of US Forces in the European Theater of Operations (ETO) and Commanding General in charge of SHAEF's (Supreme Headquarters Allied Expeditionary Force) Services of Supply (SOS), saw a growing manpower imbalance that threatened to become critical. The oversupply of black soldiers serving in supply units like the Red Ball Express and other outfits was matched by the undersupply of white replacement soldiers for rifle companies on the front lines.

Lee decided in a bold challenge to Army segregation policy to bring the imbalance to General Eisenhower's attention. The Army had been under pressure back home for years to move black soldiers into combat, and Lee's incremental solution of adding them as direct one-for-one replacements for white soldiers who'd been killed or wounded seemed like the way forward.

Lee distributed a notice offering all physically fit African American soldiers within the Services of Supply Corps, providing their jobs could be filled by limited-duty personnel, the opportunity to volunteer for infantry duty. They would be placed in otherwise white units, without regard to a quota but on an as-needed basis.[1]

Eisenhower's Chief of Staff, General Walter Bedell Smith, became alarmed and disagreed with Lee's bold new "integration" policy, believing that the Army should not do a one-for-one replacement plan. Bedell offered an alternative solution, creating new replacement platoons of black soldiers commanded by experienced white combat officers. This plan won Eisenhower's approval, and the concept of an additional "5th Platoon" of black soldiers in otherwise white infantry companies was born.

With the surprise German attack on December 16, the Ardennes Offensive, launched only days after the new black replacement platoons plan was envisioned, sped up its implementation. On December 26, 1944, the official call went out in the three-paragraph, confidential letter below disseminated to all units:

1. The Supreme Commander desires to destroy the enemy forces and end hostilities in this theater without delay. Every available weapon at our disposal must be brought to bear upon the enemy. To this end, the Commanding General, Com Z, is happy to offer to a limited number of colored troops who have had infantry training the privilege of joining our veteran units at the front to deliver the knockout blow.* The men selected are to be in the grades of Private First Class and Private. Non-commissioned officers may accept reduction in order to take advantage of this opportunity. The men selected are to be given a refresher course with an emphasis on weapon training.

2. The Commanding General makes a special appeal to you. It is planned to assign you without regard to color or race to the units where assistance is most needed and give you the opportunity of fighting shoulder to shoulder to bring about victory. Your comrades at the front are anxious to share the glory of victory with you. Your relatives and friends everywhere have been urging that you be granted this privilege.

* The term "privilege" is ironic as prior to this letter black soldiers were denied any role in combat infantry units at all. The only front-line exceptions were several tank destroyer units and black field artillery battalions.

The Supreme Commander, your Commanding General, and other veteran officers who have served with you are confident that many of you will take advantage of this opportunity and carry on in keeping with the glorious record of our colored troops in our former wars.

3. This letter is to be read confidentially to the troops immediately upon its receipt and made available in Orderly Rooms. Every assistance must be promptly given to qualified men to volunteer for this service.

The response from black soldiers in service units to the call for infantry training was overwhelming, with just over 4,500 men applying in the first two months. Unable to handle the influx, SHAEF decided to cap the number at 2,500, and in the end, 2,221 black soldiers made it through replacement training and qualified for combat duty. Willy F. James Jr. from Kansas City, Missouri, was one of those men.

16TH REINFORCEMENT DEPOT, COMPIÈGNE, FRANCE FEBRUARY 16, 1945

The bitter winter of 1944–1945 in Europe showed no signs of easing as Willy James Jr., 24 years of age, 5ft 7in. tall, and 143lb, pulled on his jacket in the stone barracks where some of the men believed Napoleon's troops last slept. James was part of the 25th Replacement Platoon; there were 47 in camp, and there would be 53 by the end of training. James didn't mind the cold. Kansas City, where he'd grown up as the only child of his widowed mother, Lillian James, saw its share of snow that blew in from the central plains. France was no different except perhaps damper.

James exited the barracks with his friend John Hemley, another Midwesterner like himself from St. Louis. Their breaths visible in the frigid air, they crunched over the hard-packed ground toward morning inspection. It was 0620 hours, and they knew once they got moving they wouldn't mind the sub-zero temperatures.

Hemley, walking beside James, flipped through a 16-page orientation booklet they'd received upon their arrival. It had a map of the local town, listings of the times of religious services – Catholic, Jewish, Protestant – and recreational activities. Hemley pointed out the two movie theaters in town, Cinema Nouveau and Cinema Pinson. James smiled and told his friend that was nice to know, but they'd never have time to go.

Infantry training at Ground Forces Reinforcement Center (GFRC) had been recently reduced from six weeks to four due to the critical need to provide front-line replacements as fast as possible. The black volunteers received training in primary weapons and tactics at the squad and platoon level. Each platoon was composed of approximately 50 men, and during the intensive month-long training they grew to know each other well.

As James and Hemley reached the inspection field and fell into formation, Bill Harden of Cincinnati arrived. The trio had met during induction. They hadn't known each other previously as they had all served in different service units.

Harden leaned in, teasing James by asking if he'd run out of stamps yet. James slightly blushed; he wrote to his wife, Valcenie, almost every other day. They'd met in a club in Kansas City, and it had been love at first sight. The couple decided to marry in September 1942, only weeks before James shipped out. They barely had a honeymoon or enjoyed much time as a family with Valcenie's two young children from a previous relationship.

James jabbed Harden right back, stating that at least he had someone to write to back home. Hemley shook his head then changed the subject. He had heard they were starting BAR (Browning Automatic Rifle) training that day, and that's what he'd had his eyes on, being a BAR man. He wanted all the firepower he could get.

James told his friend he could go "shootin' up those Krauts" all he wanted but not him; he wanted to be out on his own scouting or a Forward Observer or maybe even a sniper. Harden told James that Forward Observer was out unless he was in an artillery unit, which he wasn't.

"Attention!" All 50 men in the 25th Replacement Platoon threw their shoulders back and stood with their eyes fixed forward at the call to attention by Sergeant Sam Santo. These were motivated men in the ranks. The majority realized this was a singular opportunity, and they weren't going to squander it. There were fewer absentees and fewer disciplinary problems among the black trainees in proportion to white soldiers being retrained as infantrymen.[2]

After inspection and breakfast, three platoons, the 18th, 25th, and the 32nd, gathered in the dayroom. A Corporal stood beside a motion-picture projector at the back. Instructor Lieutenant Kelsey Harris of 1st Division at the front of the large hall introduced the BAR training film they were about to watch. Harris noted the film had been produced in 1943, but all operational principles of the Browning Automatic Rifle remained the same.

James, Hemley, and Harden were midway back in the room on folding chairs with their platoon, waiting for the film to begin. Harris called to douse the lights, and the clattering of the Bell & Howell started, and patriotic music filled the room. The projector light on the white front wall flickered to an opening title, which read *Official Training Film, T.F. 9 – 1205, The War Department*. James turned to an excited Hemley and pretended to yawn. Hemley punched him in the shoulder, attracting Harris's attention. He shouted, "Pay attention!"

By 1945 the Army had distributed hundreds of instructional films on almost all subjects pertinent to combat soldiers, everything from weapons training to the correct way to put on a condom. The Walt Disney Company was one of the largest and busiest suppliers, with over 90 percent of Disney employees devoted to producing training and propaganda films for the government during the war.[3]

At the GFRC, the instructional film viewings were followed by field training, which provided critical hands-on skills but lacked the urgency of actual combat conditions. As a result, the various divisions, which were preparing to welcome the additional black rifle platoons into their companies, assigned some of their most experienced white combat officers to lead them. The individual infantry regiments then sent their officers ahead to the GFRC for assessment and further training of their forthcoming black platoons.

One of the officers sent was 1st Lieutenant Richard Ralston, a combat veteran with the 99th Division. He was assigned to command the 5th Platoon of K Company. Upon his arrival at GFRC, he was alarmed to discover men not adequately trained for actual combat conditions. The black service troops had undoubtedly gained skills with the weapons, but Ralston immediately discerned they needed psychological training and more comprehensive field training. Ralston knew the intensity of combat would shock most of these men; soldiers were going to die, so he exaggerated the number of deaths that would occur on the battlefield. The psychological ploy was designed to scare anyone out of his unit that wasn't fit to be there. None of his men quit.

The 104th Infantry Division, one of the newer divisions, also sent experienced combat officers ahead to train their expected platoons with specific needs in mind. The 104th Infantry Division (ID) consisted of three primary infantry regiments, the 413th, 414th, and 415th. The 104th, nicknamed the "Timberwolf" Division, gained the moniker as it represented the area in which it was originally formed in 1942, the Pacific Northwest.

The division's insignia was a howling gray timberwolf set against a forest green background. Notable members of the 104th ID in World War II included eventual New York City Mayor Ed Koch, New York Governor Hugh Carey, and Willy James Jr.

The 413th Infantry Regiment (IR), James's eventual outfit, sent ahead 35-year-old 1st Lieutenant Armand J. Serrabella. He was assigned to command the 5th Platoon of G Company attached to the 2nd Platoon. "A.J.," born in Brooklyn, New York, was a graduate of Bayport high school in Bayport, Long Island, New York. He had been a tennis instructor in civilian life. With his thick New York accent, Serrabella carried the swagger of a typical Brooklynite, thoroughly convinced he hailed from the greatest city in the world. Like most gruff New Yorkers, he also had a soft underside. He was loyal to a fault and would hand a friend the shirt off his back if he knew the person needed it.

A.J. attended Officer Candidate School at Fort Benning, Georgia, and joined the 413th as a 2nd Lieutenant. He was one of the regiment's most experienced combat officers, having already received two Purple Hearts.

Serrabella arrived with Art Letherbarrow, the 1st Sergeant of G Company. Like Ralston from the 99th Division, Serrabella immediately determined that the black volunteers needed more focused training to be ready for actual combat.

Serrabella gathered James's 25th Replacement Platoon in the day room and introduced himself and Sergeant Letherbarrow. With a confidence bordering on arrogance, A.J. told his 50 men they were joining a proud division whose motto was, "Nothing in hell stops the 104th," and he expected them all to live up to that. A.J. stressed there was no time to waste; they would go right into marksman training with the M1 Garand. He motioned Sgt. Letherbarrow to his right to grab his rifle as Serrabella began, "Just like New York is the best city in the world, American riflemen are the best in the world. Why? Because they get the best training in the world."

Letherbarrow gripped the M1 in a shooting position and dropped prostrate to the floor as Serrabella continued that there were four firing positions: prone, which his Sergeant was demonstrating, sitting, kneeling, and the standing or off-hand position. Letherbarrow moved into each position as the Lieutenant counted them off. Good positions mean good scores, poor positions mean poor scores, it's as easy as that, Serrabella concluded, waiting for questions.

James and the men had listened politely but had no questions. Serrabella noted a distinct lack of engagement. It was time, he believed, to employ his New York toughness and he raised his voice, telling them they'd better f—kin' get interested. If not, they were gone. He wasn't teaching them the different firing positions so they could plaster a bunch of bullseyes on a target range. He was teaching them to kill their enemy before he could kill them. If they were going to survive on the battlefield, they had to shoot fast and straight from any position. And they had to drop into that position instantly, automatically, without thinking about it. If not, they were dead. Goodbye, sayonara.

James and the platoon were thrown back by Serrabella's dressing-down, but all came to understand during the following days that A.J. was "no bullshit"; he was simply trying to keep them alive and prevent other soldiers in the platoon from dying. There wasn't time for prejudice, and they didn't sense any from the man. Serrabella often stressed that all the white soldiers on the line wanted to know was whether the men to the left and right of them were going to have their back. If not, A.J. warned there were going to be problems – big f—in' problems.

James took to the rifle platoon training well and caught Serrabella's attention with his marksmanship. His accuracy was in the top percentage on the target range, and James was known throughout the platoon as a "damn good shot."

James's birthday was approaching on March 18, and the men were coming to the end of training. Hemley and Harden wanted to do something special for him, but the 18th was their last day in camp so they wouldn't have time to celebrate. A.J. scheduled a final pre-departure meeting with the platoon in the morning on the 18th before they set off on the train.

Hemley stopped by Serrabella's desk at headquarters a few days before the 18th and told him about James's birthday and asked the commander if he could mention it. A.J. agreed, saying it wasn't a problem.

On the morning of the 18th, Serrabella had the platoon gather in the day room. It was apparent they were not the same men who had greeted him four weeks earlier. They'd matured tremendously and now acted like soldiers. A.J. was proud of them, although he didn't let on. Serrabella opened the meeting by first thanking Art Letherbarrow for his superior work and for being the best damn 1st Sergeant in the entire regiment. He told the platoon they should count themselves fortunate training under him. A.J. began a round of applause, which the platoon joined with enthusiasm.

Then A.J. told the men this was not graduation but the first day of the rest of their service as combat soldiers in the US Army.

IMMORTAL VALOR

They'd passed the test and now were going to put those well-earned skills to good use. Serrabella finished by telling the men that generally, on a training mission, one particular soldier will stand out. This replacement training assignment, he informed them, was no exception. Murmurs began as men looked at one another.

Sgt. Letherbarrow stepped away to wheel a small steel cart forward covered by a blue cloth. A.J. waited for Letherbarrow to arrive up front then continued. With training now concluded, he said he wanted to recognize one soldier, and in fact, it was the man's birthday.

The platoon instantly knew whom A.J. was talking about, and cheers began. A.J. announced that Private Willy James, now Private First Class (PFC) James, had received the award for leadership and marksmanship, and they had had the kitchen mess bake something up.

Letherbarrow pulled the blue cloth from the top of the cart, revealing an aluminum foil serving tray containing a long chocolate-frosted cake in the shape of a rifle with a decoration of a Private First Class stripe. Men applauded as James looked embarrassed, not knowing what to say. Serrabella motioned James forward. James thanked A.J., who handed him his new PFC stripe and patted him on the shoulder. Then James turned to the platoon and told them he was sure gonna remember his 25th birthday for a long, long time. Later that day, A.J., James, Hemley, Harden, and the rest of the 5th Platoon of G Company of the 413th IR boarded an eastbound train for the two-day journey to the front.

Chapter 8

Crossing the Rhine

Arriving at dusk on the 20th at the train depot in Cologne, the men were stunned to near silence. Utter devastation surrounded them. Allied bombing had reduced the ancient Roman city to little more than a vast pile of dust and rubble, except for the blackened Cologne Cathedral, which still stood.

A.J. led the platoon through the city to the outskirts, undamaged from Allied bombing but left deserted. Along the way, several white soldiers stopped and stared at the black platoon and talked in whispers. Serrabella shouted to his men to pay the other soldiers no attention; just do their jobs on the line and they wouldn't get any flack. He'd make sure of it.

G Company had taken over several houses in the immediate suburbs of Cologne, and there was ample space for the new platoon to catch some shut-eye. In addition, the 2nd Battalion had just returned from three days in Efferen re-equipping, and Serrabella planned to distribute new rifles to his platoon later that evening.

Although at the time a *Stars and Stripes* headline had proclaimed "The 104th Takes Cologne," there was still a good deal of mopping up to do, and the area was an active combat zone. German mortar shelling in the divisional zone was relentless, and the constant bombardment rattled the newly arrived black soldiers' nerves. They tried, however, not to show it.

With the platoon settled into a large home outside the city just after 2100 hours, Serrabella and Letherbarrow carried in two long green crates with a crowbar sitting on the top one. They set the crates down on a sturdy farmhouse table in the kitchen. As James and the men gathered around, A.J. said, "Gentlemen compliments of the Springfield Armory back home." Serrabella then cracked open the top crate revealing ten sparkling new M1 Garands. Sgt. Letherbarrow directed two soldiers to bring in three more boxes from outside.

Serrabella passed out the rifles while Letherbarrow recorded the serial numbers in a logbook. As James ran his hand down the barrel of his sleek new weapon admiring it, A.J. joked, telling Pvt. James to meet his new best friend, one that was gonna keep him alive. Receiving his shiny new Garand, John Hemley turned to James with a grin, saying that it ain't a Browning; he liked it just fine.

After the guns were distributed, the Lieutenant informed the platoon the regiment would be on the move early the following day. They were headed south to Honeff for an eventual river crossing. Elements of the First Army had already crossed at the Remagen bridgehead further south over the Ludendorff bridge.

The 413th was operating under a new tactical commander, Lieutenant Colonel William Summers, from Tulsa, Oklahoma. He'd taken over for Colonel Waltz on March 4, who'd been with the outfit since their formation in Oregon. The regiment's new broad mission in late March 1944 in conjunction with 3rd Armored was to clear out the enemy east of the Rhine.

On March 21, 1944, James's platoon joined the 413th as part of the 104th ID. They jumped in 6 x 6 trucks and rolled 25 miles south in a convoy deep into the Rhine Valley. The Rhine River represented the final natural barrier into the heartland of Germany. The men traveling along the river's banks could see the ancient castles of Germany towering high on wooded cliffs on the opposite side. The river itself was smoke-filled primarily due to the engineers setting off smoke pots on both sides of the waterway to mask the construction of a pontoon bridge.[4]

With the pontoon bridge in place later in the afternoon of the 21st, the regiment crossed into Germany without incident at

Königswinter in the shadow of Petersberg mountain and Castle Siegfried. Their orders from VII Corps were to extend the Remagen bridgehead to the east. Their first action was to relieve the 26th IR "Blue Spaders" of the 1st Infantry Division.

Consolidating at the jump-off point, the 413th and 415th infantry regiments were under constant German bombardment, everything from mortars to nebelwerfer rockets to 88mm guns; anything the Germans could scrape together to heave at them. They were penned in for the moment.

Although the 413th was spinning its wheels, three soldiers in K Company in Germscheid performed yeoman service, but not on the battlefield. A German woman in the town began to give birth in the middle of the day. With no doctors available, Captain Hayden Bower, PFC Gibert, and T/5 Joe Diamond of K Company volunteered for delivery duty, but none actually knew how to deliver a baby. Soldiers hauled over an SCR300 backpack radio, and Captain Furlong, back at the battalion aid station, talked them through it. Everything went well, and they nicknamed the baby "Roger Out."[5]

On March 23–24, the 413th and the 415th Regiments were ordered to resume the offensive. Divisional command directed them to attack the high ground directly in front of them. Before daylight on the 24th, after encountering strong small arms and artillery resistance, the regiments advanced 1,000 yards and secured assigned objectives. The units also took some German soldiers as prisoners.

Third Armored with the 414th attached was directed to pass through the 1st and the 104th Division on March 25 with this breakout. Their new objective: seize Altenkirchen 25 miles to the east. The 413th and 415th would closely follow the armor, destroying the enemy within the zone. It was here on the east side of the Rhine that American troops had their first real encounter with German civilians. They stood with their arms crossed and lips pursed as the convoys rolled through. Needless to say, the black soldiers within the ranks came as a great surprise to many.

The 413th decided to fan out away from the armor-clogged highway, threading down side roads and through fields. They broke up scattered German defenders in isolated groups and captured

120 prisoners in the first couple of days. The 3rd Armored received new orders redirecting them to Paderborn 80 miles to the north as the 413th continued eastward.

German soldiers to the north started to surrender in large numbers and the 414th mounted on tanks with 3rd Armored seized the town of Marburg, where 3,000 German soldiers were captured.

An Associated Press war correspondent traveling with 3rd Armored toward Paderborn painted a vivid picture of the noose starting to tighten around the German defenders:

> Behind the greatest tank force ever massed under the leadership of a British or American Army commander in this war, Lt. Gen. Courtney H. Hodges has grouped some of the finest infantry divisions in the European theater. German soldiers by the hundreds are deserting and changing into civilian clothing, hoping to escape becoming prisoners. Other units are destroying and abandoning their equipment and then are trying to march across American lines on foot. But they still are organized as fighting units and carry enough automatic weapons to put up a scrap.[6]

Not all of the enemy was ready to give up. On April 2, the 413th encountered dug-in SS troops in the wooded mountainous areas between the towns of Rimbeck and Scherfede. There were several hundred fanatical young SS troops with concealed sniper platforms built into the trees and numerous panzerfaust squads that kept up a steady fire.

A stubborn captured SS 20-year-old Lieutenant from the 741st Jäger Regiment expressed to his American captors at the time the iron will of the German soldier and all Germany to fight back against the Allied invaders. He reportedly said:

> Whatever stretches of land you may occupy in Germany, you will never conquer or defeat the German nation. As long as there is a German alive, he will fight you. No Allied soldier will ever feel safe on German soil. A master race born to govern cannot be held down eternally. We shall never capitulate. There are thousands of fanatical German youngsters who are willing to sacrifice everything for a defeated Fatherland.[7]

With help from B Company of the 750th Tank Battalion, the 413th started to break down the resistance of stalwart SS defenders, but in the town of Scherfede, 1st and 2nd Platoon of G Company only gained a toe-hold, and it was impossible to push farther without heavy losses.

The platoons decided to employ psychological warfare, setting up a loud-speaker on a tank and blasting a surrender message to the Germans holed up in the town. Approximately 30 regular army German soldiers surrendered, but the remaining SS troops fled into the nearby well-defended Hardehausen forest. G Company commander Captain Laurance Wolfe, seeing the SS troops withdraw, thought it an excellent opportunity for his new black rifle platoon to see their first action. To their great frustration, James's platoon had been held back from combat duty with the 2nd Platoon, and this assignment would without a doubt be their trial by fire.

Lt. Serrabella received the order and brought it to the platoon. He assigned Staff Sergeant Harvey Moseley from Mansfield, Ohio, to lead the mission while A.J. remained with the Command Group. Moseley separated the remaining platoon into three rifle squads, Able, Baker, and Charlie, with 12 men apiece.*

Able would lead the assault locating the German position with two scouts, followed up by Baker with their BAR man and additional riflemen. Charlie squad would press the attack after Able had found the enemy and Baker had engaged them.

Staff Sgt. Moseley selected two scouts for Able squad, PFC Bent T. Brown of Charleston, West Virginia, whose nickname was "Big Slim" and Willy James as second scout.

Sgt. Moseley positioned the squads into a column then checked with Baker and Charlie's team leaders. The soldiers in line chafed at the bit. Their moment had finally come.

Sgt. Moseley made his way back to the Able squad to James and Brown and asked them if they were ready for this. Without hesitation, both responded in the affirmative. He then ordered them forward up into the forest. The rest of Able would follow 150 yards behind.

* After 1956 the military changed Able and Baker to Alpha and Bravo.

As Able squad set off following James and Brown, a cheer rose from Baker and Charlie, which were soon on the move as well, pursuing the hardened SS soldiers up into the hills.

White infantrymen in the 2nd Platoon folded their arms and watched the squads advance up into the forest. They looked to one another, commenting that the men certainly had confidence, they would give them that.

The squads, armed with only rifles and sten guns,* came under fire almost immediately. "Big Slim," 10 yards ahead of James, was struck in the right forearm and thigh and went down. Able squad converged as James returned fire, then shouted to Sgt. Moseley that he'd spotted the enemy location. SS troops were behind a group of pines 200 yards to their northwest. Baker squad arrived, and Sgt. Moseley directed the BAR man to the German position. An intense firefight began.

Charlie squad, staying low, fanned out to flank the location and came under intense rifle and small arms fire from a German position higher up in the trees. The men took up defensive positions and returned deadly accurate fire, wounding and killing several SS soldiers, including a sniper. The coordinated attack by the platoon proved too much for the scattered SS defenders, and after several minutes a Mauser with a bandage tied to its barrel was thrust out from behind some thick brush. Other "white flags" soon followed.

In the end, the three black squads of James's platoon captured or killed 40 SS troops by sheer determination in record time. Their action was so noteworthy it attracted the attention of Ann Stringer, a United Press war correspondent.

Stringer, a 26-year-old from Tyler, Texas, was one of the few women permitted to report from the front lines. A foreign affairs journalist for years, she took over duties as war correspondent from her husband Bill Stringer who was killed by a German tank during the Normandy invasion. Attached to the First Army, she reported the war from France, Holland, Belgium, and Germany.[8]

---

* Reporter Ann Stringer stated that the men carried sten guns, which was a British weapon and it is unconfirmed if the unit had this weapon in their arsenal.

Ann decided to spread the news of the black platoon's achievement far and wide. On April 3, she wrote in an article titled, "With the 104th Timberwolf Division South of Paderborn, Germany":

> An all-Negro platoon saw action for the first time today and licked Adolf Hitler's supermen. Within a few hours, these eager infantrymen, armed with only rifles and sten guns, captured or killed 40 crack Nazi SS troops, cleared two thickly wooded hills, and chalked up a record to make any veteran battle group envious.[9]

Soldiers interviewed for the article said the platoon nicknamed themselves the "Dusky Devastators." The successful mission secured Lt. Serrabella's untested platoon respect within the regiment, and commander Lt. Col. Bill Summers no longer kept them out of the fight. The 413th's Cannon Company 105mm howitzers subsequently pounded the southern and western fringes of the hills, firing over 160 rounds and killing at least 60 more German soldiers. The last defender in the Hardehausen forest was captured on April 4.

Organized German resistance significantly reduced by this date, and the division was hurriedly regrouped in preparation for further advance. The next natural obstruction was the Weser River, 45 miles to the east.

On April 5, the 413th relieved elements of the 9th Armored Division and the 2nd Infantry Division at Teutonia, Bonneburg, and Borlinghausen. The 415th moved into a position to the right of the 413th. Throughout the day of the 6th, patrols of the 413th and 415th probed enemy positions to the east in preparation for an attack on the 7th.

At 0700 hours on April 7, the 413th attacked to the east and overcame pockets of stubborn enemy resistance to reach the Weser River in the afternoon. At 1515 hours that day, the Germans blew the bridge crossing only minutes before the 3rd Battalion of the 413th reached the near end.

G.K. Hodenfield of *Stars and Stripes* reported the action the following day:

> The Jerries blew up the bridge across the Weser River yesterday almost right in the face of Lt. Col. Bill Summers of Tulsa, Oklahoma, But today, the doughs of his 413th Regt. of the 104th "Timberwolf Division" are across the 80-yard wide obstacle and headed east.

Chapter 9

Into the Lion's Mouth

WESER RIVER, GERMANY
APRIL 8, 1945

At 0400 hours on the morning of April 8, the remainder of the 3rd Battalion crossed the Weser in assault boats. They were followed by James and the men in the 2nd Battalion before the engineers constructed a pontoon bridge. On that fog-shrouded morning, the Weser bridgehead became the point of departure to attack and capture the village of Lippoldsberg adjacent to the river. Lt. Serrabella's platoon was selected to lead the assault to capture the town. Again, stubborn SS troops defended the village, and it would require intense house-to-house fighting.

During the morning, John Hemley noticed that James had been subdued since the river crossing, and he asked his friend what was wrong. James, who was now the first scout of the platoon, the assignment he'd desired in training camp, said he felt uneasy. Something wasn't right.

Hemley looked around at the zero visibility and said it was just the damn fog. It was making everything feel creepy. James shook him off, saying it was something more.

A.J. came upon James and Hemley and sensed something was up. He asked them what was the matter. James looked up and told him it was just the damn fog, he guessed. Serrabella checked his watch and told James and Hemley to get prepared; they'd be underway in the next 15 minutes. A.J. then gave James final instructions on the scout. Serrabella wanted him 150 yards ahead of the platoon. James was probably going to draw fire right away, but that would give up the German positions on the west entrance to the town.

As A.J. left, Hemley looked around again at the fog, shook his head, and said it was like you couldn't breathe and it was too damn quiet to boot. James and Hemley clasped hands, and James said he'd see him later. Hemley told him to count on it.

Lt. Serrabella, next to PFC James, lined up his platoon, splitting them in half on each side of the road spaced 10 yards apart and off-angle from each other. A.J. turned to James and nodded him onward. James stepped forward, disappearing into the fog alone. When he was 30 yards away from the first small stucco house opposite the river, he came under small arms and submachine gun fire.

Serrabella, leading the platoon 200 yards behind James, held up a closed fist to halt movement. The platoon heard German shouts and men running ahead of them in the fog. The squads held their rifles in front of them at the ready.

James slipped behind a long low stone wall. He had no idea how the Germans had spotted him in the fog, but it was evident that they had. Bullets ricocheted off the top of the wall above James, scattering stone dust and debris over the top of him as he crawled forward behind it.

As the temperature rose, the thick fog started to thin out. James, lying at the end of the low wall, was able to note the location of a few enemy positions. He knew there were more, but he couldn't see them from his vantage point. He felt someone coming up behind him, turned, and saw, crouching low, Lt. Serrabella moving up.

A.J. arrived and asked how the situation looked. James said there were a couple of riflemen in the first two homes, but he couldn't see that well from this position. Serrabella frowned as James offered to move further forward. He pointed to an overturned metal cart on the side of the street 20 yards from them. It could provide a better vantage point and cover. Serrabella gave him the go-ahead but then told him to get right back to the platoon with the information he'd gathered. James agreed.

As A.J. headed back to the platoon, James waited for another 15 minutes, staying absolutely still as the gunfire died down, then he made a break for it. Gunfire pelted his path, but he darted behind the metal cart as bullets pinged off the opposite side. This location had a much better field of view, and James noted several homes on both sides of the street with enemy infantry.

Within ten minutes, the German gunfire died down again, and James knew it was time to get back to the platoon. He readied himself to dash out exposed in the open toward the low stone wall. He was an excellent sprinter, and now he had to make every step count.

James drew a deep breath and bolted out from behind the metal cart as gunfire erupted again, bullets buzzing past him like angry hornets. He neared the stone wall and dove behind it unscathed.

James then made his way back to the platoon. He saw Hemley in the line who gave him a thumbs-up, then he gave Serrabella, who'd rolled out a map, all the intelligence he'd gathered. James pointed out the enemy locations to the south and east and suggested possible alternate maneuver routes. Serrabella was appreciative, and he assigned PFC James to lead the platoon forward. James nodded with a slight smile and said, "Yes, sir."

James headed out once again, with A.J. on the opposite side of the road. The men in the platoon followed in three rifle squads. Unfortunately, the fog had dissipated a great deal by this time and would not shield their movements as it had earlier. James, on the south side of the street, cautiously moved forward. He constantly checked Lt. Serrabella, who was hand-signaling the platoon 10 yards to the north.

The foreboding James had felt earlier of things not feeling right returned in greater intensity. He tried unsuccessfully to shake off the feeling. Serrabella led them on the planned attack route skirting around the main road to the north side, then closed in on one of the first small houses on the outskirts near the river.

Suddenly James heard a German shout about 100 yards ahead. The soldier called an alarm. A.J. had little time to react as a Waffen-SS soldier stepped from the doorway of the house they were nearing. A burst of muzzle fire from the German's shoulder-slung MP 40 submachine gun tore a path across Serrabella's chest. A.J. staggered backward, dropping onto the dirt road in a growing pool of blood.

James shouted, "Lieutenant!" as intense German gunfire erupted from every direction in the village. PFC James fired several shots from his Garand toward the village center, then threw his rifle over his back and raced to Serrabella's side.

As James reached the man and tried to grab his shoulders with both hands to pull him to safety, the foreboding James sensed overtook him. The sounds of gunfire seemed to die away, and James knew he was in the crosshairs of several German rifle sights. He had nowhere to escape. James stopped, looked up, and saw a sniper in a second-floor window two blocks down the street. The sniper pulled the trigger. A flash was the last thing James's eyes saw, then his world went black. He fell forward next to his commander, shot through the head.

The battle escalated, but the "Dusky Devastators," with their superior numbers, overwhelmed the hardened SS defenders of Lippoldsberg by midnight that night.

Victory had come at a high cost; four more soldiers in Serrabella's platoon died in the all-day battle, and several more were wounded. Due to Willy James Jr.'s heroism and sacrifice, the 104th Division was able to smash through the Weser bridgehead, allowing the armor to crush the will of the German people to fight on as the excerpt below from the 413th's Regimental History describes:

> That evening, 8 April, the 413th again saw the tanks and half-tracks of Third Armored roll through the lines bumper to bumper. Civilians at first stared haughtily; then, as the column filed by in a never-ending stream, they became first humble then panic-stricken. The miles of American vehicles manned by tough fighting men were too much for even the most confident Nazi.

PFC Willy James Jr. was recommended for the Distinguished Service Cross on May 26, 1945 by 1st Lieutenant Herbert G. Brown, one of the seasoned officers in G Company. Within a month, the recommendation was approved by the 413th's

2nd Battalion, regimental commanders, and commanders in the 104th Infantry Division.

In September 1945, PFC James's Distinguished Service Cross was awarded posthumously to his widow, Valcenie James, by Seventh Army commander Lieutenant General Geoffrey Keyes. In 1997 Willy James's widow also accepted the Medal of Honor on his behalf.

In 2001, Seventh Army Reserve Command in Bamberg, Germany, renamed its Bamberg Center the Willy F. James Jr. Army Reserve Center. This honor ensured a lasting legacy to his heroic sacrifice.

WILLY F. JAMES JR. MEDAL OF HONOR CITATION

For extraordinary heroism in action on 7 April 1945* near Lippoldsberg, Germany. As lead scout during a maneuver to secure and expand a vital bridgehead, Private First Class James was the first to draw enemy fire. He was pinned down for over an hour, during which time he observed enemy positions in detail. Returning to his platoon, he assisted in working out a new plan of maneuver. He then led a squad in the assault, accurately designating targets as he advanced until he was killed by enemy machine-gun fire[10] while going to the aid of his fatally wounded platoon leader. Private First Class James' fearless, self-assigned actions, coupled with his diligent devotion to duty exemplified the finest traditions of the Armed Forces.

* The History of the 413th Regiment, which was written and authorized by the regiment in 1946 and Timberwolf Tracks: the History of the 104th Infantry Division, 1942–1945 by Leo A. Hoegh and Howard J. Doyle state the battle in Lippoldsberg occurred on April 8, 1945.

PART FOUR

Edward Allen Carter Jr.

Chapter 10

Baptism by Fire

INTERNATIONAL SETTLEMENT, SHANGHAI, CHINA
JANUARY 1932

Compact, scrappy, dark-skinned Eddie Carter, aged 15, picked up a wooden bat, struck the hard earth twice, and entered the dirt-outlined batter's box in the wide alley off Nanking Road. The lanky, pale British pitcher, Squires, aged 16, Eddie's schoolmate, looked over his shoulder and nodded his outfield back. They were already backing up.

Eddie, a natural at many sports, including basketball, smiled at the distance the outfield was moving back as he tapped the dirt again with his bat.

Squires turned back to Eddie, snarled at the boy's overconfidence, wound up, and threw a winder that sailed wild.

Eddie laughed, watching the catcher scramble for the errant pitch, then taunted the British boy, asking him if he knew how to play ball.

Squires threw down his glove and stormed the batter's box.

Gathered schoolmates chanted, "Fight, fight, fight," which reverberated down the alley as Squires stormed toward Eddie.

Eddie smiled, threw aside his bat, and pulled up his sweatshirt sleeves.

The two boys crashed together, punching and kicking as their teammates encircled them. Neither could bring the other to the ground as they jostled toward Nanking Road with a crowd in tow.

Eddie and Squires stumbled out onto chaotic Nanking Road. Creaking rickshaws sailing in every direction skirted around them; drivers shook their fists and cursed in several different languages.

A nearby barrel-chested American Marine in wool khaki winter service coat and patterned winter cap, part of the 4th Marine Regiment, saw the commotion and rushed to the scene. American military planners had ordered the "China Marines" to the Far East in January 1927. Their mission – protect the lives, property, and commerce of Americans in the International Zone.

The shrill shriek of a stainless-steel whistle cowered the boys.

Eddie and Squires looked around in a daze, searching for the source of the ear-piercing noise.

Sergeant Connelly glared at the two as they released their sweaty grips on each other. They were well known to Connelly. Eddie, Squires, and the rest of the boys attended the military academy in Shanghai. Eddie's father had enrolled him to instill some yet-to-be-displayed discipline. Believing Eddie was at fault because of his history of troublemaking, Connelly collared him and dragged him back to his home to much protest.

Young Eddie Carter Jr. was part of a bustling population that occupied the International Settlement in Shanghai, China, in the early 1930s, composed of British, American, French, Japanese, and Dutch citizens. It was a chaotic cosmopolitan melting pot of missionaries and mercenaries crammed into eight square miles in the middle of a teeming Asian metropolis.

With a population of 3 million on the East China Sea coast, Shanghai had become known as the "Paris of the Orient." US dollars traveled 20 times as far, which was in sharp contrast to the United States, which was sinking into the depths of the Great Depression.

But booming, wealthy Shanghai had attracted neighboring Japan's attention. The ambitious island nation had its sights set on global expansion with the Tanaka Plan, and the Chinese knew it. Growing anti-Japanese sentiment was rampant, and the seacoast city was a virtual powder keg ready to blow.

Los Angeles-born, Eddie Carter had recently relocated to Shanghai from Calcutta in 1927 with his father and two younger siblings. Edward Sr., a missionary with the Los Angeles-based Holiness Church, was not a physically large man but his oratory skills made his presence loom larger than life.

Eddie's birth mother, Mary, whom he was very close with, was an Anglo-Indian from Calcutta who had run off with their church's treasurer while the family lived in India. The hole she left in Eddie's heart would take years to fill. In 1928 Edward Carter Sr. remarried to Mary "Marie" Westerhold, a wealthy young German woman with bright red hair.

Due to the earlier family break-up and his father's quick remarriage, young Eddie turned rebellious and distanced himself from his strict father. His dad meanwhile had become busier than ever with his new wife and building his Christian flock in Shanghai.

Eddie sulked in his bedroom in the small apartment; he heard the front door shut, signaling Sgt. Connelly's departure, and he braced himself. Beatings were a frequent part of his childhood and he anticipated a walloping this time.

Edward Carter Sr. appeared in the doorway. Eddie held his breath. He knew he was becoming too much for his father to handle; his independent streak was catching fire.

Edward Sr. quoted several passages from scripture about following a wicked path, leaving his son with a warning that he was on the wrong path and road to eternal damnation if he didn't change his ways.

After the browbeating, Eddie bowed his head, aching to scream. He longed to free himself from his father's domineering shadow. However, that time had not yet come, and Eddie looked up and offered a weak promise to try to do better.

Edward Sr. frowned, turned abruptly, and exited the room.

Eddie's eyes followed him with surprise for the absence of the beating.

Perhaps his freedom was closer than he thought.

✱✱✱

JANUARY 28, 1932

Eddie fell out of bed, hitting the wood floor hard. *What was that noise, he wondered, and why was he on the floor as he shook his groggy head awake?*

The earth-shaking noise rumbled again, a deafening roar followed by another and another. Eddie's younger sister, Miriam, in the bed across from him, sat up screaming. His brother William in the other bed continued to doze. Pictures crashed to the floor all around Eddie from the bedroom walls. It was just past midnight, and the International Settlement was under attack from a fleet of Japanese warships in the harbor.

Edward Carter Sr. shouted for his children to come as he rushed to their bedroom, followed by his new wife; he instructed them to gather their things and accompany him to the church sanctuary.

Eddie protested, wanting to know what was happening, but his father ignored his pleas and immediately ordered them all out of the home.

Eddie grunted under his breath that he believed it was the *Japs*, as he grabbed his coat and followed his family downstairs to the street.

Nanking Road was in a state of absolute panic. Fire and explosions lit up the sky. People crisscrossed in all directions, some pulled carts, others begged rickshaw drivers to carry them to safety even though the roads were too clogged to navigate, and the fare was ten times the regular price.

Residents trapped within the International Settlement found themselves under siege in what would become known as the "Shanghai Incident." The Japanese had amassed 30 warships, including several aircraft carriers and 7,000 troops outside Shanghai, and bombarded the defenseless International Zone. American historian Barbara Tuchman, author of *The Guns of August*, described the event as "the first terror bombing of a civilian population."

Hours turned into days in the shelter, and young Eddie, now a refugee, languished. His younger brother and sister found playmates, but Eddie itched to escape while his father and stepmother busily spread comfort and saw to other refugees' spiritual needs within the sanctuary.

Gunfire rang out day and night. Explosions that were too close for comfort rocked the shelter. Given the situation, young Carter felt he had no choice. War was raging, and this was his opportunity for escape and adventure. Carter had already begun marksman training at the Shanghai Military Academy. *It was time, he thought, to put his skills to use.*

Carter slipped out of the shelter one night after his family had gone to sleep. Navigating through the darkened Shanghai streets he knew like the back of his hand, he found the 31,000-strong Chinese 19th Route Army's front line, primarily the 78th and 60th Divisions in the Chapei district.

A Route Army was a type of military organization within the Chinese Republic. Although the 19th was a part of the Chinese National Revolutionary Army, they were not looked upon favorably by municipal officials. The 19th were considered a rag-tag warlord force with their cotton uniforms, tennis shoes, and signature straw hats slung over their backs. Regardless of appearance and reputation, they were well trained by German advisors and had a deep hatred for the Japanese.

Moving through the darkened street, Carter came face to face with a picket guard from the 19th who demanded in Cantonese that he halt. The guard had his Hanyang 88 rifle leveled at Carter's chest.

Having learned several Chinese dialects at the academy as well as German, Carter replied in Cantonese that he wanted to join the fight.

The guard returned his rifle to his shoulder and motioned young Carter forward. He quizzed him on his military skill level, and when Carter responded that he attended the academy, the guard laughed. The picket guard motioned him forward with a wave. The 19th were desperate for fighting men. Even a 15-year-old boy from the military academy could fill a gap in the trenches.

The Japanese's initial infantry assault targeted the rail center at Chapei. North Rail Station was a labyrinth of twisting tracks and rail sheds, Shanghai's transportation hub. Admiral Shiozawa of the attacking Japanese fleet predicted, with contempt, that his forces would take the rail hub in three hours. His prediction was premature. The 19th held off the enemy assault with snipers stationed on the train shed rooftops. The Japanese sustained many casualties and withdrew.

FEBRUARY 14, 1932

The Army put Carter to work right away – filling sandbags. He was now part of an Independent Brigade. The 19th had gained confidence holding off the Japanese attack, but they knew the enemy would return with reinforcements. Soldiers dug a vast network of defensive trenches, positioned machine guns, and focused on fortifying their position in the slums of the Chapei district.

Covered in dirt and grime, Carter finished filling a sandbag and paused to watch the steady stream of misery, the impoverished refugees fleeing Chapei. They were the poorest of the poor, the young, old, and infirm, now homeless with a bleak future ahead of them. The sight made Carter reflect. *Had he left his family behind for this?*

He returned to his shovel and sunk it back into the hard winter soil. At that moment, Carter heard shouting, turned, and saw several soldiers pointing skyward.

A single Japanese Mitsubishi biplane with the distinctive red rising sun insignia on the side circled 1,000 feet above and then swooped in low for a closer look. Scattered 19th Infantry soldiers took potshots at the plane, but it escaped their fire.

The scout plane was joined two minutes later by five Japanese bombers, which zeroed in on Carter's position. Shouted orders snaked down the line to seek cover as the bombers unleashed their deadly payload of 100lb incendiary explosives.

Refugees clogging the Markham Road Bridge across Soochow Creek had no room to move – there was no escape. What unfolded was the most horrifying sight Carter had ever witnessed as the terror-stricken refugees tried desperately to scramble over one another as the falling incendiaries ignited in their midst, burning them all alive.

Carter's ranks did not fare any better. One doomed soldier rushed toward him, a human torch, engulfed in flames, flailing his arms. As the screaming soul ran past Carter, the soldier's flailing arms fell away, still on fire, as the body continued forward.

Lost in shocked stupor a moment, Carter felt a hand grab his shoulder; he spun around, and his section commander shoved a Hanyang 88 toward him and pointed in the direction of the distant Woosung Creek. Four companies of Japanese Marines, 400 men, were embarking from the opposite shore to attack their position.

Carter grabbed the rifle then felt a strange sensation, his heart pounding in his chest. He had never felt this odd sensation of opposing emotions, fear, and excitement simultaneously. Teetering on edge between the two, Carter could go either way: flee in the opposite direction of the battle as fast as his legs could carry him or jump down in the trench, grab extra clips, and get down to business. He chose the latter.

The 19th were scrappers like he was. They had already held off the Japanese Marines once through a combination of strategy and good fortune. They had landed the lucky first punch but now had to counter a much larger retaliatory strike.

In addition, little did the front-line troops in the 19th know, but the embarking Japanese Marines were only the vanguard of a much larger infantry force, the Japanese Ninth Division more than 10,000 strong, which had landed during the night at Shanghai in seven transports.

Carter, checking over his rifle, heard his name shouted as his commander, Chaing, directed him toward a gap between men on the forward trench wall. Carter was desperate to know how near the Japanese were getting as he made sure the safety was off his Hanyang 88.

Carter slapped a five-round en-bloc clip into the bottom of his rifle magazine; he sensed a wave of excitement drifting down the line from his right. He leaned back and turned to the right and saw the reason for the rush of enthusiasm.

Moving confidently down the trench, encouraging the troops, was the Commanding General of the 19th himself, Tsai Ting-chai, beloved by the men. Ting-chai, a lanky, youthful, and somewhat circumspect commander, was a veteran of 170 campaigns yet just 39 years of age. In public statements, he made clear who his enemies were. He said, "These are my enemies: Communists, Chinese militarists, and Japanese imperialists."[1]

Ting-chai liked to consider himself as "one of the men" and dressed as modestly as the humblest Private, scorning all gold braid and ribbons.

He kept very tight order, however; violating Ting-chai's rules resulted in swift and severe punishment. Infractions included looting, disrupting morale, gambling, cowardice, and laxity in performance of duty. Six offenses were punishable by death during wartime. Ting-chai also demanded temperance in his men, and drinking samshu, the popular Chinese intoxicant, was prohibited.

The soldier to the left of Carter tapped him on the shoulder and postulated that they must be going over first and that was why the General had appeared.

Carter let the comment sink in.

As Ting-chai approached his position, the General paused and gave Carter a sideways look, "American?" he asked.

Carter, too nervous to reply, acknowledged the General with a quick nod.

Ting-chai's lip curled to an approving smile.

Commander Chaing shouted to get on the line as Ting-chai skirted away to safety, and Carter scrambled up to the lip of the trench, keeping his head low.

He could see the first elements of the embarking Japanese reaching the nearshore and hurriedly erecting mortar positions to shell the 19th's forward trenches. Other Japanese in this first wave spread out, establishing sniper positions.

An unexpected air group bombing raid from Japanese carrier *Kaga*, and an artillery salvo from armored cruiser *Izumo* suddenly descended upon the 19th's position. The ground shook as explosions tore up the earth, scattering white-hot shrapnel and debris down upon the men. In addition, deadly mortar shells began falling within the 19th's ranks from the newly secured nearshore enemy positions.

Carter peered through the smoke across the battlefield and saw that one of the 19th's machine gun emplacements, the one protecting his trench, had been breached. It had sustained a direct hit from an enemy shell, leaving behind a smoking crater.

These well-trained Japanese sailor-infantry soldiers were often called Marines. Their uniform was a shipboard winter-style blue, single-breasted tunic with a stand-up collar. Their khaki-colored steel helmet was a variant of the old Dutch MK16 in the shape of a dome with a short protruding rim all the way around. It had an anchor emblem on the front. The amphibious force's official name was the Special Naval Landing Force (SNLF). They had a reputation as a formidable force that would fight nearly to the last man.

The Special Naval Landing Force would later lead the Philippine invasion in 1941 and mount a stubborn defense against American Marines determined to take control of Betio Island on the Tarawa atoll in November 1943.

Amidst the enemy fire and falling mortars, Carter heard a soft thud and the soldier to the left of him went limp, clipped in the right temple by a sniper.

A strange sound then arose behind Carter above the battle din. He turned around and saw Japanese civilians, most likely from the International Settlement, on scattered rooftops surrounding the battle area shouting, "Banzai! Banzai!" the patriotic Japanese battle cry at the top of their lungs. They were cheering their fellow countrymen on to Carter's and the 19th's destruction.

Anger gripped Carter as his section commander prepared them to fire, and he steadied his bolt action rifle awaiting the order.

Chaing shouted the fire command.

The Independent Brigade unleashed a fusillade.

Carter's accuracy was off; his first shot sailed harmlessly into the battle mist missing the intended target, a gunner in one of the mortar companies. He paused and berated himself for not remembering his academy marksman training. His anger caused him to jerk the trigger.

His section commander shouted again to fire.

Carter snapped the rifle's bolt back, took aim, slowed his breathing, exhaled, and on the pause squeezed the trigger. The 8mm rimless round tore into the chest of one of the soldiers in the Japanese mortar crew some 300 yards away, and he dropped instantly.

Carter's section was having some success holding the enemy assault back, but the Japanese would not disperse. He knew the order would come soon to attack, which meant exiting the trench and charging headlong into close infantry combat.

Carter peeked over the lip of the trench again and saw the enemy infantry forming lines preparing to launch their coordinated frontal attack. The time had come. Commander Chaing raised his whistle, shouted to prepare to advance, then BLEW.

As the shrill, high-pitched squeal of the whistle melted away, Carter rose with 300 other men in his trench section and scrambled over the top.

As he cleared the lip of the trench, the cacophony of battle stilled, and he felt fellow soldiers almost fade away as he advanced through the battle murk alone. Carter entered another world where time slowed, and fear was nonexistent.

Moving forward, he and his comrades in the 19th found little cover as he coolly advanced and fired. The enemy line 300 yards distant was a smoky blur interrupted by muzzle flashes. Carter wasn't sure if he'd struck anything; he just targeted their fire.

Halfway across the field, he ran out of ammunition clips and crouched to grab the rifle of a dead soldier just ahead of him. As he did, an advancing Japanese Marine appeared out of the smoke and aimed his rifle at Carter but was instantly cut down by a soldier in the 19th bringing up the rear.

Carter, still crouching, nodded thanks, then peered forward across the battlefield. The smoke was clearing, and he could see the Japanese lines faltering as scattered enemy troops began limping away.

As they retreated, the Japanese were hit by Chinese artillery, which had relocated a mile to the rear and was now fully engaged.

Carter looked back toward his trench and saw Chaing waving them rearward to their defensive position away from the killing field. There was no need to pursue the trapped Japanese on the nearshore; the artillery would finish the job. Throughout the Chinese Army's ranks, it was becoming well known that although the Japanese Special Naval Landing Forces were fierce fighters, they struggled to take and hold ground.

The *New York Times* would describe the battle that occurred on February 14, 1932, as "the most desperate fighting that has taken place since the hostilities have broken out between the Japanese and Chinese on January 28."

Nearly a draw, casualties were equal in number on both sides, although official Chinese reports of the total number killed or wounded were later revised upward.

It was Carter's baptism by fire in his first battle, and his courage and calm did not go unrecognized. The fact that he was an American fighting with the Chinese Army also enhanced his stature. He stood out for all the right reasons, and being an African American to the Chinese only made him more exceptional. A short time after the hard-fought battle, a remarkable event, which would cement his reputation, unfolded.

Carter turned his coat collar up against the biting February wind and returned to cleaning his rifle. He sensed someone approaching, and he lifted his gaze and saw Corporal Hong, a member of Chaing's headquarters staff, coming toward him at a brisk pace.

Hong informed Carter that the commander needed to see him immediately. When Carter asked what for, Hong glared in response to the question. A soldier does not question a request or an order. Carter still had a few things to learn.

Carter slung his rifle over his shoulder and followed Hong to the bombed-out headquarters building. As they entered, Carter saw Chaing at a desk reviewing correspondence. The commander gazed up as Carter saluted and, surprisingly, motioned him to a chair in front of the desk.

Chaing commended Carter for his bravery in the recent battle and remarked on his "fighting spirit." The commander then informed him that General Shek had moved the 88th to Kiangwan, and the 19th would be providing several brigades in support.

Carter, attentive, nodded at learning of the new troop movements.

Chaing then announced that Carter would be among the soldiers he dispatched, reassigned to the 155th but not as a Private.

Carter leaned forward, unsure of what this meant.

Chaing reached in a desk drawer, withdrew a shoulder patch with a single bar, and told Carter that he was promoting him to Lieutenant, and he would lead a section. Chaing pushed the patch across the desk and sat back, satisfied.

Carter stared at the Lieutenant patch a moment, then lifted it slowly and shoved it in his pocket.

Carter stood and saluted, struggling to find words. The promotion was extraordinary for an African American boy still in his teens, who had only been in China for five years.

Chaing dismissed Carter with a wave and a hint of a smile.

Carter turned crisply and exited headquarters with rising pride in his step. The elevation in rank was the first military recognition of Carter's courage under fire, but it would not be his last.

Chapter 11

A Mercenary Man

Carter's promising future in the 19th would not endure. On a bright spring day just before Carter's redeployment to fight under General Chiang Kai-shek at Kiangwan, Edward Sr. arrived at 19th Army headquarters.

Amid refitting his forces, commander Chaing had little patience or time but agreed to meet with Carter's father out of respect for his newly elevated Lieutenant. Heated and frantic, Edward Carter Sr. explained how his family had discovered Carter missing from the church sanctuary and searched for him for weeks. Only recently had he heard rumors that his son had joined the military.

Chaing reassured him that his son was not only safe but performing exceptionally well and about to be redeployed. Carter Sr. was relieved but undeterred in seeking to remove his son from harm's way. He stunned Chaing by announcing a salient fact, of which the commander was unaware – Carter was only 15 years old and underage for military service.

As Chaing brought a hand to his temple to massage a beginning migraine, he shouted for Corporal Hong to summon Lieutenant Carter to headquarters at once.

✳✳✳

Corralled, Carter returned to his studies at Shanghai Military Academy, none the worse for wear but seasoned vastly beyond his years in combat experience and military tactics. It would not take long, however, before he was itching to get back into the fight. By 1935 a potential avenue opened up, which presented another opportunity to escape his father's domineering grasp.

In the fall of 1935, with his country suffering under the global Great Depression's ravages, Benito Mussolini sought land and mineral resources for his starving fellow Italians. The Italian leader set his sights on Abyssinia, now Ethiopia, which bordered neighboring Italian Somaliland. Abyssinia, one of the few independent states in European-dominated North Africa, had fended off colonization and defeated Italian forces at the battle of Adowa 39 years earlier, in 1896. The defeat had wounded Italian national pride and, with a desperate need for resources, presented the perfect target of opportunity for the fascist dictator to claim.

Without warning and without a declaration of war, on October 3, 1935, 200,000 Italian soldiers attacked from Eritrea, an Italian colony, against the unsuspecting soldiers and civilians of Abyssinia, then ruled by Emperor Haile Selassie. The aggression sent shockwaves reverberating around the world, which soon reached Shanghai.

Carter, now 19, headed over to the Kalee Hotel on Jiangxi Road, where the American consulate conducted business, and he formally requested to fight against the Italians in Abyssinia. The crisis in Abyssinia was being handled by the League of Nations, of which the United States was not a member. Isolationist America had voted down joining the organization years earlier for fear of being drawn into international entanglements where the country had no vital interests at stake. The Italian war in Abyssinia was a perfect example of this.

American officials at the consulate were stunned by Carter's brash request and explained that America was not at war with the Italians and therefore could not grant his demand. They offered instead to secure a Merchant Marine position for the young man on a freighter.

Although not combat, the Merchant Marines opportunity would serve as the escape route Carter desperately desired. He accepted, and surprisingly his father offered no objection. Perhaps Edward

Sr. knew that he could not hold onto his son forever and finally let him go. Carter would now begin to make his way in the world and find a new life for himself.

Carter served several uneventful months in the Merchant Marines, sailing to ports of call, including Japan and the Philippines. He eventually docked in Los Angeles, where to his surprise, America was limping through the darkest days of the Great Depression. With its thriving international trade, Shanghai had not experienced the economic downturn that much of the world suffered during the first half of the 1930s.

Times were bleak in the United States, and there was little to no work for a black man seeking employment. Carter languished picking up odd jobs here and there to survive but nothing upon which he could build a future. He was still young and seeking adventure; in the summer of 1936, news from Spain offered that promise.

Trouble had been brewing in Spain since 1931 when the liberal Republicans won the national election that April and abolished the centuries-old monarchy. The new government immediately faced a raft of problems. First, the country was reeling from the effects of the global Great Depression, and Spain's agricultural-based economy's two leading exports, olive oil and wine, withered, sending prices falling. Second, with unemployment soaring, both Catalonia and the Basque regions sought their independence, believing they could better navigate the economic crisis by governing themselves.

Turmoil grew and, by July 1936, a successful right-wing military uprising in Spanish Morocco, led by General Francisco Franco, called for the overthrow of the leftist Republican government in Madrid. In short order, the Franco-led military uprising captured Morocco, much of northern Spain, and several key cities in the south. Franco's Nationalists, as they called themselves, instituted martial law. Within days both sides sought foreign aid and support.

The United States remained neutral, but coverage of the war flooded America. Newspapers were ablaze with daily war journals. American movie-goers watched trumpeting newsreels of the Spanish conflict preceding their Saturday afternoon matinees. Readers of *Life* magazine, which began publication in November

1936 and created the era of photojournalism, were captivated by Robert Capa's haunting photos of the destruction and misery on the distant European battleground.

Young Americans, nearly 2,800 strong, including Edward Carter Jr., seeking adventure, stirred by the compelling imagery and anti-fascist ideology, decided to take up arms in support. Carter sided with the embattled loyalist Republican forces. He had seen firsthand how fascism had become a significant military threat. Using his Merchant Marines connections, he quickly found shipboard passage first to Africa and then to Spain.

Upon Carter's arrival in Spain, he found himself one of the few American volunteers with substantial military experience. A diverse group of college graduates surrounded him, mainly Jewish and some African American recruits as well as young intellectuals perhaps influenced by writers such as Ernest Hemmingway. The iconic American author's writings had romanticized the war in Spain.

War was anything but romantic to Carter, and he was taken aback by the naivety of the majority of his comrades in arms, including his commander, Robert Hale Merriman. Merriman, a lanky 6ft 4in. 27-year-old American doctoral student, had never experienced combat. Still, due to his Reserve Officers' Training Corps (ROTC) training at Cal Berkeley, he was elevated to command of the 428-strong Abraham Lincoln Brigade, also known as the Lincoln Battalion. The unit consisted of two infantry companies, a machine gun company, medical and kitchen staff, and an armory section.

Merriman was an avowed Communist and believed that defeating the fascists in Spain would prevent a second world war. The International Brigades, of which the Lincoln Brigade was a part, were recruited and coordinated by the Communist Party in Paris. Carter didn't realize it at the time, but fighting on behalf of the Communists would come to haunt him later in his life.

Carter mustered in at International Brigades headquarters at Albacete in the southeast of the Iberian Peninsula and encamped at the village of Villanueva de la Jara. As he watched his fellow recruits train, a sense of creeping dread swept over him. They were ideological and enthusiastic but woefully ill-prepared for the realities of combat.

By this time, in January 1937, well-trained German and Italian forces substantially supported Franco's Nationalists. Germany supplied around 16,000 men, nearly 100 planes, and $215 US million to the Nationalist cause. However, this was surpassed by the Italian contribution of 75,000 men and 600 aircraft. It is believed that Hitler's motivation in backing the fascist Franco had much to do with promoting a favorable balance of power in Western Europe and using a Nationalist-run Spain to weaken France with the Spanish conflict as the precursor to World War II.

Carter, amidst the inexperienced Lincoln Battalion, prepared for his unit's baptism by fire in mid-February 1937 outside Madrid. Thus far Franco had been unsuccessful in taking the capital city. The International Brigades' objective, of which the Lincoln Battalion was a part, was to prevent Nationalist forces from taking the Madrid–Valencia road.

Carter and his fellow soldiers in the battalion loaded into trucks on February 15, headed for the Madrid front at Jarama; they had no idea of the scene of carnage that awaited them along the way. Three days earlier, the 600-man British Battalion had attempted to hold a strategic hill. Four hundred were killed or wounded, and their bodies added to the thousands of dead that already lay rotting in fields along the route or buried in hastily dug graves.

The Americans, gripping their newly issued Mosin-Nagant rifles, grew silent as the miles of corpses passed. Carter in his section did what he could to keep spirits up until near Morata when a German squadron of Heinkel He 51C light ground attack biplanes swooped low and strafed the convoy. All dove for cover but soon realized there was nowhere to hide.

The unnerved soldiers of Carter's battalion arrived at the reserve line at Jarama on February 16. They began digging a low trench into a hillside facing irregularly placed enemy fortifications, and several machine gun emplacements 50–200 yards away. The battlefield the battalion would cross consisted of a grove of shattered olive trees with absolutely no cover.

Franco's attack had stalled, and the Nationalists' rear guns commenced a continuous bombardment of Carter's entrenched position. On that windswept hill trench under constant enemy fire, Carter watched his surrounding ill-prepared, ill-trained, and combat-green comrades slowly come unglued.

A trembling soldier, Jon Tisa, beside Carter, gripped his helmet to his head so tightly Carter could barely see his face. When Carter reached a hand over to the man's shoulder to calm him, the man shrieked and jumped a mile. After that, Carter focused on what he had to do to keep himself alive. His mind drifted back to the trenches at Chapei, but the resistance here at Jarama was much stiffer and unrelenting.

The Nationalist bombardment lasted five long days, and, on the 23rd, the brigade received the orders to attack. Carter's section commander, Captain John Scott, came through the lines encouraging the men, urging them to stay low and follow him.

Carter knew what he was facing, but none of these men did, and they wondered what they had gotten themselves into. He heard a man several yards down the line shout, "What the hell am I doing here!" as Capt. Scott blew his brass whistle, the signal to go over the top.

The Lincoln Brigade scrambled over the top into their first attack. Immediately enemy machine guns ripped men apart, and the lines began to melt.

On the right flank, Carter looked over to the center and saw Capt. Scott rushing forward, kneeling and firing his rifle. Following him in an almost tragic comical fashion, he saw about six or seven men behind Scott imitating his every move. Carter continued rushing forward and found shelter behind a wide olive tree, aiming and firing when the enemy machine guns paused.

After a few minutes, Carter noticed a frantic fellow soldier nearby in the open, digging furiously into the hard soil with bloodied hands to create his own trench, a hole in which he could disappear. A Nationalist's bullet to the man's head ended the struggle.

The futile attack faltered when Capt. Scott was mortally wounded. The attack had accomplished nothing, and 20 men from the brigade lay dead. Sixty more were injured and lying amidst the grove of splintered olive trees. When night fell, survivors, including Carter, crawled back to the trench line. During the following days, enemy snipers put an end to the misery of the dying wounded.

Prevailing wisdom dictated that it would be foolhardy to attempt another frontal assault. Sadly, in the Lincoln Battalion sanity did not prevail. On February 27, reinforced by 70 fresh arrivals, some still in street clothes, the Lincoln Battalion was ordered to attack a Nationalist stronghold at Pingarrón from their trenches.

From his diary, Robert Merriman painted the picture:

Early on February 27, weather bad and the attack was put off until 10 AM. We waited without promised machine gun support, without telephone, artillery going to the left and not helping the 24th Brigade or us either. Finally got on the telephone ourselves to headquarters. I said machine gun fire on our boys was too heavy for any action. Coptic [Vladimir Čopić, the commissar of the Brigade] bawled me out for failing to move at 10 o'clock and told me to go.[2]

Merriman was left with no choice; the men had to attack, and he intended to lead the charge himself. Giving the signal to go over the top, Merriman scrambled out of the trench and into the slaughter. Before he could take a full step, his shoulder was shattered in five places by machine gun fire, and he crumpled in a heap.

The attack quickly disintegrated, and by the following day, only 150 of the 263 men who had gone into battle were left standing.[3] However, the overall effort was successful, albeit at a high cost, and the Republicans achieved their objective of keeping the Madrid–Valencia road out of Nationalist hands.

✳✳✳

Carter's military skills by this time had become apparent to everyone, and his marksmanship was first class. With six years' prior service in the US Army, his new commander, Martin Hourihan, replaced the seriously wounded Merriman and acknowledged Carter's combat experience. Hourihan selected Carter as the only black man to help lead a 12-man reconnaissance patrol probing enemy defenses during the July 1937 offensive in the Brunete sector. The overall

The American infantry in this photo are facing similar terrain and weather conditions as they encountered at Climbach. (Signal Corps/NARA)

Charles Thomas being awarded the DSC. (Allene Carter)

Vernon Baker with Edward Carter III. (Allene Carter)

Sandra Holiday and Vernon Baker.
(Allene Carter)

Vernon Baker from *Ebony* magazine.
(Allene Carter)

Soldiers from the 92nd Infantry Division, 1944. (NARA)

Valcenie James with President Clinton. (Allene Carter)

A sketch of Willy James Jr. (Allene Carter)

Valcenie James with the sketch of her husband. (Allene Carter)

Edward Carter Jr. (on right) at Fort Benning, 1942. (Allene Carter)

Another photo of Edward Carter Jr. at Fort Benning. (Allene Carter)

Edward Carter Jr. (Allene Carter)

Edward Carter Jr. shows his sons his DSC. (Allene Carter)

Russell Blair and Allene Carter. (Allene Carter)

White House ceremony. (Allene Carter)

Edward Carter Jr. receiving his DSC. (Allene Carter)

Above Sgt. Carter's reinternment at Arlington National Cemetery. (Allene Carter)

Right Allene Carter and Mildred Carter at Arlington National Cemetery. (Allene Carter)

Hall of Heroes event at the Pentagon where the Army formally apologized to Sgt. Carter. (Allene Carter)

Santalia and Corey Carter, Sgt. Carter's grandchildren. (Allene Carter)

George Watson prior to World War II.
(Allene Carter)

USNS *Watson*, named for George Watson.
(Allene Carter)

SMA Gene C. McKinney accepting the Medal of Honor on Watson's behalf. (Allene Carter)

Ruben Rivers. (Joe Wilson Jr.)　　　　Ruben Rivers with another soldier.
(Joe Wilson Jr.)

SERIAL NUMBER	1. NAME (Print)			ORDER NUMBER
4972	Ruben	Rivers		1410
	(First)	(Middle)	(Last)	

2. ADDRESS (Print)
815 North Harvey　Oklahoma city,　Oklahoma,　Oklahoma
(Number and street or R. F. D. number)　(Town)　(County)　(State)

3. TELEPHONE
2-15-66
(Exchange)　(Number)

4. AGE IN YEARS
21 years.
DATE OF BIRTH
October 30. 1918
(Mo.)　(Day)　(Yr.)

5. PLACE OF BIRTH
Tecumseh.
(Town or county)
Oklahoma
(State or country)

6. COUNTRY OF CITIZENSHIP
U. S. A

7. NAME OF PERSON WHO WILL ALWAYS KNOW YOUR ADDRESS
Fred Foster
(Mr., Mrs., Miss)　(First)　(Middle)　(Last)

8. RELATIONSHIP OF THAT PERSON
Employer

9. ADDRESS OF THAT PERSON
815 North Harvey　Oklahoma city　Oklahoma　Oklahoma
(Number and street or R. F. D. number)　(Town)　(County)　(State)

10. EMPLOYER'S NAME
Fred Foster

11. PLACE OF EMPLOYMENT OR BUSINESS
815 North Harvey　Oklahoma city　Oklahoma　Oklahoma
(Number and street or R. F. D. number)　(Town)　(County)　(State)

I AFFIRM THAT I HAVE VERIFIED ABOVE ANSWERS AND THAT THEY ARE TRUE.

REGISTRATION CARD
D. S. S. Form 1
(over)　16—17105

Ruben Rivers.
(Registrant's signature)

Ruben Rivers' draft card. (NARA)

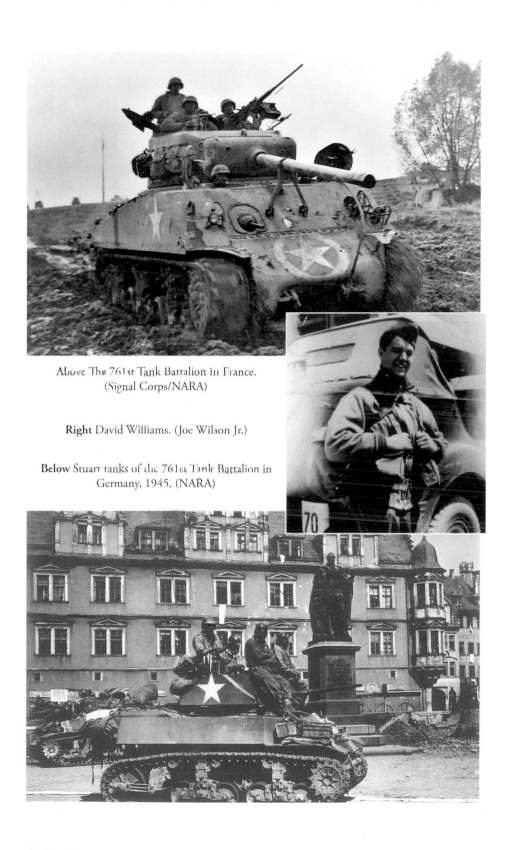

Above The 761st Tank Battalion in France. (Signal Corps/NARA)

Right David Williams. (Joe Wilson Jr.)

Below Stuart ranks of the 761st Tank Battalion in Germany, 1945. (NARA)

David Williams in 1997. (Joe Wilson Jr.)

John Fox. (© Sandra Fox)

John Fox's friend Otis Zachary. (Solace Wales)

Sandra Fox, Cassandra Charles and Arlene Fox in Sommocolonia, (© Sandra Fox. Photo: Solace Wales)

Arlene Fox and President Clinton. (© The White House / 1997)

Arlene Fox, Grace Rivers, Valcenie James and Mildred Carter. (Allene Carter)

Adm Chester W. Nimitz pins the
Navy Cross on Steward's Mate 3rd Class
"Dorie" Miller. (NARA)

Ashli Carter with five out of the seven medals
at the Honor Deferred Exhibit. (Allene Carter)

Honor Deferred Exhibit at the National WWII Museum. (Allene Carter)

Republican objective was to lift the siege of Madrid by clearing out all the fascists from the surrounding area and dislodging them from their artillery positions to end the shelling of the city.

Carter waited at the perimeter of the camp. He checked his watch with a lighter in the inky morning blackness, 0430 hours. Men began arriving, groggy but ready for the patrol mission, which would set off at 0445. Within five minutes, Carter assembled his entire reconnaissance patrol. As the last man arrived, Carter pulled out the grid map and pointed to the area of suspected enemy entrenchments. Carter directed the men to make sure they loaded their Soviet-supplied M91/30 type Mosin-Nagant rifles. Republican forces carried both the bolt action Mosin-Nagant and the Mexican-made 1936 Mauser. Both were accurate and reliable and could get the job done.

Their objective was almost two miles distant through the hilly region on the outskirts of Brunete. It was challenging terrain as there were many blind spots, and the men had to tread cautiously in the early morning light.

After trekking a mile and a half, the road began to slope upward. Carter waved several men forward to scout. He noted the dead stillness as the patrol followed the forward scouts up and over the rise in the hill.

The patrol had not gotten 20 yards down the other side when muzzle flashes lit up the darkness, and machine gun fire shredded the patrol. It was crack German troops from the Condor Legion who flanked the road with cross-positioned MG-34 machine guns firing 900 rounds a minute.

The patrol was decimated; men crumpled down into the dirt in pools of their own blood. Carter could do nothing but shout to fall back then scramble rearward himself up over the rise.

As Carter cleared the top of the rise, he grabbed two grenades from his vest, pulled the pins, and lobbed them over the slope toward the German positions. Crouching back down and scanning his immediate area, he noted none of his men made it back with him. They all lay dead or dying on the other side of the hill. Bursts of machine gun fire instantly silenced the wounded who dared cry out.

Carter got to his feet, keeping low, and a searing pain shot from his left foot. He stumbled forward and examined the back of his torn boot; he had been grazed in the heel by one of the German shells. There was no time to attend to the wound as enemy voices grew louder coming up the opposite side of the slope. Carter struggled, put his weight on his rifle, and limped back the mile and a half to the Republican line, the only man to survive from the ambushed patrol.

The subsequent battle at Brunete inflicted heavy casualties on the Lincoln and Washington Brigades, primarily composed of Americans. The Republicans declared victory due to capturing some ground; it was anything but, as the rout inflicted a heavy blow to the International Brigades' morale. The territory gained was also shortly recaptured.

A third decisive battle at Teruel in December 1938 would turn the tide of the conflict in Franco's favor for the remainder of the war. A final offensive by the Nationalists in March of 1939 forced the surrender of all Republican forces. Although they still held Madrid and 30 percent of the country, Britain and France determined the effort hopeless and recognized the Nationalist Franco government. Fighting ceased by April 1, 1939, and Franco ruled Spain as a military dictator until he died in 1975.

Returning to the States in 1940, 24-year-old Carter turned his thoughts from war. He unexpectedly ran into his father and stepmother near Central Avenue in the heart of Los Angeles. Edward Sr. and his wife had fled war-torn Shanghai during the Second Sino-Japanese War in 1937.

Recognizing his father from a distance, now grayer, Carter paused and debated whether to turn away. Instead, he exchanged pleasantries, although little remained in common between them. His preacher father did not understand the younger Carter's passion for the military.

Carter avoided his father after the chance meeting. He was very much his own man now and bristled at being judged for the choices he'd made. Instead, Carter focused on building his new life and soon met the woman he would marry, Mildred Hoover. A beautiful and educated woman whom Carter charmed immediately, Mildred was a widow with two small children.

Mildred would become Carter's rock and fill the void left by the absence of his mother. They did not marry right away but became inseparable and soon had a child on the way, Edward "Buddha" Carter III, born March 27, 1941. The large, rotund child reminded Carter of the revered spiritual figure and founder of the religion of Buddhism, and the nickname stuck. Carter was as proud as any doting father could be and assured Mildred he planned to marry her once he was established, often referring to her as Mrs. Carter.

***

Carter's lack of a civilian career, in addition to the swirling winds of war in Europe, directed his thoughts back to the military. He knew it was only a matter of time before America broke from her isolation and joined the growing global conflict. After talking it over with Mildred, he decided to enlist on September 26, 1941, just short of three months before the Japanese attack on Pearl Harbor. The military was the life he knew best, and he planned to put his heart and soul into making himself a success.

Carter, however, would encounter more than enemy combatants on a distant battlefield; he'd grapple with deeply entrenched racist attitudes in the American South. The segregated environment came as a shock to Carter when he arrived at boot camp in Camp Wolters, Texas. In Shanghai, where Carter had grown up, black people were respected and admired, and there was no segregation of black soldiers in the Spanish Civil War. In that conflict, approximately 90 African Americans served side-by-side with white soldiers, even commanding them in combat. Oliver Law, a black soldier from Texas, had replaced a wounded Martin Hourihan and led Lincoln Brigade troops at the battle of Brunete.

Carter felt for the first time in his life like a second-class citizen at Camp Wolters, but he was wise enough to keep quiet and stay focused. He only expressed his frustration in letters home to Mildred: "Conditions here are pretty bad. Only the damned live here in the rotten South. They don't treat you like soldiers; it's more like slaves. When this war is over, you'll see plenty of tough and bitter boys coming home."[4]

Despite the conditions and treatment, Carter excelled. He confounded and amazed his instructors with near-perfect scores in marksmanship and natural military discipline. Carter was proficient with all types of weapons, including his favorite, the Thompson submachine gun. After basic training, however, he was assigned to the 3535th Quartermaster Truck Company at Fort Benning, Georgia, where his weaponry skills were not required. From Fort Benning, he continued to express his irritation in letters to Mildred: "The officers down here tell us they don't need niggers in the Army. Then why in the hell don't they let us go. After all, a mop, bucket, and a broom are not worth giving one's life for."[5]

Although his letters to Mildred conveyed his disgruntlement with military life, he also expressed his continuing devotion and desire to marry her. Mildred, who had been reluctant due to her previous marriage, finally relented and traveled to Georgia, where she and Carter were married on June 10, 1942.

The newlyweds settled with their son "Buddha" in a small house off base in Columbus, Georgia, and soon a second baby was on the way. Although pleased with his domestic life, Carter remained frustrated that his unit remained Stateside. With his training and combat experience, it was not what he had envisioned when he had enlisted, but with his willingness to work hard, he rose to the rank of Staff Sergeant in less than a year.

Carter's situation changed, however, in the fall of 1944 when Allied Command ordered the 3535th to the European Theater of Operations. The Quartermaster Truck Company arrived first in England, then quickly departed for southern France, arriving there on November 13, 1944.

Chapter 12

March to the Rhine

From the moment Carter arrived on European soil he maintained his focus on joining the infantry. He volunteered daily for combat duty, but the Army continually turned him down. Many Allied planners had hoped that the war would be over by Christmas, "End the War in '44" had been on everyone's lips since the recapture of Paris in August. With Hitler's retreat back into Germany, no one could have imagined that the Führer had spent many months planning a new bold offensive in the Ardennes, one he believed would split the Allies in half and decimate their forces.

Operation *Wacht am Rhein* (Watch on the Rhine), Hitler's codename for what would become the largest land battle fought by the US Army on the European continent, is remembered by the world as the Battle of the Bulge. The Germans launched the surprise attack in the early morning hours of December 16, 1944. It had an immediate and lasting impact on the role African Americans would play during the remainder of the war.

General Eisenhower needed reinforcements desperately in the ranks, and color no longer was a factor. Circulars were issued soliciting volunteers for combat units, which read, "volunteers would be accepted without regard to race or color." Nearly 5,000 African Americans applied, with less than half being accepted.

Eddie Carter Jr. was one of the soldiers accepted for training. He had to surrender his rank of Staff Sergeant and return to being a Private, but he took the demotion in stride. Combat was the reason he had enlisted, and now he would have the opportunity to utilize his well-honed skills in support of the cause for freedom.

Carter began training with other black volunteers in January 1945 during the wind-down of the Battle of the Bulge. He was subsequently assigned to the 12th Armored Division, 56th Armored Infantry Battalion, D Company on March 12.

1st Lieutenant Floyd Vanderhoef of the 56th Infantry stood next to his Executive Officer (XO), Russell Blair, at the edge of an expansive open field north of Saint Avold, France. This area in subsequent years would become the largest United States military cemetery, Lorraine American Cemetery, with the bodies of the brave men who were about to embark on the final push east. Vanderhoef was awaiting the arrival of newly trained black combat volunteers assigned under his command. As the deuce and a half trucks began arriving, Vanderhoef turned to his XO and commented that now they'd see what they'd gotten themselves into.

Carter and fellow black soldiers poured from the trucks with an air of wild excitement and expectancy. Carter chafed at the lack of discipline in his fellow combat volunteers, and he shouted at them to settle down and get into order.

Vanderhoef and Blair noticed. Carter, now 28, radiated confidence and natural solid leadership, and the men around him obeyed and fell into lines. Others followed suit as Vanderhoef and Blair approached. Blair called the soldiers to attention, and all instantly straightened up.

Vanderhoef surveyed the eager volunteers a moment then ordered them at ease. He began by introducing himself and his Executive Officer and informing them they were now "Hellcats," and they'd better damn well live up to the name. They had a big job ahead of them, and if the volunteers were looking to kill Krauts, they'd come to the right place.

Men in the ranks grinned at the comment as the Lieutenant continued. Floyd told the men they were expected to fight just as hard as the white soldiers, and men in the 56th looked out for one another and it didn't mean a damn thing what color they were. He concluded by telling them to get what rest they could as they'd be moving out shortly for Siereck Les Baines. The battalion was linking up with Third Army and XX Corp, and, yes, they were headed into Germany.

Carter and the men were now part of the last major Allied campaign of the war, the Rhineland Offensive, which was, in fact, a series of operations: *Veritable, Grenade, Lumberjack*, and *Undertone*. Supreme Allied Commander Dwight D. Eisenhower intended to occupy the lands west of the Rhine River in Germany to allow British Field Marshal Montgomery with the 21st Army Group to make the main assault north of the Mosel River against the vaunted Siegfried Line.

Eisenhower left the Ninth Army under Montgomery's command but shifted most American troops to cover Montgomery's right flank, including Patton's Third Army, which would continue the drive toward the city of Trier and the Saar River basin. The 12th Armored Division on the move was reassigned from Seventh Army to fight under General Patton on March 17, 1945.

On that day, the division rumbled into the French river village of Siereck Les Baines, where General George Patton was there to welcome them. The regiment passed orders to assemble in a field north of the town where the Third Army commander would speak. Carter admired Patton, and he conveyed this in letters home to Mildred: "General Patton, as you already know, is our leader. One thing I like about him is that he has plenty of guts. He is a regular G.I. Joe."[6]

As Patton mounted the hood of a deuce and a half, he shouted his welcome to the 12th and continued that now he had the men and might to make it a real horse race to his objective, the Rhine. He planned to leave old Monty in the dust, and he drove home his point by concluding, "I'll reach the Rhine first if I have to take a 6-by-6 Mack Truck to haul back the dog tags!"[7]

Carter would discover one of the first orders issued by Patton concerning his division when a Corporal was dispatched to D Company to locate Carter and bring him to Lt. Vanderhoef. Upon the Corporal finding him, Carter asked if there was a problem. The Corporal didn't know.

Carter trailed the soldier to the 12th Command Post (CP) area near the center of the town. Traversing the route, Carter saw several crews with buckets of olive drab paint covering over white unit markings on idling trucks and numerous parked jeeps in a staging area. Part of Patton's orders were to conceal the 12th's identity.

Arriving at the CP, Carter saw Vanderhoef and Blair conferring over a map rolled out on the hood of a jeep. Carter, getting their attention, saluted crisply and said, "Sir."

The officers turned from the map and ordered him at ease, and Blair dismissed the Corporal.

Vanderhoef began by saying that he and Blair had been discussing assigning squad commanders within Dog Company before reaching the Trier jump-off point. They decided that Carter fit the bill, noting his leadership potential, and notified him of his added responsibilities.

Carter welcomed the assignment with understated pride as Vanderhoef informed him that General Patton assigned the 12th as the spearhead in the push to the Rhine. They'd be traveling with little to no cover, exposed in unconquered enemy territory, and had to be on their toes. Carter acknowledged him with a sober nod as the commander relayed that a new uniform order would be disseminated shortly. All shoulder patches were to be removed for secrecy. Patton wanted the Germans to believe that the 12th Armored remained with the Seventh Army.

From this moment forward, the 12th Armored Hellcats gained a new moniker, "Mystery Division," coined by a *Stars and Stripes* article. Patton intended the Mystery Division to be used as a covert tool to confuse the enemy, and the unit would make planned stealth moves at night, although that was not always possible.

Carter and the 12th Armored rumbled out of Siereck Les Baines the next day, March 18, 1945, and paralleled the Moselle River north into Germany on their way to Trier, the jump-off point. The Rhine, the last natural barrier into Germany, was their objective. Still, they had to cross over 125 miles of hostile territory to reach it, moving unsupported into the heart of Nazi Germany.

The division was organized into three combat commands: tanks, armored infantry, and artillery. Carter, part of the 56th Infantry, was integrated into Combat Command B (CCB). As CCB moved into Germany, they captured hundreds of German POWs, and destroyed and abandoned German equipment clogged the route. Their first main objective was to locate an unmined, intact bridge crossing. As they pressed into Germany, they met scattered and stiff pockets of resistance, especially around the area of Freinsheim. The Germans blew the first bridge Combat Command B reached at Ludwigshafen, so the CCB bivouacked nearby.

The next day, March 22, they were ordered south along the Rhine to attack and capture the crossing at Speyer. Vanderhoef received intelligence that a formidable German force was dug in among thick woods along the route. As they entered the area of the reported heavy German presence the following day, CCB discovered that the enemy had withdrawn during the night.

Carter and D Company, part of CCB, were then pulled back to join the main attack on Speyer. As Carter and his squad rode atop a tank en route on a bright and clear March 23 day, the ear-splitting recoil of a panzerfaust from a nearby abandoned warehouse rocked the vehicle in front of them.

Carter leaped off the tank with his squad, taking momentary cover from German machine gun fire. Carter, ignoring the MG-42, immediately volunteered to lead a three-man team across the field to see if they could ascertain the location and strength of the enemy position.

Carter, calm, cool-headed, born for the fight, inspired confidence in the soldiers under his command. Self-assured, he told them they would take it out; they hadn't come this far to let some German die-hards stop the mission.

The 150 yards between the road and the warehouse contained virtually no cover except a road embankment, tall grass, and various mounds of upturned earth. Not exactly the best terrain to charge a machine gun nest, but Carter was undaunted as he cradled his trusted Thompson submachine gun and checked his jacket for an extra 30-round box magazine.

Carter crawled up behind the road embankment with his squad and waited several minutes for a lull in the enemy fire, which would provide enough of a chance to make some distance across the field. He hand-signaled his three-man patrol to fan out ten yards apart to make the dash. Carter signaled forward, and intense enemy small arms fire erupted again as the patrol left the embankment. Carter turned his head to the right and saw one of his men jerk as the soldier's machine-gun-riddled body crumpled. The German fire continued without pause. Carter, not yet 10 yards across the field, turned and shouted above the intense enemy fire to his other men, "Cover me, fall back to the road."

Carter kept low, scanning forward through the tall grass as bullets like hornets hissed angrily past his head. He turned around to the road and saw the second of his men struck; a sickening gush spurted from his neck, his eyes rolled back, and he fell lifeless. Five yards farther back, his other man was struck as well, his right shoulder tearing open from German fire just before he made it behind the road embankment.

Carter knew from seeing his comrades go down there was no retreat; that was never his plan to begin with. He had a mission and intended on completing it, but the odds stacked against him with every step forward, alone in the middle of the field.

He had no choice but to advance, and he leaped up, zig-zagging his way forward as German machine gun fire carved up his left arm, hitting him three times. However, he was still on his feet and continued moving forward until a sharp stabbing pain in his left leg toppled him from his feet. Carter, struck by small arms fire, opened up a top pocket on his uniform and gobbled some sulfadiazine tablets to diminish the pain and prevent infection. As he washed the pills down with water from his canteen, a bullet cut clear through his left hand, knocking the canteen to the ground. Stunned, he stared at his empty hand a moment then over to the canteen. Carter quickly tore a section of bandages with his teeth and wrapped his bloody hand.

Still exposed within the enemy's sights, he had to keep moving and decided to crawl several yards to better terrain where the grass was taller. He shimmied forward as low as he could and got to within 30 yards of the abandoned warehouse where he could hear German shouts. German was a language he had learned well in his time at Shanghai Military Academy. From the sound of it, he determined these soldiers were just as dogged as he was but possessed the added emotion he did not feel, fear.

He decided to wait them out, and he lay on the ground for two hours listening to them. He knew the Germans had sent out a patrol to locate him, and he waited patiently for his moment. He still had enough ammo in the Thompson that he gripped under his chest as he lay face down playing dead.

The German voices grew louder as the patrol drew nearer, but Carter could not determine the number of men in the patrol. But no matter the number, he would have the element of surprise but only get one chance. When they were almost upon him, Carter waited for one of them to alert the others upon finding him on the ground. Then Carter heard a soldier shout, "Hier! Amerikanisch!"

The two hours of waiting had given Carter enough time to rehearse his move in his mind. He thrust the Thompson out, threw all his weight on his right leg to push himself up, then kept his finger on the trigger as he executed his plan. In seconds six Germans fell dead as Carter grabbed the shaken and stunned remaining two soldiers who'd raised their hands in surrender.

With superhuman strength, ignoring his pain, Carter pulled one soldier in front of him and the other behind him, using them as human shields to make his way back to his position on the road. Both German and American soldiers looked on in awe, disbelieving what they were witnessing.

Vanderhoef had given him up for dead due to the relentless enemy fire. Still, here Carter was, bleeding, bringing two prisoners back from what could accurately be labeled a suicide mission. It was one of those moments in war that made even the most grizzled combat veterans pause.

Arriving safely back behind the lines, men secured the Germans to take them away. Carter shouted, "No, they got information we can use." As confused men in D Company who did not speak

German looked to one another, Carter began, "Wie viele Truppen? Was sind ihre Positionen?"

Vanderhoef and Blair, seizing the opportunity, sighted an observation post in a nearby abandoned building, and Carter climbed up with the prisoners and continued his interrogation in German, a language that no one knew Carter spoke fluently. The POWs cooperated, pointing out hidden enemy strongholds ahead.

Carter, growing weaker, refused evacuation until he was satisfied he had gleaned all the intelligence the prisoners had. The information they provided was accurate regarding the number and disposition of German troops. It allowed the 12th Armored to clear the road and continue advancing into Speyer with minimal loss of life.

✳✳✳

Carter wrote to Mildred as he recovered in a hospital in Luxembourg:

> Dear Lover, just a line or two to let you know that I am still able to kick. I guess the War Dept. has written you concerning my getting shot up. A little. A Jerry machine gun hit me in my left hand; three holes in my left arm, one hole in my left leg, two holes in my right leg, and one hole in my right foot. And also one in the head. I have nine bullet holes in all. Not so bad at that, is it? I hope that I'll get well in time so that I can get back to my outfit.[8]

Carter did get back to his outfit. One month later, he slipped out of the hospital and hitched a ride with a Captain from the 10th Armored back to the front near Bad Tölz, Germany. When Carter arrived in camp, Executive Officer Blair, now a Captain, was shocked to see him and simultaneously got a message from the hospital that Carter had gone AWOL. Captain Blair wired the hospital back, reassuring them that there was no problem; Carter was back at the front on active duty where he belonged.

One of the last acts by Captain Blair before Dog Company was deactivated was to sign a recommendation for the Distinguished Service Cross for Carter's actions at Speyer. Although in comments after the war Blair revealed that he believed Carter deserved the Medal of Honor, he feared that Army command would turn down the recommendation due to the racial climate.

Carter was one of the honored VIP guests at a "Welcome Home Joe" dinner for GIs in Los Angeles in December 1945. In an interview with reporter Fred Vast at the event, Carter summed up his feelings about the war and reflected on his future:

> We fought for the recognition of our people, and we found
> democracy in the front lines. We fought because Hitler was the
> worst of two wrongs; worse than racial discrimination at home.
> We liberated Europe, but here at home, we are not free. I just
> want a chance to earn a living, and I want to help finish the
> fight for freedom.[9]

Edward A. Carter Jr. died in 1963 and was buried in California. In 1997 his son Edward Carter III accepted the Medal of Honor from President Clinton on behalf of his father. The day following the White House ceremony Sgt. Carter was reinterred at Arlington National Cemetery. A hero had finally come home.

In June 2001 in Norfolk, Virginia, Edward Carter's family was on hand at a renaming ceremony for a 950-foot ammunition ship. The M/V SSG *Edward A. Carter Jr.* was rechristened that month and currently serves as part of the US Navy's Military Sealift Command based in Diego Garcia in the Indian Ocean.

EDWARD CARTER JR., MEDAL OF HONOR CITATION

> For conspicuous gallantry and intrepidity at the risk of his life
> above and beyond the call of duty: Staff Sergeant Edward A.
> Carter, Jr. distinguished himself by extraordinary heroism in
> action on 23 March 1945. At approximately 0830 hours, 23
> March 1945, near Speyer, Germany, the tank upon which Staff
> Sergeant Carter was riding received bazooka and small arms
> fire from the vicinity of a large warehouse to its left front. Staff
> Sergeant Carter and his squad took cover behind an intervening

road bank. Staff Sergeant Carter volunteered to lead a three-man patrol to the warehouse where other unit members noticed the original bazooka fire. From here they were to ascertain the location and strength of the opposing position and advance approximately 150 yards across an open field. Enemy small arms fire covered this field. As the patrol left this covered position, they received intense enemy small arms fire killing one member of the patrol instantly. This caused Staff Sergeant Carter to order the other two members of the patrol to return to the covered position and cover him with rifle fire while he proceeded alone to carry out the mission. The enemy fire killed one of the two soldiers while they were returning to the covered position, and seriously wounded the remaining soldier before he reached the covered position. An enemy machine gun burst wounded Staff Sergeant Carter three times in the left arm as he continued the advance. He continued and received another wound in his left leg that knocked him from his feet. As Staff Sergeant Carter took wound tablets and drank from his canteen, the enemy shot it from his left hand, with the bullet going through his hand. Disregarding these wounds, Staff Sergeant Carter continued the advance by crawling until he was within thirty yards of his objective. The enemy fire became so heavy that Staff Sergeant Carter took cover behind a bank and remained there for approximately two hours. Eight enemy riflemen approached Staff Sergeant Carter, apparently to take him prisoner, Staff Sergeant Carter killed six of the enemy soldiers and captured the remaining two. These two enemy soldiers later gave valuable information concerning the number and disposition of enemy troops. Staff Sergeant Carter refused evacuation until he had given full information about what he had observed and learned from the captured enemy soldiers. This information greatly facilitated the advance on Speyer. Staff Sergeant Carter's extraordinary heroism was an inspiration to the officers and men of the 7th Army, Infantry Company Number 1 (Provisional) and exemplify the highest traditions of the military service.

PART FIVE

George Watson

Chapter 13

Picnic at a Hanging

George Watson, approaching one and a half years old, lay peacefully in his crib as his mother, Madgie, cut vegetables for lunch in their farmhouse kitchen. Older brothers W.B., aged four, and John, aged seven, were running under foot. It was mid-morning on a picture-perfect but sweltering Friday in early August in Starkville, Mississippi. Today had been declared a holiday in the town, although it is doubtful that George or his siblings knew it.

Two miles distant across the vast cotton fields in a hollow on the outskirts of town, a chilling, dark-carnivalesque scene was unfolding that featured the worst of humanity on display. And practically all the reporters in Mississippi and several from across the nation were on hand to cover it.

Promptly at 11.25 a.m., two black men, Dit Seals and Peter Bolen, were led in shackles toward an enormous crowd by Sheriff Nickels, his deputies, and two black preachers, Reverends Winburn and Hutchins. The overflow crowd was perched atop rolling bluffs encircling the hollow. The masses, estimated to surpass 5,000 people including many children, had been gathering since 9 a.m. Some had even camped out the night before.

Rising from the center of the hollow, looming before Seals and Bolen, was a specially constructed double gallows on an 18ft-high platform allowing the crowd of picnickers with their baskets of cucumber sandwiches, hard-boiled eggs, and pie an excellent view.

It was Seals' and Bolen's day of reckoning, but they weren't alone. The day had been dubbed locally as "Black Friday" because several other black men were being hanged in Mississippi that day and four others across the state line in Alabama. This "celebration" in Starkville, however, was the largest. The two accused had been charged with murdering a black porter, Willie Taylor, for his $25 railroad pay in a crime which only one of the men admitted.

As Seals and Bolen neared the gallows, they noted two pine coffins being offloaded from a wagon. Then they glimpsed county politicians exhorting the masses, not allowing the opportunity to secure primary votes to go to waste. The politicians stationed themselves at soda fountains, passing out free drinks and popcorn to all, making sure the voters remembered their names.

Just three minutes after their arrival, the two doomed men were atop the gallows as Sheriff Nickels, who also served as executioner, placed the 2in.-thick nooses around their necks. With solemnity to match the occasion, the Sheriff asked the condemned men if they had anything to say before justice sent them into the bowels of hell.

Seals craned his neck to Bolen, and both agreed that it might be nice if the crowd joined them in a hymn. The Sheriff thought it a splendid idea and asked which particular one. Bolen suggested one of his favorites, "There is a Land of Pure Delight."

The crowd knew it well and put down their chicken wings, wiped their mouths, and stood in reverence to join the soon-to-be-expired men in verse:

There is a land of pure delight where saints immortal reign;
Infinite day excludes the night, and pleasures banish pain;

By the sixth and last stanza of the 1709 hymn by Isaac Watts, many impatient picnickers wanted Nickels to move things along. They'd been wilting in the hot sun all morning, and many had a noon-time service to catch at First Baptist Church.

The Sheriff didn't disappoint. Before the last line of the hymn echoed away and a rushed prayer from Reverend Hutchins, Nickels turned to the men and announced, "May God have mercy on your souls," then pulled the lever opening the trap doors.

"They dropped instantly and writhed for a moment in the air," a reporter for the *Chicago Tribune* wrote. What the reporter failed to add, which we can only assume, is the thunderous cheers which rose from the crowd.

The *Semi-Weekly Leader* in Brookhaven, Mississippi, reported that after the pair were pronounced dead ten minutes before noon, "people clamored for pieces of the ropes, and many fragments were carried away by the crowd as souvenirs."

The brutal Deep South world into which George Watson was born had changed little since the Civil War. The Watsons themselves were sharecroppers who only a generation earlier had been former slaves. George Watson Sr., aged 24 in 1915, had married Madgie Everett six years earlier in 1909 and settled down into a back-breaking life.

Not only did the physical labor take its toll, but the sharecropping system crushed the soul. Under the scheme, sharecroppers rented their land for 30 to 50 percent of the crop they raised. They secured farming tools on loan from the landlord's store and paid the money back at exorbitant interest rates. At the end of the season, sharecroppers settled up their crop sales with the landlords and kept the difference as profit. There were seldom any profits, and most tenant farmers never got out of the hole.

It was slavery by another name and contributed significantly to spurring on the Great Migration of black citizens moving north, which began in 1910. There was a direct train line from Mississippi to Chicago. The *Chicago Defender* newspaper urged black people to migrate north and lobbied the railroad to offer group ticket rates to those relocating from the state.[1] By 1919, over a million black citizens had migrated to northeastern cities, including Detroit, Chicago, and New York.[2]

The Watsons were one of the families who stuck it out and the boys W.B., John, and George joined their father picking cotton in the fields. By 1920 two younger sisters, Eula and Mary, had been born and, eventually, another brother, Lawyer Watson, arrived in 1922.

As George grew, turning six in 1920, he began attending a Rosenwald school in Starkville. Here he discovered a love of learning and an aptitude for math. The Rosenwald "black" schools across the Jim Crow south were funded by a matching-grant endowment established in 1917 by Julius Rosenwald. The philanthropist was a Sears senior executive who served as president of the Chicago-based department store from 1908 to 1922. Rosenwald had great concern for the plight of education in the country, especially in disadvantaged communities across the Deep South.[3]

Most weekend afternoons when George was not in school or completing chores or out in the sweltering fields, he spent time fishing with his older brothers. The trio would don their denim overalls, pack up their bamboo poles, and head out barefoot for Oktibbeha County Lake. The 513-acre lake featured plentiful largemouth bass, crappie, and bream, which the boys hauled back often for dinner.

While fishing, the oppressive Mississippi heat would ultimately wear on them, and the boys would strip down to their drawers and cool off in the county lake. All of them were excellent swimmers. George, however, for reasons W.B. and John couldn't figure out, was by far the best. There was a sunken tree a quarter of the way out in the lake that they would challenge each other to reach. Nearly every time George would tap the tree trunk first and head back to shore, his winded brothers bringing up the rear. Eventually, the races were abandoned; George had no competition.

Through those bucolic but desperately poor times, George and his family had to stay ever vigilant to a growing menace that saw a resurgence in 1915. During the release of the film *Birth of a Nation*, which portrayed the Klu Klux Klan (KKK) in a favorable light, the Klan was officially relaunched by Atlanta-based Methodist preacher William J. Simmons. The self-proclaimed Imperial Wizard was also a savvy marketer and tied the Klan's rebirth to the *Birth of a Nation* film premiere in Atlanta.

During the film's run, he took out ads in the *Atlanta Journal* announcing the reemergence of the secret society, which was clearly no longer a secret. On the night of the premiere, he and about 50 men marched through the streets to the Atlanta Theater at Hurt Plaza and Exchange Place in Klan robes and regalia. They fired their rifles into the air upon their arrival in celebration.

Simmons's recruitment criteria were simple: the new KKK was a "whites-only," Christian patriotic organization. The preacher emphasized that race-mixing of any sort would undermine the vitality of true (white) America. In his manifesto, he went further:

> We avow the distinction between races of mankind as same has been decreed by the Creator, and we shall ever be true to the faithful maintenance of White Supremacy and will strenuously oppose any compromise thereof in any and all things.[4]

The Klan was active in the Watsons' state of Mississippi throughout the early 1920s, spreading terror, except for a single town on the Delta, which stood up to it. In 1922 LeRoy Percy, a progressive attorney and politician in Greenville, Mississippi, made an impassioned plea to disavow the organization at a KKK recruiting session at the Greenville County courthouse.

Percy wanted to keep the delicate balance in race relations, which had allowed the town to flourish. He argued if the Klan were to infiltrate Washington County, the African American exodus would lead straight to the economic ruin of Greenville's economy.[5]

The citizens agreed and voted on a resolution condemning the Klan, and Percy emerged as a national hero to many for standing up against racism. Due to Percy's stand and several scandals and internal corruption, the Klan's popularity waned in Mississippi by mid-decade.

However, many prominent politicians were Klansmen or former members, including Mississippi governor Theodore Bilbo, who was elected governor in 1928 and ultimately served as a US senator from 1935 to 1947.[6]

Toward the end of the 1920s, George was growing restless. He envisioned a suffocating future on the farm as he witnessed his father's daily struggles just to provide for the family. George wanted no part of that life. He had ambition and longed for an education. However, he saw no way to make that happen in Starkville.

Ironically Starkville was the home of Mississippi A & M, which later became Mississippi State, but the college was not open to black students. Surprisingly, it was not until 1965 that the first black student was admitted to the state university.[7]

In 1930 when George turned 16, there were many mouths to feed in the Watson household, including his older brothers, W.B. and John, and his younger sisters, Eula and Mary, and youngest brother Lawyer. A niece, Jennie, aged five, also lived with the family at the time.[8]

Just before the Great Depression tightened its grip on the country, Watson decided to leave for the big city, Birmingham, Alabama. In 1932, at age 18, he moved in with his widowed grandmother, Emma Gains, 59, who lived in Birmingham, two and a half hours away. She had a small apartment, which she rented, and supported herself by working as a maid in a private home.

Watson was extremely fortunate in the midst of the country's severe economic downturn to find work as a janitor at a private club on First Street in the city. Birmingham was reeling from the effects of the Great Depression. The statistics were bleak, with only 8,000 of the 108,000 local workers employed. President Roosevelt called Birmingham the "hardest hit" city in the country.[9] In his janitorial job, Watson earned about $624 for the year working full time, the equivalent of just over $11,000 in today's dollars.[10]

MAY 1935

Watson turned 21 in 1935 and had stuck with the janitorial work as employment of any kind was difficult to come by. One day, entering the club's foyer on his way to start work, he saw a slender young woman in a gray smock carrying a basket of laundry descending the wide mahogany main staircase. Her hair was pulled up and back, and her features were striking. Watson stopped to admire her until he became self-conscious and realized he was staring.

Most of the maids in the private club were approaching 40 years old, and Watson had never given them a second glance. This woman floating down the stairs, however, was a vision and near his age. Watson gave himself a quick once over, then wiped the sweat from his palms on his trousers. If he had had a hat, he would have removed it. As she reached the landing, he nodded hello, introducing himself, and asked her name.

The woman didn't acknowledge Watson but kept on walking, heading to the first-floor laundry. Watson scrambled after her asking again for her name. The woman turned back abruptly, saying she heard him the first time, but she wasn't interested in giving it to him.

Watson smiled and, with pretended confidence, told her not to worry; she would be interested. The woman cocked her head, confused, as Watson smirked then walked away, leaving the attractive woman staring after him. Watson called back without turning, "You'll tell me your name."

After he rounded the hallway corner away from the attractive maid's view, he leaned back against the wall and exhaled. His older brothers always advised him that to impress girls, he had to act confident. Watson had never gotten the opportunity to try the strategy out until now.

Later that week, in the downstairs hall of the club, Watson was slipping on his jacket, preparing to leave at the end of his shift when one of the club members, who were all men, burst through the front door. Mr. Carmichael was trying to settle his sobbing five-year-old daughter with blond curls. She was crying and holding her knee. The dark-haired, 35-year-old father was not the picture of compassion as he tersely instructed young Lydia to stop whining and just rub it and it would be fine.

Watson approached and asked Carmichael if everything was all right. Carmichael, who knew Watson well, said all was fine; his daughter had just tripped on the sidewalk.

His more significant concern was his ex-wife, who was 20 minutes late to pick their daughter up. Carmichael had a pressing business dinner engagement and glanced at a pocket watch. While the girl was inconsolable, Carmichael chastised her not to be hysterical, like her mother. The comment sent Lydia over the edge.

Watson knelt to the girl and smiled. He was comfortable fixing bumps and bruises.

The attractive maid Watson met earlier in the week stepped out from a first-floor bathroom and saw Watson down the hall comforting the girl. The maid stepped back behind a pillar and lingered.

Watson had gotten the little girl's name from her dad and said to Lydia he thought they had some bandages in the office that would make her feel much better. The girl's sobbing slowed, and she wiped her nose on her arm. Watson asked her if she wanted him to get her a bandage.

Lydia nodded sweetly between sniffles as her father looked down at Watson and told him he had quite a touch. Watson shrugged it off, telling Carmichael he had younger sisters he used to care for, not much bigger than his daughter. Watson smiled at Lydia again, and she brightened.

The attractive maid spying the unfolding scene from behind the pillar softened. She thought, *maybe there was something to this man after all.*

After Watson went for the gauze, the ex-Mrs. Carmichael blew through the door, a peroxide blond in clattering heels, and she scowled at her former husband. Lydia rushed and clung to her mother as Mr. Carmichael admonished that it was about time she arrived. Lydia's tears began again as Watson arrived with the bandages and handed them to the girl.

The mother, confused, asked what had happened, and Watson told her it was just a scraped knee, but Lydia was going to feel much better, giving a smile to the young girl. She agreed, sweetly gazing up at him as her mother hauled her out the door. Mr. Carmichael muttered that he needed a drink and pushed forward toward the bar, leaving Watson alone in the hall, or so he thought.

As Watson finished putting on his jacket, the attractive maid approached. Watson turned, surprised, as she said, "It's Nannie. My name's Nannie."

Watson grinned and told her all right then. He was pleased to make her acquaintance. Watson realized she had watched him comfort the young girl and instantly felt a nervous pang. He decided he'd better leave before he fumbled the ball. Watson told Nannie he'd look forward to seeing her the next day as he turned for the door. Nannie, suddenly demure, nodded then watched him through the window as he navigated down the street.

Nannie Hood, who had just turned 18, was cautious around men. She had returned to work recently after her daughter, Kay, turned one year old in April 1935. Kay's father was not in her life, and Nannie wanted nothing to do with him.

Mother and daughter lived with her parents, Will and Barbara, in the South Titusville section of the city. Nannie's older sister Hattie watched Kay while she was at work.

Nannie and Watson's romance blossomed as they got to know each other. She had been concerned at first and waited to tell him about Kay, but he embraced the child. Nannie was thankful that her instincts were correct about Watson when she had seen him comforting the young daughter of the club member.

As they grew closer, Watson grew tired of his work at the club. He had been saving for college for a long time, but he was not nearly where he wanted to be in terms of funds. The janitorial job didn't pay much, and dating did cost money. The solution to his financial dilemma came in the form of a newly announced city initiative.

A year earlier, in March 1934, an enormous fire had destroyed Loveman's Department store on 19th Street, and the damages totaled over 3 million dollars. It was the costliest blaze in Birmingham's history and drew national attention. An official with the National Board of Fire Underwriters, William Straiton, investigated the fire and commended newly sworn-in Fire Chief Bryon "Boots" Hargrove. Straiton praised Hargrove and his staff for their "untiring efforts" in preventing the fire from spreading and protecting the crowds of onlookers.[11]

The national notice prompted a public investment initiative, and Hargrove went on a hiring spree. Walking to the grocery in his neighborhood one Saturday morning, Watson saw a recruitment sign seeking full-time firefighters outside his local fire station, Station No. 6. He wasted no time and entered the double-bay red-brick firehouse on 15th Street North and applied that day. Several days later, he was contacted at his grandmother's house, offered the job, and began training. The pay was much better than at the club, and being a fireman instilled a great deal of pride in Watson. He had an instinct to be of service and help people.

Watson and Nannie had settled into a routine, and he'd grown close to her daughter. They all spent as much time together as often as they could. After several years as a couple, in 1939, Nannie began dropping hints about how they should plan for the future. Watson could see a life with Nannie, but he wanted to become better established. To him, that meant an education, and the dream Watson had of getting an engineering degree persisted in his mind. He felt the dream slipping away, however, as he celebrated his 25th birthday in March.

Every time he brought the subject up, Nannie would become quiet. Watson knew she thought it was an impossible pursuit in the difficult times of the depression. She believed the money Watson had saved would allow them to move out of their homes and get a place of their own with Kay. Watson saw college, however, as a way to better his life if he ever planned to support a family.

All came to a head one Sunday afternoon in May 1939, while the two were taking a walk with Kay in Green Springs Park, later George Ward Park. Attending college was now on Watson's mind so frequently he became distracted, and Nannie decided to confront him. She accused him of being distant and perhaps dating another woman because he certainly wasn't paying attention to her.

Watson was shocked at the accusation and pleaded his innocence, saying he had no time for anyone else and loved her only. Nannie wanted him to prove it. She told him that if he truly loved her after these years of dating then he would be man enough to stand next

to her at the altar. It was either marriage, or she was moving on –
essentially handing him an ultimatum.

Watson froze in indecision at being backed into a corner.
Nannie was his first love, but he could sense she meant it. Watson
didn't want to lose her. He struggled awkwardly in the moment
but knew a decision had to be made. Finally, Watson chose love,
praying somehow he could make it work; Watson knelt and
proposed. Nannie began crying and threw her arms around him,
saying "yes" before he even finished the proposal. It was her dream
come true – a family.

Watson and Nannie were married a short time later on July 31,
1939, in a small ceremony, which his grandmother and Nannie's
parents and siblings attended.

Watson's grandmother, Emma Gaines, was not entirely happy
with the blessed union. She felt that Nannie was just trying to
snag a father figure for her daughter. Emma had seen the type
before, and her grandson was not wise to the ways of the world yet.
Grandma Gaines felt he was too earnest for his own good, and she
hated that he was giving up on a college education. She knew it was
his dream, and she didn't want him to grow old, bitter, and poor
without at least giving it a shot.

Shortly after the wedding in mid-August, when Watson and
Nannie were looking for a place to live, and Watson had not moved
out of her home yet, Emma decided to make him a special Sunday
supper: Watson's favorite, creamed chipped beef.

After finishing the meal, when they were relaxed and still at the
small kitchen table, Emma casually asked him how much he had
saved up for college. Watson's mood became sullen, and he asked
his grandmother why she had asked him that. Emma explained
that she didn't want to see him throw away *his* dream and that there
was still time. How much money did he need?

Watson had the figures memorized and told her that to attend
the school he wanted out west, Colorado A & M; he needed
another $965 for a second year in their Engineering program. He
explained that tuition was $400, room and board was $520, and
books another $45. Watson said that the first year's tuition was

saved but not the second. Watson wanted to make sure that he could at least continue if he ever started school; otherwise, what was the point?*

Emma grinned and reached for her pack of Camels that was always nearby, lit a cigarette, leaned back, and began to propose an offer. She asked her grandson what he thought about her paying for the second year. And perhaps if he were doing well, Emma would help him with the rest. That was only *if* he was doing well; she wasn't going to waste her money.

Watson glanced off into the distance, thinking about what he would tell Nannie as he considered the offer. Emma, reading his mind, didn't want him going soft. She told him this offer was *only if* he started right away, this fall. Otherwise, he could forget all about it, and she meant it.

Watson sighed. He'd come to know his grandmother well, and if she said something, she was a woman of her word. Watson knew Emma wouldn't make the offer again. Silence hung between them a long moment as he came to his decision. The word "yes" was coming out of his mouth before he could pull it back. Watson's voice grew stronger as he repeated it twice more and Emma thrust her Camel cigarette in the air in triumph, saying "yes" right along with him.

Watson mailed his application to Fort Collins, Colorado, the following day. It had been sitting filled out for a few years. Watson decided not to tell Nannie anything about it until if and when he was accepted. He also stalled moving out of his grandmother's house.

A couple of weeks later, after checking the mailbox every day, finally, the letter came. Watson opened it slowly, his hands trembling, and read the words, "pleased to offer admission…." Watson's heart soared. Growing up as close to poverty as one could get, then rejecting that life, striking out on his own, getting married, and now he became the first one in his family to go to college. Watson believed it was as close to a miracle as any divine event that

---

* $965 in today's dollars is $17,954.

had ever occurred. His joy didn't last long. Watson had to tell the new Mrs. Watson the "wonderful" news; Watson closed his eyes and shuddered at the thought.

Nannie was utterly devastated and retreated to her room, weeping. Watson felt helpless. He knew it was the right thing to do for himself *and* their future. He wished there was some way he could convince her; make her understand.

The clock ran out, however, as September arrived, and Watson had to head west for his first semester at Colorado A & M. The couple spoke little in his remaining days in Birmingham. Watson didn't know this, but Nannie had decided that the marriage was over. She felt Watson had gone back on his commitment to her and their future. He was spending his savings on school, and those funds were meant for starting their new married life. The break was irreparable.

Watson attempted to talk with his wife several times, but she refused to see him every time he arrived at her parents' doorstep. Watson tried one last time on the way to Terminal Station. Will, Nannie's father, answered the door this time, and Mr. Hood held out a letter from his daughter. Watson took it as his father-in-law wished him well and closed the door. Watson stuffed the letter in his jacket and headed for Terminal Station and his new life.

Chapter 14

Off to War

The separation from Nannie became permanent as Watson remained in Colorado during the next several years to finish up his degree in the summer of 1942. Watson had done well enough to stay, and Emma helped him with the tuition as promised. With the country now at war due to the Pearl Harbor attack, Watson faced an uncertain future. That uncertainty was resolved at the end of the summer when Watson was drafted on September 1, 1942 and sent to Camp Lee, Virginia, for basic training.

Camp Lee was the home of the Quartermaster School and had been since the end of 1941. Quartermaster School and the Quartermaster Corps, which Watson would subsequently join, were responsible for procuring and delivering various supplies to units in all theaters of operation. No other area proved to be more challenging than the war in the Pacific Theater with its lengthy supply lines where Watson would eventually be stationed.[12]

The Quartermaster School grounds at Camp Lee covered 507 acres and training areas adequate for the 5,000 students attending the school, staff, and faculty numbering 362 officers, 1,373 school troops, and 195 civilian employees.[13]

The physical training of Quartermaster entrants was critical from the beginning of the Army training program. Rigorous military training included weapons training and other physical combat skills. This regimen included crawling through simulated battlefields, taking refuge in foxholes they dug themselves.

Watson was a natural athlete and embraced the physical training. The Quartermaster Corps also emphasized analytical skills, making technical decisions regarding rations, and learning every aspect of ammunition supply points (ASPs).[14] With Watson's studies in engineering and his love of math, these duties suited him well.

At Camp Lee, Watson trained for 12 weeks to become a laundry specialist on mobile laundry machines, joining the 2nd Battalion in the 29th Quartermaster Regiment (Truck). It was no small operation. Laundry units in the Quartermaster Corps were made up of three officers and 85 enlisted men. Mobile laundries resembling semi-trucks containing up to six mobile laundry units each could wash approximately 125lb of clothes each hour.

Men paid 50 cents per bundle to have their clothes washed as, surprisingly, legislation to provide free laundry service to soldiers failed to pass.[15] Watson was then sent to Charleston, South Carolina, for final training before heading up to Virginia to ship out on December 27, 1942.

At Newport News, VA, Watson boarded the USS *Hermitage* (AP-54), a former Italian luxury liner, the SS *Conte Biancamano*, launched in 1925. The troop transport had just arrived back from Casablanca on December 11.

Embarking on the 27th, the *Hermitage* sailed south with over 10,000 men en route through the Port of Cristobal, Panama, where it docked on January 2 and spent four days. Onboard the ship, Watson met and befriended Sergeant James E. Guilford Jr. from Boston, Massachusetts.

Guilford was extroverted and what they used to call an "operator." He seemed always to have some deal going aboard ship to make spare cash, from gambling to selling trinkets and soap. Guilford covered all the bases. To him, it was all about the dollar. He viewed Watson at first as an easy mark, an earnest man whom he could easily take advantage of. However, for reasons Guilford didn't fully understand himself, he decided against doing that with Watson. He admired the man and wanted to know what made him tick.

Watson, in turn, realized Guilford was an operator, but he loved the man's street-smart humor. Guilford kept Watson in stitches, doubled over laughing nearly the entire trip. It helped Watson forget about the lingering pain of the marriage he had left behind. The journey to Brisbane would eventually last more than a month with Watson, Guilford, and the rest of the battalion's arrival in Australia on January 31, 1943.

The 29th Quartermaster (QM) Regiment had been activated at Fort Leonard Wood, Missouri, in 1941 as an African American unit with three battalions and 12 lettered truck companies.

The regiment had earlier deployed to Australia on April 7, 1942, sailing out of San Francisco as part of the US Army Forces in Australia (USAFIP). In early March 1942, General Douglas MacArthur had received direct orders from President Roosevelt to move his command from the Bataan peninsula to Australia. On March 17, 1942, MacArthur's B-17 touched down at the RAAF Batchelor Field, located 45 miles south of Darwin. He was accompanied by his wife, his child, the child's nurse, and 13 of MacArthur's senior staff officers.[16] His officer staff entourage was nicknamed "The Bataan Gang."

MacArthur's arrival was met with great fanfare and support from the Australian people. He outlined his mission with a press statement at the time: "The president of the United States," MacArthur said, "ordered me to break through the Japanese lines and proceed from Corregidor to Australia for the purpose, as I understand it, of organizing an American offensive against Japan."[17]

To say MacArthur was treated like royalty would be putting it mildly. The Australians welcomed him with open arms everywhere he went, and a dinner was held in his honor on March 26 at Parliament House in Canberra. At the affair, his oratory rose to heights worthy of Churchill: "There can be no compromise," MacArthur stated. "We shall win, or we shall die, and to this end, I pledge you the full resources of all the mighty power of my country and all the blood of my countrymen."

On April 18, 1942, General MacArthur formally assumed command of the Australian armed forces. MacArthur now commanded 100,000 members of the 2nd Australian Imperial Force (AIF) and 265,000 Australian Militia in his role as Southwest Pacific Area Supreme Commander.[18]

By late January 1943 and Watson's arrival in the Southwest Pacific Theater docking in Brisbane, Australia, the Japanese were licking their wounds from recent losses in the Guadalcanal and Papuan campaigns. In early February 1943, the Japanese hatched plans to fortify their depleted positions in the Solomons and New Guinea.

A large Japanese seaborne convoy was assembled and began sailing for their intended position at Lae, New Guinea, which was sighted by planes of the Allied Air Forces, Southwest Pacific Area. In addition, codebreakers in Melbourne, Fleet Radio Unit Melbourne (FRUMEL), and in Washington, DC, had decrypted and translated messages indicating the Japanese convoy's intended destination and date of arrival on March 2.[19]

The codebreaker's intelligence breakthrough resulted in the battle of the Bismarck Sea. It was an unmitigated disaster for the Japanese. Out of the 6,900 enemy troops aboard the convoy, only a little over 1,200 made it to Lae, New Guinea. Allied aircraft sank a total of 16 Japanese ships, half being troop transports and the other half destroyers.

The victory was a propaganda boon for the Allies, especially MacArthur, who inflated the enemy losses to enhance his reputation further. He issued a communiqué on March 7 stating that 22 ships, including 12 transports, three cruisers, and seven destroyers, had been sunk along with 12,792 troops.[20]

The battle of the Bismarck Sea serves as the backdrop and context in which Watson was operating and why the Japanese resorted to desperate tactics to exact revenge on Allied South Pacific forces.

Chapter 15

Operation *Lilliput*

The 29th QM Regiment 2nd Battalion was headquartered at Port Moresby, New Guinea. In early February, Watson and Guilford boarded a train on the Queensland's rail system for the 600-mile journey south to Sydney, their port of embarkation.

The 2nd Battalion was part of the ongoing Operation *Lilliput*, which had begun in December 1942. It was a seaborne convoy operation ferrying troops, weapons, and other supplies in a regular transport service between Milne Bay and Oro Bay, New Guinea. The objective was to build up resources in anticipation of the US Army's 32nd Division capturing the Japanese beachhead at Buna-Gorda.

In the *Lilliput* convoy, Watson was assigned as laundry specialist to the US Army Transport (USAT) *Jacob*, sometimes referenced as *s'Jacob*, a US Army-controlled Dutch freighter. The 325-foot vessel was constructed in Rotterdam, Netherlands, and launched in 1907. The Army pressed it into wartime service at the start of the Pacific War.

In February 1943, USAT *Jacob* departed Sydney harbor with 165 souls aboard, including George Watson and James Guilford. The vessel, transporting troops, weapons and medical supplies, was escorted by the Australian corvette HMAS *Bendigo*.

The transport and escort ship stopped briefly at Townsville on the northern coast of Australia and then again up the coast at Cairns before crossing 520 nautical miles north to Port Moresby, New Guinea, in late February.

Port Moresby was a military debarkation point located on the southern coast of New Guinea on a peninsula that includes Paga Hill, Ela Beach, and a wharf area. Port Moresby was code-named "Teak" by the US Army and was targeted constantly by Japanese aircraft. The port ultimately sustained over 100 enemy bombing attacks from January 1942 to September 1943.

By January 1943, the Japanese had 164 army and 190 navy aircraft on their base at Rabaul and the surrounding airfields of Kavieng and Vunakanau to use to attack Port Moresby and any approaching Allied shipping.[21]

On March 8, near one o'clock after Watson had finished lunch in the galley with his friend Guilford, they decided to go topside. Guilford joked that hearing the sun was out, he needed to get himself some rays. It was a clear day; the sun was indeed shining bright and it was 78 degrees Fahrenheit.

USAT *Jacob* was sailing north parallel to the southeast coast of New Guinea from Milne Bay toward Oro Bay rounding Cape Nelson when shipboard alarms rang out. Panic set in on the ships as American pilots providing air cover were alerted; the convoy was under attack. The alarm was not a drill.

Two squadrons consisting of nine Japanese G4M1 Betty bombers escorted by 12 fighters of the 751 Kokutai and 705 Kokutai flown from Kavieng and Vunakanau airfield were fast approaching in a V-formation. USAT *Jacob*, approximately 13 nautical miles offshore, was entering Porlock Bay. The mainland was barely visible as a strip on the horizon.

As Watson and Guilford wandered amid the confusion near the stern, they heard the approaching planes and watched the skies in horror. One Japanese squadron peeled off and attacked their escort ship, which already had their three Oerlikon 20mm cannons engaged on the enemy planes as well as their long-barrel 40mm British Bofors antiaircraft gun.

HMAS *Bendigo* was able to stave off damage from the first squadron with several near misses while the second squadron zeroed in on USAT *Jacob*. Japanese bombers flew low, scoring three direct hits in succession, rocking the transport. One bomb entered the number three hatch while another bomb exploded near the smokestack. Still another erupted toward the bow, causing structural damage, tossing sailors overboard and setting the ship ablaze.

An initial effort by the Dutch Captain was made to save the vessel. However, when it was realized the water pumps had malfunctioned, preventing any effort to extinguish the fire, the Captain gave the order to abandon the ship.

Lifeboats had already begun to be lowered, but Watson and Guilford felt the *Jacob* listing to starboard within minutes and knew it was time for them to abandon ship. Knowing that the vessel was about to sink, the crew released all floatable materials, such as hatch covers, rafts, and barrels for life-saving aids.

Guilford grabbed two life jackets and handed one to Watson, who told him to give it to someone who needed it as he was a strong swimmer. Taken aback, Guilford handed the "extra" life jacket to a crewmember who was rushing by. It was pandemonium and very much every man for himself.

Watson and Guilford ran to the rail and leaped over, falling 40 feet to the water toward the rope raft. Guilford could not swim and plummeted farther into the ocean than Watson had. Upon seeing his friend struggling, Watson swam down and pulled Guilford back up. Guilford gasped for breath as he broke the surface.

As Watson assisted Guilford to the rope raft, they heard a deep twisting metallic sound then felt a spray of water as USAT *Jacob* rolled over, and the bow rose high out of the water.

Watson could see crewmen still trying to leap off the ship and others floundering in the water, and he left Guilford's raft and swam toward them. Grabbing men one at a time who were frantically paddling to stay afloat, Watson pulled them to rafts and other floating debris surrounding the ship. Some distant sailors he could not save; he watched them disappear below the ocean surface.

Thankful enlisted men and officers watched Watson tirelessly rescue one man after another but started to see him tiring, dipping below the surface several times. His friend Guilford, who'd now pulled himself together after nearly drowning, saw without question Watson was in trouble as the HMAS *Bendigo* began to pull men aboard.

Guilford shouted for Watson to come aboard the raft. Watson heard his friend in the distance but turned back and saw one more struggling man. The sailor was waving his arms, and his head kept dipping below the water near USAT *Jacob*. The vessel was almost entirely submerged. Watson swam toward the struggling sailor, but it was too late. At 1.16 p.m. the 3,000-ton ship gurgled its death gasp and sank beneath the waves.

The sinking of the enormous ship created a powerful vortex of suction that dragged Watson and the men near the vessel instantly under, deep into the ocean's depths. They were powerless against the suction-force the descending ship created, similar to being caught in a whirlpool riptide from which there was no escape.

Five men were lost in the sinking, including George Watson, and a total of 153 were rescued, with two of the men dying en route to a military hospital. James Guilford noted in his book, *The Saga of George Watson*, that one of the men Watson saved was the white Lieutenant who was in charge of their detail.

For Watson's heroic efforts in saving his comrades and his commanding officer, with utter disregard for his own life, he was posthumously awarded the Distinguished Service Cross (DSC) on June 13, 1943. He was the first black American service member to receive the award in World War II.

On Saturday August 14, 1943, Watson's grandmother, Emma, received a knock on her apartment door at 1085 North Britain Street in Birmingham. Waiting outside was Army Major General Harry F. Hazlett, commanding officer of the Army Ground Forces Replacement School in Birmingham. He presented a tearful Emma with Watson's Distinguished Service Cross. In making the presentation, he said, "George died in the shining splendor of high courage and utter unselfishness, true to the best traditions of the American soldier, an inspiration to every real American."[22]

Watson's courage and selflessness shone like a beacon through five decades. He was finally awarded the country's highest military honor for valor for his heroic sacrifice when President Clinton elevated his DSC to the Medal of Honor on January 13, 1997. Sergeant Major of the Army, Gene C. McKinney, accepted the award on behalf of the family. The medal is displayed at the US Army Quartermaster Museum in Fort Lee, Virginia. Watson was further honored on July 26, 1997, when the Navy named a newly constructed ship in the Military Sealift Command, the USNS *Watson*, in his honor.

Although George did not live a long life, he achieved a great deal considering the circumstances of his birth and the realities of the world. Although born as a sharecropper's son, he believed he was destined for much more. Amid widespread racial prejudice, Watson dared to strike out on his own during the harshest economic times the entire world had ever faced. He had the intelligence and drive to better his future in gaining a college education, the first one in his family to do so.

However, what ultimately set him apart was his concern and care for his fellow man; the color did not matter. He saved the lives of both black and white sailors, including the commander in charge of his own detail. He demonstrated the best of what we all can aspire to and serves as a model of what the Medal of Honor, America's highest military honor, stands for.

GEORGE WATSON, MEDAL OF HONOR CITATION

For extraordinary heroism in action on 8 March 1943. Private Watson was on board a ship that was attacked and hit by enemy bombers. When the ship was abandoned, Private Watson, instead of seeking to save himself, remained in the water assisting several soldiers who could not swim to reach the safety of the raft. This heroic action, which subsequently cost him his life, resulted in the saving of several of his comrades. Weakened by his exertions, he was dragged down by the suction of the sinking ship and was drowned. Private Watson's extraordinarily valorous actions, daring leadership, and self-sacrificing devotion to his fellow man exemplify the finest traditions of military service.

PART SIX

Ruben Rivers

Chapter 16

Black Gold

Young Ruben Rivers, aged seven, wiry, full of kinetic energy, in brown overalls, bolted onto the porch of his family's farmhouse. The rusted screen door slammed shut behind him, jolting awake his grandmother who had been snoozing in her nearby wicker rocker. Jane, 71, berated Ruben for the number of times she'd told him *not* to slam the door.

After a monotone apology, Rivers peered down the road, shielding his eyes from the searing Oklahoma sun. His distinctive Cherokee almond-shaped eyes scanned the prairie horizon, searching in vain for his father's 1920 Ford Model T pickup. There was no sign of it.

Disappointed, Ruben glanced over to the side yard and saw his nine-year-old sister Gracie, twirling around in a large tractor tire on the tree swing. Taunting, she reminded him that their dad never got home till after dark.

Defiant Ruben countered, not always.

Gracie shot him back a frown then returned to twirling.

Ruben sized up the tire swing and the tree and proclaimed he bet he could swing higher and faster than she ever could.

Gracie, who lived in the tree swing, laughed then snorted disagreement.

Ruben dared her to show him how high she could swing.

Gracie grinned with great expectation of winning the bet, walked the tire back, and jumped back in. She kicked her legs high, swinging the tire in an impressive long wide arc.

Ruben yelled to his brothers to come out and see him swing higher than Gracie.

Robert, eight years old, and Dewey, aged four, sprung onto the porch, letting the rusty door slam hard, nearly off its hinges. Grandma Jane jerked awake again, picked up her cane, rapped it on the porch floorboards, then shouted something everyone ignored.

Gracie swung as high as she could then dragged her feet on the ground to slow herself. She jumped off, threw Ruben a contemptuous look, and walked to the side triumphant.

Ruben laughed, then mocked her, asking if that's all she got. Approaching the swing like an Olympic champion, he walked the four-foot tire back, nodded to the judges – his siblings – then hopped in. He didn't sit in the tire like Gracie; he stood in it and held onto the rope. Ruben pushed his legs down, pumping the swing higher and faster till it almost went perpendicular touching the lower branches of the old oak tree.

His brothers, impressed, gasped, "Whoa."

Jane screeched to Ruben to stop acting like a damn fool; he was going to get hurt. Robert laughed and reassured her, Ruben wasn't scared of nothin'. They'd all learned, perhaps except for stubborn Gracie, not to challenge or underestimate Ruben at anything. He was fearless, and he always won.

The kids all heard a truck backfire, turned, and saw the tell-tale rising dust cloud from their father's Ford pickup coming down the road. Ruben, seeing the pickup, leaped off the tire, and they all raced each other to the gravel driveway. Gracie yelled in to her mother that Dad was coming.

The siblings were especially excited. It was market day, the day their father sold the family's surplus crops. He'd always bring special treats back from Earlsboro for the kids on market day.

Willie Rivers, father of the brood, aged 33, had migrated from Conway County Arkansas to Hotluka, Oklahoma near Earlsboro in 1912 to tenant farm cotton and wheat. After arriving, he met Lillian

Thompson, three years his junior, in Earlsboro. She had also moved to Oklahoma from the south. She'd resettled with her family from Moscow, Alabama, northwest of Birmingham, and worked at the dry goods store in town. The two met, fell in love, and were married on March 1, 1915. Ruben was their third child, born on October 30, 1918.

The Rivers had been scratching out a living on their hardscrabble tenant farm on Rural Rte 1 for the past ten years. The last five had been especially difficult since Prohibition became law. Earlsboro, the market for their crops, was a wild frontier town with 90 percent of its economy based on liquor sales, especially whiskey.

Prohibition wiped out the town's economy, and a majority of the population moved on. Willie and Lillian had been considering doing the same. Not only had their market dried up, but crop prices hovered at all-time lows.

Times were so desperate in Pottawatomie County it drove one poverty-stricken Oklahoma farmer just west of Willie and Lillian to a life of crime. The "Robin Hood of Cookson Hills," better known as "Pretty Boy Floyd," left Oklahoma farm life far behind and began a life of crime, committing a series of robberies in the late 1920s and early 1930s. During bank heists he often burned people's mortgage documents, eliminating their debts. The act elevated Floyd to mythic status, and he was perceived as a folk hero by the public.

Whether the Rivers viewed Pretty Boy Floyd's exploits favorably or not is unknown. Undoubtedly, their bleak economic prospects and accompanying financial woes were taking a toll on their marriage. On this warm March day, however, Willie Rivers was bringing home news that would turn the family's fortunes around.

Gracie shouted again for her mother, and Lillian emerged onto the porch past a snoozing Grandma Jane. She let the screen door close softly as she cradled sleeping infant Bernice in her arms. Mrs. Rivers, a striking, slender woman with high cheekbones, had deep-set frown lines, revealing she was aging before her time. She waited on the porch, apprehensive, as Willie turned the old black Ford into the driveway.

Willie shut the door of his pickup, grabbed a vegetable crate of groceries from the back, and came around the cab looking like a man reborn. His tall frame had a spring in its step. All the Rivers noticed his beaming smile – unusual for him. Lillian cocked her head and told her husband he looked like the cat who ate the canary; what on earth had gotten into him?

Willie chuckled as the kids pawed at the overstuffed grocery crate. He told them to hold their horses as he approached the porch. Willie kissed little Bernice on the forehead. "Lil," he announced, "you're never going to believe this." The kids shouted in unison, "what?!"

Willie hushed them so as not to wake the baby. Then he continued saying that when he was at the feed store, Mr. Drucker came busting in the door and announced they'd struck oil in town, right outside Earlsboro.

Lil couldn't believe it. Finally, people would be coming back to the town. They'd have more customers for the crops, lots more money. It was what they'd long been praying to happen.

Ruben and the rest of the children weren't sure what it all meant. However, Ruben's younger brother Dewy, with the honesty of a four-year-old, tugged at his mother's dress and asked if this meant she was "gonna stop being mad all the time?" The comment elicited loud laughter and a nod from Lillian to the relief of them all.

That oil strike and subsequent well was the Earlsboro Sand. On March 1, 1926, the drill had penetrated to 3,557 feet, and oil started flowing at a rate of 200 barrels a day. According to one historian, the Earlsboro Sand oil well was part of the more significant Seminole oil boom across east-central Oklahoma, which "swung the United States' oil reserves from scarcity to surplus."[1]

The town and the Rivers' fortunes changed overnight. At the start of March 1926 there were little more than 400 people in Earlsboro and Hotluka combined. Within three months, the population soared to an estimated five to ten thousand people. Main street was lengthened from one block to five with numerous side and parallel streets. Doctors, lawyers, engineers, and geologists sought office space. Shotgun houses and tents occupied almost every available space.[2]

In the years that followed, Willie and Lillian had several more children amidst the petroleum prosperity. By 1931 times were so good and the money so plentiful in Earlsboro and the surrounding communities that notorious Pretty Boy Floyd targeted the Earlsboro Bank and Loan.[3]

The heady times, like Pretty Boy Floyd's life of crime, were not to last. By 1932 oil production in Earlsboro slowed to a trickle, leaving the city high and dry with huge debts from a municipal bond issue. The debt eventually drove the municipality into bankruptcy. The boom and bust of east-central Oklahoma had distilled important lessons into Ruben. Living through his family's daily struggles and strife during the Great Depression, he turned self-reliant, toughened up but remained fearless.

Graduating from Earlsboro High School in 1938, he went right to work for the local railroad. It was a hard-pounding labor-intensive tough job that was preparing him, although he didn't realize it, for the coming rigors of the military.

Ruben eventually registered for the draft in Oklahoma City on October 16, 1940, listing his height at 6 feet and his weight at 168lb. He had moved to Oklahoma City to be near his brother Robert who had married in March of 1938. Robert had taken a job with the Universal Mercantile Company. In 1940 Dewey Rivers began working and living at a CCC (Civilian Conservation Corps) Camp in Konawa 30 miles south of the farm.

***

By early 1942, after the attack on Pearl Harbor the previous December, the Rivers brothers had all registered for the draft. Robert would later serve in a supply unit in France while Dewey would enlist in late October 1942 and serve with the engineers in New Guinea. The draft board ordered Ruben in January 1942 to Camp Claiborne, Louisiana, assigned to a new black tank battalion that was forming.

On the train ride to Louisiana, Ruben Rivers had his first significant brush with discrimination heading into the Deep South. Like Vernon Baker on his train ride to Texas, Rivers, shortly after he boarded, was escorted by the porter to the train car for black passengers, mostly black military recruits. It was a sweltering hot, smoke-filled, overcrowded space up near the engine. Occasionally a smoking coal ember would sail through a window into the train car, which they had to stamp out.

Rivers wedged himself in between two other young black men with duffles who were also heading off to basic training. Between catnaps, Rivers watched several men play poker. Despite the oppressive conditions, almost all were in high spirits.

The train finally pulled into Alexandria, Louisiana, 20 minutes by car north of the army camp. Rivers asked a nearby man with a watch the time. It was just past noon. As the black recruits disembarked with their duffles, their smiles quickly faded. The town felt especially unwelcoming as they saw numerous "whites only" signs hung in store windows.

Rivers and the small group of men decided to try to find a place to grab a bite to eat. As they walked down Lee Street, residents glared at them. They were unaware of the southern custom of stepping off the sidewalk to let a white person pass. The hostile atmosphere convinced the men to forgo lunch and find their way to the bus station. They had instructions to take the Forest Hill bus south to camp.

When Rivers and his fellow nine enlisted men boarded the bus, they saw black passengers bunched up at the back with many empty seats between them and the driver. Rivers paused a second, eyeing an open seat near the front, but the overweight driver motioned with a chubby thumb to the back, sneering, "niggers to the back."

The recruits were unaware that two months earlier, on January 10, 1942, the largest Army race riot during World War II had erupted in Alexandria. The town was a popular Liberty Weekend destination for soldiers from Camp Claiborne and Camp Livingston. The riot was reportedly triggered by a white MP discharging his sidearm at a black soldier for allegedly assaulting a white woman. The shooting caused unarmed black soldiers to retaliate against the MP and local authorities with bricks and whatever else they could find.

Two to three thousand people jammed the Lee Street entertainment district that Saturday night, with the overwhelming number being African American. With tempers flaring, the incident quickly spun out of control. Law enforcement, unlike the soldiers, had an arsenal of weapons at their disposal and began shooting black soldiers indiscriminately.

Although the military coordinated with the local paper, the *Daily Town Talk*, to cover up the severity of the violence, reporting that "there were no deaths," scholars including Dr. Bill Simpson, a former history professor at Louisiana College, have subsequently come to a different conclusion. Simpson's multi-year investigation published in 1994 determined that at least 10–15 black recruits died that January night. In the aftermath of Simpson's publication of his findings, the *Daily Town Talk* acknowledged its complicity publicly in the now demonstrated cover-up.*,4

Camp Claiborne, named after Louisiana's first governor, William C.C. Claiborne, was built after the Louisiana Maneuvers in 1940 within the Kisatchie National Forest. Although geographically remote, by the time Rivers arrived in March 1942, thousands of soldiers were training within its confines. Claiborne was the first home of the 82nd Infantry Division reactivated that month with Major General Omar Bradley commanding. Soon after, the 82nd ID was reconstituted as the Army's first Airborne Division under General Ridgeway and moved to Fort Bragg, North Carolina.[5] A short time later, the 101st Airborne got their start at Camp Claiborne as well.

Rivers would not be parachuting into battle, but he was there to join a new outfit formed from black soldiers of the 758th. This new black battalion was the 761st, officially getting its start on April 1, 1942.

Entering the camp, Rivers was impressed by its massive size, being a world unto itself. As he checked in with an officer, a green bus idled outside the main administration building, waiting to take him and a small group of other black recruits to their new barracks. Rivers and the other fresh recruits laughed and joked and scrambled onto the bus. 1st Sergeant Sam Turley greeted them. Turley, a powerful hulking black man with jet black eyes, silenced the men by his menacing presence without even uttering a word.

---

* The events in Alexandria would cast a pall over the entire community for years to come. Looking back on it from today one cannot help but be repulsed by the attitudes of the townspeople and what little value they placed on black lives.

When he did speak, his voice was gruff and rasping. He told the soldiers to "listen up M—fkers" mommy wasn't there to take care of them no more; they were in the Army now.

No one dared speak, but Rivers would get accustomed to the profane epithet. In fact, "M—fkers" somehow worked its way into every other sentence in camp from there forward.

The Army temporarily assigned Rivers and the other recruits to the 758th Tank Battalion, but Rivers would soon transfer to Able Company of the 761st. Both black battalions were located at the far end of the sprawling camp a mile from the main gate.

As the shuttle bus lumbered forward on the paved main camp road, it passed pristine drill areas, motion picture theaters, post exchanges, wooden barracks, and immaculate training areas. It slowed to a crawl after about five minutes upon reaching the main camp's outskirts, jostling the men out of their seats as the smooth pavement changed abruptly to a rutted cow path. Rivers and the other recruits bouncing around in the bus turned to look back at the disappearing main camp as if they were watching civilization fade away.

The bus arrived at a rise overlooking a valley, which was a former mosquito-infested swamp. Outstretched before Rivers and the other recruits was a bleak scene reminiscent of sepia-toned Civil War photographs. Row upon row of sagging canvas squad tents with wooden duckboards between them served as their new home. The original white canvas tents had darkened from mold in the suffocating Louisiana humidity.

As Rivers and the open-mouthed men scanned the depressing site, a gaseous fecal stench filtered into the bus, gagging them all. They coughed and held their noses. The black section of the camp was adjacent to the facility's enormous sewage disposal plant. The men's watery eyes looked at each other in disbelief as Sgt. Turley rose to chortle, "Welcome to your new home, M—fkers."

At the same time Rivers was settling into Camp Claiborne and the 761st, a white 2nd Lieutenant, David J. Williams, was beginning his journey in the same unit. Rivers' and Williams' lives would intertwine almost in a predestined way that no one in 1942 could have imagined or predicted. The two would not formally meet, however, until early 1944.

Williams grew up in Pittsburgh, Pennsylvania, the son of a wealthy industrialist, and had prepped at Phillips Academy in Andover, Massachusetts. He was attending Yale when the war broke out. He had served in the Army's 70th Tank Battalion during peacetime and graduated at the top of his Officer Candidate School class at Fort Knox, Kentucky, in January 1942.

Arriving at Camp Claiborne on April 11 that year as a buttoned-up liberal-minded officer, he was assigned to the 758th Tank Battalion. Williams, tall with dark wavy hair, could not have been more different than the "good ol' boy" officers surrounding him. At his first awkward meeting with Charlie Company commander Captain Barnes, his commanding officer asked him point-blank what an educated man like him was doing in a Negro hell hole like this. Williams, filled with back east idealism about training black soldiers, had no answer for him.

At this same meeting, Barnes' 1st Sgt. Sam Turley reported in. Williams made, in Barnes' eyes, the grave mistake of shaking the black man's shovel-sized hand after saluting him.

After sending Turley away, Barnes leaned over his desk, jabbing his finger at Williams, asking what the hell he thought he was doing putting himself on the same level as a "nigger" enlisted man, even if Turley was his Topkick.* A white man, he admonished, never puts himself on the same level.

Williams slunk away with his tail between his legs, and less than a month later, Barnes handed Williams transfer papers to Charlie Company of the 761st. During their last meeting, Captain Barnes wished Williams well in a sarcastic tone, saying he hated seeing him go. Williams' now-former commander finished up by telling him he thought he could've made a Christian out of him before long.[6]

In 1942 the 761st was a long way away from being the pride of Third Army as Patton's Black Panthers and recipient of the Presidential Unit Citation. The three "letter" companies plus Headquarters Company were commanded by white Captains mainly from the Deep South who believed they knew how to "handle the Negros."

* Military term for 1st Sergeant.

One of the first orders of business each of them did was select a ball-buster like Sam Turley as their 1st Sergeant to handle discipline, reflective of their attitudes that you had to be "mean to keep these boys in line." Punishments meted out included cancellation of passes, two-hour runs in full packs, digging stumps, and shoveling mud from one pile to another for hours.

Despite the harsh treatment and threats, the black enlisted men remained slovenly and undisciplined. Unsurprisingly, morale was low, and venereal disease rates were high. None of them, including Rivers, believed they would ever be allowed to fight. They were just passing the time. Junior officers like David Williams rarely stayed longer than a month before they transferred out, although Williams vowed to stick it out. It was a revolving door for others – a place for young white officers to get as far away from and as fast away from as they could.

Rivers' training schedule consisted of Reveille at 0600 hours followed by an inspection, then close-order drills, falling in, falling out, learning to salute correctly, and standing at attention. There was more to it than he thought; shoulders back, head up, stomach in, fists slightly closed, the thumb resting behind the seams of the pants, heels touching, and toes spread apart at a 45-degree angle.

The outfit's primary weapon was the M5 Stuart "light" tank. It carried a crew of four. Powered by twin Cadillac engines, it could reach a maximum speed of 40mph and had an open-road cruising range of 172 miles. It was armed with a .30cal machine gun mounted to fire along the same axis as the tank's main armament, a 37mm cannon.[7]

Rivers was one of the few attentive soldiers in the company, and 761st Able Company commander, Captain Charles W. Calvert, a red-haired, kind, knowledgeable man, a rarity among the white officers, noticed. Rivers rose to a Sergeant's rank as the companies gained three new black 2nd Lieutenants in early summer, one in each of the letter companies. Ivan Harrison joined Charlie, Charles Barbour was assigned to Baker, and Sam Brown became the first black 2nd Lieutenant in Able Company.

As the summer progressed, excitement built toward the first scheduled week-long maneuvers at Camp Livingston, August 23,

1942. All companies of the 761st joined a 32-mile road march to Camp Livingston for the training. The 761st was considered a light tank battalion as they utilized the M5 Stuart. In the march, the Stuarts kept a 20-yard spacing between them as a safety barrier. The maneuvers went off without a hitch as Rivers in Able Company with his platoon practiced fire and movement tactics against fortified positions that the 78th Division had set up. 2nd Lt. David Williams commanded the 1st Platoon of Charlie Company. Seeing the black tankers in action, he felt encouraged. They compared favorably to the white tankers in his old 70th Tank Battalion.

With the battalion back from maneuvers in early September, Williams became involved in an incident that contributed to him eventually leaving Charlie Company. After finishing up overseeing first echelon maintenance on the tanks and other Charlie Company equipment, he decided to head over to the officers' mess.

Arriving earlier than usual, he saw few people in the mess but caught sight of the three new black 2nd Lieutenants who'd joined the battalion earlier in the summer. Without thinking, after getting his food, Williams went over and sat down with them. Ivan Harrison served with Williams in Charlie Company, and Williams had met Charles Barbour and Sam Brown on the recent maneuvers. He considered them able and intelligent officers.

Williams didn't register their surprise that he had sat down to eat with them, which, in retrospect, he should have noted as shock. He attempted to make small talk, but they weren't responsive, just nodding yes and no to his rambling conversation.

Before long, Williams felt someone standing behind him as he looked across the table at the three black officers who appeared frozen in fear. Behind him stood Tilmer Davidson, the battalion S-3 and the officers' mess officer. Williams turned and saw Davidson's hard stare and piercing eyes. Davidson yelled down at Williams that he was out of line, his place was over in the white section, and he'd better never forget that.

Williams did not move fast enough for Davidson, so the mess officer raised his voice much higher, telling Williams to get his ass over there NOW, and that was an order. He was in charge of the dining facility.

The sting of the embarrassment Williams felt was sharp, but he felt worse for the humiliated young black officers. At that moment, the idealism he'd carried into the 761st died. Williams realized the system was too entrenched. No matter what good intentions he'd come in with to break down the color barrier, they'd all been for naught. Williams began planning his transfer out of the 761st that evening.

As fall descended and the weather grew crisp, the war unexpectedly heated up. On an overcast Sunday, Rivers, in the tent he shared with four other men, started hearing radios click on throughout the barracks area. Corporal Homer Bracey stuck his head into Rivers' tent and told him that old Ike had invaded Africa and a big battle was raging.

This was Operation *Torch*, the invasion of French North Africa. In the end, the amphibious invasion would feel like a warm-up for the assault on the beaches of Normandy. However, in the early days for troops under the command of Brigadier General Lucian Truscott, nothing went right, as Truscott recalled:

> As far as I could see along the beach, there was chaos. Landing craft were beaching in the pounding surf, broaching to the waves, and spilling men and equipment into the water. Men wandered about aimlessly, hopelessly lost, calling to each other and for their units, swearing at each other and at nothing.[8]

Later that month, on November 24, David Williams was promoted to 1st Lieutenant. He'd been working at Group Headquarters with Colonel Faye Smith and performing well as morale officer. He arranged boxing matches and other diversionary activities that kept the men's minds off not being called to the war.

As 1943 began, Rivers and fellow black tankers were shut out of a big USO show coming to camp. The show, on January 27–29, was called *Hellzapoppin*, a former Broadway production that featured comedians Olsen and Johnson. This USO version featured 16 white dancing girls called the Roxyettes. There was great concern on the part of the Camp Claiborne brass that they didn't want "the

Negros" stirred up by the dancing girls and didn't want them to ogle the girls during the show, which was, of course, exactly what the white soldiers did.

This was just another example of blatant racism. It was also incredibly shortsighted in terms of the wider war effort. As to be expected, morale in the 761st suffered as a result of being denied entry to the show. Now a Staff Sergeant, Rivers was on the receiving end of many of the complaints, which, of course, he felt were entirely valid. When the black 2nd Lieutenants arrived, the hope of equality rose but was soon dashed. The enlisted men felt the black officers treated them worse than the white officers. Ivan Harrison's nickname in Charlie Company was "Court-Martial Slim" for his adherence to strict discipline. But Rivers knew it was because the black officers were shown little to no respect by their white peers and overcompensated by trying to outshine them.

In March 1943, events took an almost disastrous turn for the 761st as a whole and for David Williams personally. Williams had outlived his usefulness at Group Headquarters and Col. Faye Smith, for reasons he kept to himself, transferred Williams to command a mortar platoon in Headquarters Company, which in a tank unit was like being sent to Siberia. No officer in the tank battalion wanted the assignment.

Of much more potentially disastrous consequence was an incident that unfolded after the first week of March. Tensions were coming to a head as the men spent less and less time on weekend leave in Alexandria. The hostility toward black soldiers there was at a fever pitch.

Just past 1900 hours, as it was getting dark on Saturday night, the 13th, Rivers heard a commotion several tents away. Writing a letter home lying on his bunk, he stopped then exited his tent. Rivers saw a group of angry men gathered. He recognized Leo Smith and Bill McBurney. They were comforting several upset soldiers who had just returned from Alexandria bruised and bleeding.

Rivers asked what the hell had happened, and the bleeding men told him they'd just been beaten up in town and were lucky to get out of there with their lives.

Rivers probed for more details.

The men were close-mouthed and instead asked Rivers if he'd heard about the soldier who'd been killed.

He hadn't.

Smith and McBurney told him that the story was all over the camp; a black soldier from Camp Livingston was dead. His body had been discovered severed in half on the railroad lines in Alexandria. The MPs were telling everyone that the soldier was drunk and had passed out on the tracks. Rivers thought it tragic but didn't see why the men were so upset.[9]

McBurney and Smith revealed that they knew the soldier who was killed. He was a strict Baptist and never drank. He was as straight up as they come. Smith said his friend must have been beaten up and left on the tracks, and they intended to do something about it.

More angry soldiers began milling around. Rivers could see several were glassy-eyed from moonshine. The growing group simmered with fury, itching to exact revenge. Word had spread, and now all in camp had heard the story. Loud voices in the angry group were demanding justice. Rivers felt the situation spinning out of control and wanted no part of it. He told McBurney and Smith they'd better think long and hard about what they were doing because it would mean court-martial or worse.

The outraged mob wouldn't listen; it had become a full-blown mutiny. Approximately 30 soldiers stormed toward the tank park; several climbed into the Stuarts and started them up. Rivers chased after them shouting for them to stop. The furious soldiers ignored him as they commandeered six tanks and a half-track and started rumbling out of the tank park toward the main gate, heading for Alexandria.

Most of the white officers were away on leave, including David Williams. The only white officer on duty that weekend was Charles Wingo, commander of Charlie Company. Sam Turley and Rivers ran to locate him and alert him to what was happening.

Wingo, upon hearing the news, dashed, unarmed, across the camp toward the main gate. Halfway into the white section of camp, Wingo stopped and stood astride the paved road waving his arms for the tanks to stop. He didn't move an inch as the convoy rumbled toward him. The Charlie Company commander stood defiant as the tanks finally rolled to a halt a couple of feet from him.

After they halted, he waved the men forward out of the tanks to come to him. They did. He found the perfect measured tone and spoke to the men, first telling them to kill the engines so all could hear him. The men, still boiling mad, listened as Wingo told them he was with them. He wasn't going anywhere, but if they wanted to get killed, this was just the invitation for the white infantry soldiers to come to try out their new machine guns. They'd be justified, and all this would amount to nothing.

As muttering began in the mob, Turley pushed his way to the front and stood firm beside Wingo, telling the men to listen to their commander. They were just begging to be sent to the Burma road with a pick and shovel. They were lucky just to be here. Now it was time to get their black asses back in the tanks and get 'em back to the park. He shouted for them to MOVE and warned them he wasn't going to repeat it.

Wingo couldn't top the intensity of Sgt. Turley. He nodded to his 1st Sergeant and said if they listened to the Sergeant, he'd do all he could to smooth things over with Colonel Wright and tell the battalion commander this was all simply a big misunderstanding.[10]

The men grumbled but listened, turned the tanks and half-track around, and headed back to the tank park. Wingo and Turley had put down the insurrection, but the anger lingered as the unit approached its first anniversary on April 1, 1943.

On that anniversary, a ceremonial gathering was held, and Colonel Wright, commander of the battalion, announced what had long been a latrine rumor; they were going on maneuvers at Camp Polk. The Colonel didn't mention the recent mutiny. The Army filed the incident away like it had never happened, but it had come close to being the end of the 761st Tank Battalion.

David Williams returned from his weekend leave appalled upon hearing the news of the mutiny. For him, it was the last straw. He told his barrack-mate David Walkery he was done with the lousy outfit and had decided to transfer out.

On April 8, 1943, the 761st joined the 85th ID and the 92nd ID for Third Army Maneuvers at Camp Polk. It would be their most intensive training yet and last for almost two months. During the exercises, the men conducted combat simulations with infantry for the first time. They learned to coordinate with ground forces to take positions and practiced communications, including hand signals. They also did night maneuvers and learned to live off rations, and performed other tasks, which brought them as close to feeling like they were in combat as possible.[11]

The 761st returned to Camp Claiborne in late May with a road march of 83 miles. After barely putting his duffle down, David Williams headed to see Captain Storch, the transfer officer. Williams tried to put in for a transfer to an airborne unit. Storch convinced him, however, the way to go was pilot training. There was a directive out requesting more pilots in the Air Force.

Williams didn't care either way. He told Storch he'd transfer to the Salvation Army if that were possible just to get the hell out of the nightmare he was living. Storch empathized; Williams was seemingly just another in a long line of young white officers from the 761st who came through his door requesting a transfer, and he wouldn't be the last.

Williams made a point of saying goodbye to Sam Turley before he left, telling him he'd tried his best, but it hadn't made any difference. They both wished each other well amidst the frustrating situation as Williams prepared to board a train for San Antonio and his preflight training. Williams was gone before July 4, 1943, but it would not be permanent.

Rivers was impacted by the mutiny incident as well. Everything had boiled to the surface in that one frustrating night, and he knew in his bones, despite the recent maneuvers, they were never going to let black soldiers fight. They all knew it. The men were just passing the time playing war as second-class soldiers. The country would be no different, he figured, for any of them when the war ended.

Chapter 17

A New Esprit de Corps

In May 1943, a new man took full command of the 761st Tank Battalion who would become beloved by all in the ranks and turn what had been a listing, rudderless ship entirely around. Colonel Paul Bates was a tall, athletic, handsome man who had risen through the ranks of the 761st. Born in Los Angeles, he was a star football player at West Maryland College, where he had graduated with an economics degree. Bates had been a Captain at Group Headquarters when David Williams worked directly for Col. Faye Smith.

One of Colonel Bates' first actions was to become visible in training exercises leading the men from the front. He fully intended to command the black tankers into battle, and he let that be known. Bates' confidence in the men improved morale and instilled a new esprit de corps within the 761st. Black tankers started tilting their barracks caps to one side and developed a confident tanker swagger.[12]

On September 15, 1943, Rivers and the 761st were ordered to Camp Hood, Texas, to train on M4 medium Sherman tanks. On October 29, 1943, the War Department made it official. The 761st went from being a light tank battalion with the M5 Stuart to a medium with the M4. The Sherman, the Army's newest land weapon, was heavier and more mobile than the Stuart, which was underpowered for combat with German tanks. The M4 Sherman was reliable and easily repaired in the field. Its structural weakness, which the men would unfortunately later discover, was its relatively paper-thin armor. The German infantry's shoulder-fired panzerfaust (tank fist) could easily penetrate the Sherman in close combat with a shaped-charge projectile, leaving death and destruction in its wake.

In late November 1943, David Williams returned to the 761st at Camp Hood and not by choice. He had intentionally washed out of pilot training as he hated it, plus his instructor realized he had no desire to fly. Williams expected reassignment to 1st Armored when his new orders came with his many years of tanker experience. Instead, he was shocked when he read the battalion number on his orders, 7 6 1. The 761st was the last place he wanted to be stationed, but he had little choice. Williams was initially assigned to command the 3rd Platoon of Dog Company, the only company in the battalion still using the Stuarts.

After he arrived at Camp Hood, Williams met with Captain Wingo, now the battalion's Executive Officer, to get the lay of the land. Wingo conveyed that Colonel Bates had completely turned around the unit's attitude, but there were still areas that needed improvement. Williams took the comment to heart. He carried anger to Camp Hood that he'd been sent back to an outfit that he despised. That acrimony transformed into a zeal to see these men become thoroughly disciplined soldiers if he ever got the opportunity to command a company.

On January 27, 1944, Colonel Bates called Lt. Williams into his headquarters. Solemn behind his desk, Bates informed Williams that it was indeed time that he commanded a company and he would be taking over Able Company from Sam Brown, one of the black 2nd Lieutenants who had risen to command of a company.

It would be a delicate situation for a while, the Colonel cautioned, in replacing the black company commander, but he was confident Williams would handle it. Bates finished the meeting by telling Williams that he wanted these men ready for combat.

Williams emerged from the meeting with mixed emotions. The promotion meant Captain's bars, but he wondered what disarray Able Company was currently experiencing. The directive, however, from Bates was clear: get the company in shape for combat. Combined with Williams' anger and training zeal, Bates' order was about to send Able Company reeling.

Williams made Sam Brown Executive Officer. He had two other black Lieutenants, Barbour and Griffin, and a white 2nd Lieutenant, Joseph Carlson. His 1st Sergeant was Hubert House, and Ruben Rivers was one of the Staff Sergeants.

The reaction in the ranks was shock and dismay. They all knew Williams had left and most likely didn't want to be there. Worse, he had replaced a black commander. Williams went right to work on spit and polish. He ordered Reveille at 0630 every morning, except Sundays, officers included, in class A uniforms. He insisted that the beds were to be made so tight during barrack inspections that if he dropped a dime on them, it would flip-flop.

At the company's first full inspection, the enlisted men appeared sloppy, and some soldiers even talked among themselves in the ranks. As a result of numerous infractions and insubordination Williams ordered a two-hour quick time march at 1500 hours that afternoon. At the second morning inspection, there was marked improvement except for one man.

Inspecting the ranks with 1st Sgt. House and Lt. Brown, Williams arrived at the last row where he came to a man who barely fit into his uniform. The buttons on his blouse strained, two buttons were open on his fly, and the man's shoes were untied. The man had to tip the scales at least 300 pounds. As Williams stood face to face marveling at the overweight, unkempt soldier, the man appeared as if he was about to burst into tears. Williams turned to Sgt. House blank-faced and motioned to the chubby soldier.

House jumped in and introduced Williams to Pvt. Howard Richardson, but he added that they all just called him "Big Tit." Williams raised an eyebrow and addressed the soldier as "Pvt. Tit" and told him his presentation was untidy and did not pass inspection.

Williams directed Sgt. House to assign the soldier extra kitchen duty for the infractions. Alarm flashed in House's eyes as he protested that the kitchen was the last place to post Big Tit; he'd eat all the food, and there'd be none left for the rest of the company. Williams, suppressing laughter, directed his Topkick to find some other suitable punishment not involving food.

Big Tit from Chillicothe, Ohio, eventually became Williams' trusted jeep driver out of necessity. The man was too big to fit inside a Sherman tank. Several times in drills he'd gotten stuck climbing in and out of the hatch. Williams would come to rely on and appreciate the man. Despite appearances, Tit was tough with little to no fear. Big Tit was also wise in his own way; he often said, "You can't tell the price of pork chops by looking up a pig's ass." No one, however, was really sure what that meant.

Captain Williams continued to push the company hard, drilling in every type of weather, and he enforced strict discipline. He judged good progress by the increasing number of sullen faces at morning inspections. The more downcast they became, the more Williams' spirits rose.

By the final Friday in February 1944, after a month in command, Sgt. House approached Williams tentatively and informed him that all the Sergeants wanted a meeting with him. Williams, indignant, asked what the hell their issue was. House pleaded that Williams hear the men out.

The following day Williams met with all Able Company noncoms in the day room and was formally introduced to Staff Sergeant Rivers. The men had grievances they thought were valid; the overriding concern was that Williams was riding them too hard because they were black.

The accusation incensed Williams, and he asked if they wanted racist Captain Barnes back and some of the older prejudiced officers who'd left. Williams confided that the old guard didn't respect them at all, while he was at least attempting to make them soldiers with self-respect.

Comments flew back and forth, and finally, Rivers raised his hand to speak. Williams noted his athletic bearing. Rivers spoke out in support of what Williams had said about respecting them, but he questioned why he couldn't serve under Sam Brown. Williams reminded Rivers of date-of-rank being the deciding factor. Then he asked Rivers if he would have objected to his replacing Sam Brown if he were Negro?

Rivers had no answer but smiled and said that Williams sure showed his true self, and he gotta respect that. He was straight out with them, Rivers said, "showin' his ass." The group of Sergeants broke into laughter at the comment, and Williams did as well. When the laughter died down, Williams said that he wasn't exactly sure if Rivers' comment was complimentary, which drew more laughter.[13]

The meeting, for better or worse, was one which had to occur for David to begin cultivating trust and a bond with his company. Williams had completely overlooked the importance of this by attempting to be a strict disciplinarian. This gathering, however, began building the bridge that needed to be there if they were ever going to fight as a cohesive unit and rely on each other in combat.

June 6, 1944 was a monumental day in the war's progress with the invasion of German-occupied France, but June 9 for the 761st almost matched it. It was a date they would never forget. More than a month earlier, General Patton had sent an urgent message to the War Department requesting more tankers. Apparently the response back to him was "that the only ones left were the Negro tankers." Reportedly he said "who the hell asked for color? I requested tankers."[14]

At 1100 hours on June 9, Colonel Bates called Williams and the other company commanders to meet with himself and Charles Wingo, now a Major. Bates announced that the battalion had been alerted for movement overseas to the European Theater of Operations (ETO).

Bates was grim to match the seriousness of the announcement, saying that he always knew this day would come. He directed the commanders to return to their companies, assemble their men, and read the Articles of War. The 761st was now on high alert, everything from here forward was top secret, and the unit would be censoring all mail. Bates closed the meeting by informing them that expected debarking for the battalion would be sometime in August.

In the day room Able Company assembled, and Williams read the Articles of War, making sure to raise his voice on the punishment section for desertion, disobedience of orders, and cowardice in the face of the enemy, which was death by firing squad. The men remained unmoved, but the atmosphere retained a seriousness.

After Williams was through reading the articles, Rivers stood waving his hand with a question. Williams acknowledged him and asked what was on his mind.

Rivers, somewhat in disbelief like most of the men, asked his Captain if they were really going to fight. Rivers continued that they'd been hearing rumors that they were simply going over to unload railroad cars somewhere. Williams responded that that was always possible, but he understood that Patton needed tankers, and they were the only ones left. So more than likely, they were indeed heading into combat.

The excitement began to build in the run-up to August and embarkation for Europe. Esprit de corps in the battalion was high, culminating with a speech in late July by Brigadier General Ernie Dawley, commander of the tank destroyer battalion. He said in part:

> Men of the 761st tank battalion, you have performed your
> mission here in a superior manner. You will carry on in the
> same fashion when you reach the ETO. When you get close
> to the enemy, I want you to do something for me, put a high
> explosive shell in the breech of your tank and fire it at the
> Krauts for an old Brigadier General named Ernie Dawley.[15]

Not all the soldiers in the 761st would have the opportunity to fire an HE (high explosive) shell for the old General. One soldier, in particular, would be staying behind.

Williams, the officer of the day on a hot, humid, early July night, was alerted by Sgt. Ted Weston that Colonel Bates wanted him to go immediately to the camp stockade. The Colonel wanted Williams to retrieve a Lieutenant in the 761st who'd been locked up.

Williams rushed over to the stockade and found 2nd Lt. Jack "Jackie" Robinson handcuffed and shackled. Robinson, who would later break the color barrier for black baseball players with the Brooklyn Dodgers, had seemingly been involved in an incident off base.

The MP who had brought Robinson out from his cell to Captain Williams said that the boy had been mighty unruly. He was charged with threatening a civilian and using profane language in a public vehicle.

Leaving the colored officers' club at Camp Hood earlier that night, Robinson had boarded an army shuttle headed for McCloskey hospital 30 miles from the camp. He was being evaluated there for fitness to travel overseas due to an earlier ankle injury.

Getting on board, Robinson sat down four rows from the front with a woman he knew. Having none of it, the bus driver walked down the aisle and ordered Robinson to the back of the bus; when Jackie refused, citing a new Army policy eliminating segregation on military posts, the driver promised he'd make trouble for him.

The driver made good on his promise. He steered the bus to a transfer station, and two MPs duly appeared. Robinson was immediately cuffed, and court-martial charges were filed. Colonel Paul Bates, knowing Robinson and his character, refused to sign the court-martial paperwork. Bates' superiors pressed the case, transferring Robinson to the 758th, where they knew he would be court-martialed, which he was. The future Hall of Fame player was subsequently acquitted but not in time to rejoin the 761st.[16]

The only upside to the depressingly familiar tale of institutional racism within the Army was that Bates' refusal to sign Robinson's court-martial endeared him to the men. After the 761st completed training at Camp Hood, Bates was offered but turned down an elevation in rank to full Colonel. He wanted to stay with the 761st, the disciplined unit he had remade into a supreme fighting machine, which he now considered to be the finest tank battalion in the Army.

In mid-August, the battalion spent two weeks preparing for departure overseas at Camp Shanks, the 2,000-acre military camp just northwest of New York City in Rockland county. During the course of the war 1.3 million soldiers passed through the military installation, including 75 percent of the soldiers who took part in the D-Day invasion.

The 761st boarded the *Esperance Bay* in New York City on August 27, 1944 bound for England. Aboard was future Medal of Honor recipient Lt. Charles Thomas and the 614th Tank Destroyer Battalion, which had also been at Camp Hood.

David Williams felt the ship, an old Australian luxury liner, must have been last commanded by Captain Bligh because of the stench. But the ten-day voyage across the Atlantic was uneventful, and the men were on their best behavior. The unit even received a commendation from transport commander Captain Peter Jacoby. It read in part:

> I commend your unit for its discipline, military courtesy, high morale, and soldierly conduct throughout the voyage. My staff and I wish you God's speed in your future missions and the best of luck and success to final victory.[17]

After arrival at Avonmouth, in the United Kingdom, Rivers and the 761st traveled directly to Wimborne, Dorset, to receive equipment and further orders. The battalion of nearly 800 men was staying at a large estate on a plateau overlooking the quaint English village of Wimborne.

The unit's shoulder patch was a fearsome black panther with the words "Come out fighting" underneath, taken from a quote by boxer Joe Louis. At a hastily called company officers' meeting with Colonel Bates, however, Major Wingo suggested that perhaps their motto should be "Come out fornicating." Enlisted men were sneaking out of camp down to the village of Wimborne in droves, consorting with the fairer sex.

This behavior did not sit well with Colonel Bates, and he instituted a new severe disciplinary policy. Court-martial would be the punishment for even the slightest infraction.

After this episode, the battalion received new Sherman tanks just before heading over to France. They were the new long-barrel, 76mm, high-muzzle-velocity M4A3 version. The unit had only several days' practice with them before they headed to the point of embarkation, Weymouth, for the channel crossing.

The 761st had arrived at the moment Rivers had doubted would ever come – even when they received the new tanks. Rivers bed down that night, reflecting on the long journey he'd taken from Oklahoma to get there. Surveying the men, they were nervous but not afraid. They were scrappy, underestimated underdogs who got back up every time they got knocked down. Now they were going to show the Army and the world what they could really do.

Chapter 18

Patton's Panthers

The muddy and tired 761st completed their breathless six-day, 400-mile dash across France in record time to catch up with Third Army at Saint-Nicolas-de-Bliquetuit. The battalion had come ashore at Omaha beach less than two weeks earlier, four months after the Normandy invasion. They were now operating in an active combat zone, and distant low rumbling like a summer thunderstorm subdued the atmosphere. The 26th Infantry Division had suffered 400 casualties the week earlier, nearby in a place called Moncourt Woods.

November 2 dawned gray and cold, and there was drizzling rain throughout the area. Col. Bates ordered the entire battalion to assemble in a semicircle mid-afternoon at the railroad crossing house. A half-track was parked up front and just to the right of the men, which would serve as a speaker's platform for a very distinguished officer.

Staff Sergeant Rivers, standing in formation, stifled a yawn with eyes half-closed due to lack of sleep, waiting with the rest of Able Company of the 761st. He considered the scuttlebutt they'd heard about the afternoon's famed speaker. Rivers wondered if the man they awaited matched the myth. The soldier-slapping incident in Sicily was widely known.

Captain Williams, wearing his raincoat, stood in front of Able Company 10 yards back from Colonel Bates, who waited in the middle of the road near the half-track. All heads turned at the rumble of a small jeep convoy approaching. Bates peered down the road then called the battalion to attention. All men threw their shoulders back and stood with eyes fixed forward as a mud-splashed jeep with the fluttering Third Army flag and stars on the grill jolted to a stop 20 yards in front of them.

Rivers caught his breath, as did many in the ranks upon seeing a General with three stars on his helmet emerge from the lead vehicle. Patton's reputation for good or ill preceded him everywhere, but the 761st drew immense pride that the legendary commander had summoned their outfit to fight under his command. Fighting under Patton, the 761st knew they were sure to be in the thick of the action.

Patton, at this time in early November 1944, was deeply frustrated. He had raced Third Army 400 miles across France from Normandy to the Lorraine region but was bogged down by severe fuel shortages, muddy roads, and fresh enemy reinforcements in the German 1st Army opposite him.

After noting the pearl-handled pistols, David Williams studied the General as his gray eyes penetrated the 761st's ranks. He felt Patton with his beaked nose appeared like a hawk atop a fence post eyeing a barnyard filled with young chickens. The newspapers called the commander of Third Army "old blood and guts," but the men in the ranks referred to him as the "Green Hornet."

Patton strode over to the half-track and was assisted up onto the hood by Colonel Bates. Patton ordered the men at ease, cleared his throat, and began:

Men, you're the first Negro tankers to ever fight in the American Army. I would never have asked for you if you weren't good. I have nothing but the best in my Army. I don't care what color you are as long as you go up there and kill those Kraut sons of bitches. Everyone has their eyes on you and is expecting great things from you. Most of your race is looking forward to your achievements. Don't let them down, and damn you, don't let me down.

Rivers struggled to hold back a grin as Patton climbed off the hood of the vehicle, satisfied he had gotten his point across with his brief pep talk. Williams felt newly inspired as he watched Bates salute the Commanding General. Patton turned back to the ranks as he marched toward his vehicle and paused within earshot of Williams, and growled at lanky Corporal E.G. McConnell in the front row: "Listen, boy; I want you to go up there and shoot up every Goddamn thing you see. I want you to shoot haystacks, church steeples, graveyards, old ladies, children; every damn thing you see. This is war. You hear me, boy?"[18]

McConnell stammered out a "Yes, sir," and saluted awkwardly. Patton stormed back to his jeep. Colonel Bates dismissed the men, and Williams saw Big Tit approaching him, his eyes like saucers.

Williams asked his driver what the problem was.

Tit responded that the old man was crazy as hell, asking Williams if he saw how the General's eyes rolled around in his head. Tit said there was no bullshit about the Hornet for damn sure, and Tit was more scared of that crazy old man than any Kraut.

Rivers smiled as he fell out of formation, now knowing the myth about the man was no idle talk. It was the absolute truth. In that moment the 761st transformed fully into Patton's Black Panthers.

Several days later, a runner found Captain Williams, at daybreak, at his company headquarters and told him to report immediately to Colonel Bates' headquarters. Arriving, Williams noted Intelligence Officer Nelson and Major Wingo were present. Wingo appeared petrified and was trembling. Bates motioned Williams to sit and told him to take notes.

"Tomorrow, Company A will depart at 0500 for a village called Bezange Le Grange," Bates began. The three tank platoons of Able Company were being attached to the 104th Infantry Regiment (IR) and reporting to Colonel Colley, regimental commander. He would convey instructions and the mission. Able Company would be going up alone, which surprised and somewhat shocked Williams. Reading his mind, Bates reassured Williams that he had great faith in his company but cautioned him to be deliberate in thinking decisions through. He did not want Williams to act on impulse.

Word spread like wildfire through the company that they'd been assigned their first mission. Rivers carefully cleaned his .45-caliber to pass the time and settle some nerves. All his life, he had never allowed fear close to him. Now he felt its presence all around him. He sensed it when he looked at some of the men, the ones who were quiet, who'd never been silent before. He also saw it in the men who were writing letters home enclosing keepsakes. Rivers felt those men had already made the decision they weren't going to make it. That wasn't the way to think, and Rivers knew it. He had a job to do, and he planned to do it as his dad used to say, come hell or high water. All indicators were that hell was precisely where they were headed.

NOVEMBER 8, 1944

Captain Williams' orders were for all to be in their tanks at 0400. In his rubberized leather tanker's helmet with goggles above the brim, Rivers emerged from his Sherman and stood in the turret. The weather was damp and sharply cold. It had been sleeting most of the night. Rivers looked at his watch; it was just past 0415 hours and deadly silent.

The 761st was anticipating the opening two-hour Allied artillery salvo Col. Bates had told them would initiate the attack. At precisely 0430, an ear-splitting howl and whoosh of hundreds of 155mm howitzer shells and other long-range artillery turned the night sky into day. The screams of the outgoing shells were soon followed by the distant high-impact explosions behind the German lines.

In his headquarters tent giving the maps and final instructions to his officers, Williams looked over to a smiling Big Tit. Williams commented, "Well, Tit, if the Germans were asleep, they're sure awake now."

Tit's smile broadened as he said, "No Captain, they ain't awake they dead."[19]

By daybreak, Able Company was on the move, averaging approximately two to four miles per hour following the infantry path. Williams crouched in the turret with his head sticking out of the hatch. At Camp Hood, they'd learned to keep the hatch open most of the time. The reason was that if the tank got hit by armor-piercing shells, they could quickly scramble out. Hatches had a nasty habit of sticking shut when closed, and men could become trapped or burn alive if the tank caught fire.[20]

Able Company's mission objective, received from Colonel Colley, was to get across the Seille River, a tributary of the Moselle, as quickly as possible. One platoon of Able Company with five tanks was temporarily reassigned to the 101st IR from the 104th. This higher command decision left Williams leading only 12 tanks in two platoons of his company for the main assault. Colley had assigned Williams' tanks to the 1st Battalion under a commander known as the "Fighting Irishman."

Williams ordered his tank commanders to maintain radio silence until they reached their objective at Bezange Le Grange. Their tank "handles" would be their first names. Williams was in the lead tank, designated as A-17, with Williams' own handle D.J., the initials of his first and middle name. Rivers, with his first name as his handle, commanded a tank midway back in the column.

Radio silence was broken when they reached the outskirts of Bezange Le Grange, about a mile from the town, at 1115 hours. At that time, Williams in the lead tank hand-signaled for the column to halt. Williams checked in with all his tankers and told them to keep pressing forward to Vic sur Seille.

Rivers in his turret watched the infantry fan out on the left flank parallel to a distant low ridge. Rivers determined they were trying to get around an obstacle up ahead. He decided to pull his tank forward and past Captain Williams' tank. Williams jumped on the radio and asked Rivers what the rush was, for Christ's sake. Rivers responded on the radio that he was going to get them going on in a hurry. Just as Rivers finished his response, German shells began whistling to explode around them, tearing up the road and throwing men, mud, and debris everywhere.

In his anxiety, Williams' gunner, John Lane, loaded two "cans" in the breech of the tank's bow gun by mistake. It was inoperative for the moment and had to be cleared. Williams radioed in a maintenance team; then, he peered forward from his turret into the smoke and explosions. Rivers' tank was 200 yards ahead behind a small brick wall next to a cemetery, and he came on the radio for Williams. "D.J.," he said, "There's a roadblock right ahead. Mines on it. Doughs in the ditches getting shelled. Out."[21]

Williams clicked his radio mic and told Rivers to help the doughs and fire HE for effect.

The German shelling intensified as the Shermans answered with counterfire toward the direction of the incoming shells. Another new problem surfaced; Williams had lost contact with the 1st Battalion commander of the 104th nicknamed the Fighting Irishman. They were operating blind.

Events back at the jump-off point were also unraveling. A German patrol crept through the forest back to where Colonel Bates stood fully exposed on the hood of his jeep, watching the battle through field glasses. The German patrol sprayed the Colonel's jeep with a submachine gun, knocking him to the ground and seriously wounding him in the leg. The commander, who had instilled pride and developed his black tankers into a fearsome fighting unit, was now himself knocked out of action on the opening day of battle.[22]

Command devolved to Major Wingo, who was hastily brought forth in a tank. Williams had already noted fear in Wingo's eyes in the commanders' meeting a day earlier. With the battle now engaged, Wingo was near to becoming a psychiatric patient.

Corporal E.G. McConnell, waiting for Wingo to arrive at the front, received a disturbing report from Sgt. Smith, who'd brought the commander forward in a tank.

Smith told McConnell, "Wingo went nuts, he might not be plumb chicken, but he sure got henhouse ways. He gets out and looks down there and starts shaking all over like a stray dog passing razor blades in the rain. He took off in a Jeep to the rear."[23]

Although Wingo had not seen combat, he was evacuated for "combat fatigue" and disappeared, leaving the battalion void of leadership. Lt. Col. Hollis E. Hunt subsequently transferred from another battalion to assume command.

Back at Vic sur Seille, Rivers was taking matters into his own hands. He told his gunners to cover him as he jumped out of the turret surrounded by exploding mortar and artillery shells and small arms fire.

Williams had not been watching Rivers' tank but ended a radio call with Bill Griffin, who'd relayed a message from Colonel Colley asking about their status. Williams informed Griffin that intense enemy fire pinned down the infantry, and a mined roadblock held up their advance.

Williams, popping his head from the hatch, saw to his disbelief that Rivers was calmly uncoiling the tow cable on his Sherman and directing his driver. Rivers fastened the line around the large tree trunk studded with mines that made up the roadblock.

Williams brought his field glasses up to his eyes, his mouth hung open, and he whispered, "Rivers, you beautiful son of a bitch."

The Germans had Rivers square in their sights and adjusted their fire. Mortars started crashing 20 yards away all around him, and small arms fire pinged off the side of his tank. Rivers jumped back on the front of the Sherman and leapt in the turret, the tow coil secured. Williams saw the tank pull the tree trunk back slowly to the side. Several mines exploded as it cleared the road, but the column was able to resume the advance.

The 12 tanks in the two platoons of Able Company entered the village of Vic sur Seille after the 104th had endured an intense firefight with the Germans. The dead and wounded lay scattered everywhere and 30 German prisoners were being held in the basement of a building.

All was disorganized confusion, and Williams discovered the reason why. The Fighting Irishman had had a mental breakdown and was incoherent. He was being attended to in a barn being readied to be sent to the rear. That explained why Williams had not heard from him during the entire battle.

Soon Williams received orders from Colonel Colley's headquarters to keep the advance moving forward to Moyenvic. They were to link up with the 101st Regiment and Williams' other platoon of tanks commanded by Lt. Barbour. The plan was to establish an antitank defense and support the infantry advance.

Rivers, riding in the turret of his Sherman, scoped out the village they were approaching. It appeared deserted. It felt like both sides had withdrawn to lick their wounds. Williams parked his tank on the outskirts and jumped in a jeep beside his driver, Big Tit. Williams had been ordered to report to Colonel Hanford of the 2nd Battalion of the 101st Regiment.

Meeting with Hanford just past 1900 hours, the commander directed Williams to notify his tankers that they would be staying there the night. Williams informed Hanford they had ten tanks left in his two platoons; two tanks had struck mines. Hanford relayed the objective for the next day. They were going to take the town of Château Salins as quickly as possible to protect the left flank of Task Force A, which was going to try to come through the north of them at Morville.

Early next morning, Col. Hanford, Williams, Big Tit, Rivers, and two other Able Company tank commanders hiked a short distance to a ridge overlooking a valley where the village of Château Salins lay in ruin. Nearly the only building left standing was the church, and they used its steeple as a reference point. The tanks were going to head in ahead of the infantry and after a bombing run by P-47s.

By midday, eight P-47s appeared in the western sky and pounded the village. The men of Able Company were already in their tanks, with Rivers commanding a section of two tanks. Twenty minutes of heavy artillery bombardment followed the P-47 bombing run to soften up German resistance even further.

The armored attack strategy was to enter the village in a line on the road rather than a wedge. Four to five infantrymen would ride atop each tank, keeping a watchful eye ready to pick off any panzerfaust squads.

After the Allied artillery salvo subsided, Williams clicked on his radio mic: "Okay Joe, Bob, Ruben, move on down the avenue and lay down some larceny." It was slang Williams had picked up from his black tankers. Lt. Joe Kahoe, Lt. Robert Hammond, and Staff Sgt. Rivers were all commanding separate tanks. As the tanks got moving, Big Tit came on the radio, razzing his Captain saying to D.J. that he wasn't shit with that jive talk but to keep tryin' and he'd be hep. Williams laughed even though Big Tit had no business butting in on the radio like that.[24]

The attack was a success, almost textbook at specific points; Williams felt like they were on maneuvers back at Camp Hood. Williams later discovered the reason for the light enemy resistance. The Germans had concentrated their forces to the north to stop Task Force A and had nearly wiped it out.

Colonel Hanford subsequently informed Williams that Charlie Company of the 761st had run into a tank trap, and the Germans had destroyed 13 tanks. Charlie Company's Shermans had got bogged down behind a cleverly concealed antitank ditch 15 feet wide, four feet deep, and studded at the bottom with steel spikes. Williams hung his head upon hearing the news. It was a disaster.

Williams learned later that Sgt. Sam Turley, his friend from Charlie Company, had gone down fighting. In heavy snow, his tank had been hit first and, after exiting the burning Sherman, Turley had organized a dismounted combat team that was immediately struck by a ferocious counterattack. Turley ordered a fighting retreat covering his men's escape with machine gun fire.

War correspondent Trezzvant Anderson, a member of the 761st, who witnessed the action, described Turley's last moments:

> Standing behind the ditch, straight up, with a machine gun and an ammo belt around his neck, Turley was spraying the enemy with machine-gun shots as fast as they could come out of the muzzle of the red-hot barrel. He stood there covering for his men and then fell, cut through the middle by German machine-gun bullets that ripped through his body as he stood there firing the machine gun to the last.[25]

The 101st IR received word that night at Château Salins that the 4th Armored Task Force was making good progress toward Guébling. Colonel Hanford ordered Williams' tanks forward to Château-Voué immediately. Williams placed Ruben Rivers as the lead tank in the column, and in moving past Obreck, Rivers destroyed a German Mark V Panther with just two shots.

Upon arriving at Château-Voué, Major Ed Reynolds informed Captain Williams that General Paul had awarded the Silver Star to Ruben Rivers for his heroic action at Vic sur Seille, clearing the mine for the armored advance. Williams felt Rivers well deserved it, and he realized he was coming to depend on his fearless fighter from Oklahoma. Rivers greeted news of the award with surprise, remarking that he had just been doing his job.

Williams took Rivers with him and several other men on a daybreak scouting mission to survey the village of Guébling, which sat in a valley. They talked in whispers as they looked down at the town from a ridge. Rivers noted that the bridge in the village looked blown. Williams swung his field glassed over to it and saw twisted concrete and two destroyed American tanks near it. Williams said that intelligence reported a battalion of the 11th Panzer Division was heavily patrolling the area now. The objective of taking this town was the most challenging one they had yet faced.

Able Company were in their tanks on the outskirts of the town the following morning at 0400, waiting for the American artillery salvo to commence. Williams again placed Rivers as the lead tank. The temperatures had dropped to below freezing, and men shivered inside the tanks wrapped in blankets. The artillery barrage began precisely on time at 0430 and lasted for 20 minutes.

Before Williams could give the order on the radio to advance, mortars and high-impact artillery shells hit the column from German 88mm guns. Williams watched in horror as Joe Kahoe's Sherman was struck and spun around, catching fire. Williams keyed his microphone, shouting to get out, but four men were already scrambling out of the burning wreck. One man had to run back for Big Tit's cousin, PFC Harold McIntyre, who was semi-conscious, and dragged him out of the loader's compartment.

If the tanks stayed there, they were sitting ducks, so Williams ordered the column forward. Rivers led the way, and as his tank neared a railroad crossing, an ear-splitting explosion rocked his Sherman from a hidden teller antitank mine. The blast blew off the right track, the volute springs, and the undercarriage, hurling the tank sideways.[26]

Williams was on the radio in an instant. He shouted for Tit to send up Ray, their medic. Then, Williams had his driver Lomas steer A-17 to Rivers' location. Within minutes Williams was there.

Rivers was on the ground behind his tank holding his right leg, his face tight. Williams jumped out of his tank, shouted for everyone to stay back, and asked Rivers if he was all right. Williams examined the wound. Shrapnel had cut Rivers' leg from knee to thigh. There was a hole in his leg where part of his knee had been, and bone protruded through Rivers' trousers.[27]

Brakes squealed from Big Tit's jeep as it jolted to a stop with medic Sgt. Ray Robertson and Cpl. Homer Bracey. Robertson went right to work without saying a word. He painted the wound with antiseptic. Williams noted that Rivers' face betrayed no pain or emotion.

Sgt. Robertson then broke the seal on a syrette of morphine and was preparing to administer it when Rivers pushed it away, saying just tape and bandage. Robertson brushed the wound with sulfur, then he and Cpl. Bracey bandaged it.

Robertson turned to Williams and said he would take the Sergeant back. Rivers' eyes flashed upon hearing this, and he pulled himself up to a standing position. He said to Williams, "I'm not going back, Captain. You're gonna be needin' me around here pretty soon."[28]

Williams was taken aback but became firm. He called Rivers by his rank, Sergeant Rivers, and he told him he was going back with the medics and not to waste any more time.

At that moment, several German mortars fell, exploding about 25 yards from them, throwing up earth and debris. Rivers pushed past Williams and hobbled toward a tank 20 yards away. Williams watched Rivers pull himself up on the tank in 30 seconds and signal to the tank commander to exit. The tank commander got out of the tank, and Rivers jumped in. Williams shook his head, but they had to keep moving. He directed Big Tit and the medics to take cover and come in after the tanks had moved through town.

Jumping back in his tank, Williams keyed the radio's microphone and asked Rivers again if he was alright. Rivers said, "D.J., I told you I was alright. Over."[29]

Williams frowned then told everyone on the radio that he would lead the column over the railroad and into town. That afternoon Williams met with Colonel Lyons of the 101st IR, who was grim. The engineers hadn't finished the Bailey bridge yet, and German tanks had decimated F Company of his infantry. All the officers were killed, and the enemy had taken the remaining men prisoner.

Lyons ordered Able Company to stay there for the night and wait until the bridge was finished. Williams went around to visit all his tankers and especially to check on Rivers. Despite everything they all remained solid as a rock, including Rivers and Big Tit, who still had his unflagging sense of humor.

That night Williams did something he had promised he would do but for which he had never set the time aside. He found some yellow-lined paper and a pencil and began recording his experiences from the war commanding his tank company. His first entry was reflective. He wrote:

> How could I have ever doubted these men? Despite everything, they had fought their guts out and stayed in their tanks, which were like iceboxes, at night. They had smelled the stink of frightful lumps of human flesh lying in the fields and on the roads and in the villages. Would that Captain Barnes, Tilmer Davidson, Colonel Wright, and the whole goddam bunch from Camp Claiborne were here with me and these negro tank soldiers waiting for the bridge to be completed. Let those white bastards come with us to Guébling. Let them call the men niggers now.[30]

Early the following morning, while Williams was pouring coffee into a paper cup at headquarters, Big Tit came and found him. His face filled with worry, he told D.J. that he'd better come quick. It was Rivers, and he was in a lot of pain.

Williams followed Tit around several tanks over to where Rivers was leaning back against his tank. When Williams saw the pain on Rivers' normally poker-faced countenance, he became very concerned. Williams was emphatic, saying, "look, Rivers, enough of this; it's time you went back. The bridge will be in pretty soon, and once we get over to the other side, there won't be any coming back."

Rivers listened and let his Captain finish.

Williams continued telling his fearless fighter from Oklahoma that he had every right to go back. The 11th Panzers had many tanks somewhere on the other side, and he'd gotten a nasty wound. It was time to go.

Williams watched Rivers' lip curl into a slight smile, and he said it was only more reason for him to stick around. They'd be through the worst of it in a couple of days, and he'd go back then.

Williams then asked how his pain was.

Rivers' lips widened into a broader smile, and he said, "My Negro side says it hurts my Indian side say it doesn't, so I'll make it alright."[31]

The engineers completed the Bailey bridge at 1545 hours that afternoon, and Williams gathered his two officers and two Sergeants together in Col. Lyons' office. Williams ordered Rivers to take his section of two tanks up the hill right in front of the village and take cover in the brush. He also directed Rivers to search for targets in Bourgaltroff and the outskirts of Guébling. He ordered his other tank section to go around to the right of the hill. Williams' tank and Ted Weston's tank would move up the main street and take cover at the far end of the town. Then Williams asked if there were any questions; there were none.

Colonel Lyons, who'd been listening nearby, stepped forward with a grim face. He told the men to listen to him carefully and exercise great caution. Bourgaltroff had multi-barreled 20mm guns and antitank guns, probably 75mm ones, plus German tanks were patrolling. He concluded by saying that he called for a platoon of tank destroyers to back them up.

Able Company got across the Bailey bridge successfully and entered the town of Guébling, which showed the evidence of the engagement the 4th Armored had been involved in days earlier. Two American half-tracks still smoldered in town, and a Sherman was turned sideways on the road into town. E Company of the 101st Regiment was well dug in around the village.

As night fell, it became deathly quiet, and heavy snow began. Williams rotated men out of their tanks to try to get warm inside headquarters, which had a stove going. Men who came in to get warm reported seeing distant 20mm tracer fire from the German lines.

Rivers' condition was still on Williams' mind, and he grabbed Ray Robertson, who'd set up the medical station in the church, and had Big Tit drive them up the hill to Rivers' concealed tank section of two tanks. The snow had stopped, but it was still bitter cold.

When the jeep arrived, Rivers got down from his tank and limped severely toward them. He had seen them coming up the road. Robertson moved right in and told Rivers to sit down, and asked him about the pain.

Rivers said he didn't feel anything; it was too damn cold.

Ray changed the bandages on Rivers' leg and turned grim-faced to Williams. The smell coming from the wound indicated gangrene was setting in. Ray said that Rivers should go back now. Williams agreed and told Rivers that he would send John Lane up from his tank crew and let Corporal Hilliard take over. Lane could act as the gunner. Rivers could go back in an infantry medical jeep. Williams patted Rivers' shoulder, but Rivers pushed his Captain's hand away, becoming angry.

He said how in the hell could he go back and leave them all there. The damn leg didn't hurt and a couple more days ain't gonna make no difference.

Big Tit leaned down to Rivers and said with encouragement that he had a million-dollar wound and he could be back in his little town in Oklahoma in a month, and if he didn't go, he was plain crazy as hell.

Rivers pulled himself up from his sitting position and said firmly that the three should head back to headquarters. The Germans were about to say good morning to them with screaming meemies.*

Williams looked at Robertson, then at Big Tit, then back at Rivers. He could not pull this man off the line. Maybe a couple more days wouldn't matter. Williams decided there and then he would not ask Rivers again to evacuate. The soldier had made his choice, and he

---

* The Nebelwerfer was a German rocket launcher known by the Allied forces as a "screaming meemie" due to the screaming noise made by the approaching rockets.

had to respect that, and Williams needed his best tanker right where he was. The three left with the promise to send up chow when it was ready.

NOVEMBER 19, 1944

As day broke, American artillery plastered the village of Bourgaltroff. The explosions were so intense they shook Colonel Lyons' headquarters. An hour earlier, Williams crept up to Rivers' tank section and gave them their attack orders. Rivers and his companion tank were to move forward and open fire with high explosive shells on the outskirts of Bourgaltroff. Williams conveyed flanking orders to his other tank sections. Lieutenant Hammond's section was to push through the orchard and wipe out machine gun positions, and Williams and Ted Weston and two other tanks would move up the road into town in a column.

The day was clear of clouds, and a bright sun shone down, making the surrounding destruction of twisted metal, rubble, and scattered dead American and German bodies in Guébling even more surreal. As the sun warmed the air, the stench of rotting bodies, smoldering plaster, and metal and manure from the fields combined to such pungency to almost take one's breath away.

Rivers' tank rolled forward down toward the town and opened fire first. Ted Weston's tank moved ahead of Williams' at two miles per hour heading out of Guébling. Williams heard a loud zipping noise and then a loud metallic crash, and Weston's voice came over the radio, "D.J., we've been hit."[32]

Tracers were pelting Weston's tank, but he was able to reverse it to safety behind a house as other tanks backed up behind Williams. That's what they had been trained to do. Williams asked for Weston's status, and he came back saying that the gun messed up the turret.

"Move back, Rivers!" Williams yelled over the radio.

"I see them. We'll fight them," Rivers responded as shells flew back and forth between him and the enemy. Just then, 75mm enemy shells came crashing down, exploding all around Williams' tank, pinning his movement.

Rivers ordered his driver to roll forward as tracers ricocheted off the front of the tank. Rivers shouted to his gunner to steady on the target. They were 200 yards away from German guns. They would get no further.

According to a war correspondent witness, two German HE shells were fired point-blank at Rivers' tank. The first shot hit near the front of the tank and penetrated. The explosion cracked the Sherman like an egg and killed Rivers and his crew instantly. A second high explosive shell followed the same path, slicing through the tank and emerging out the back.

Williams shouted into the radio for Rivers' tank to fall back. It was too late. All was confusion as smoke and tracers obscured Williams' view of Rivers' tank section. Williams ordered his driver Lomas to get him a field of fire and keep his damn head down. Lomas wheeled the tank around, and Williams shouted the order, "Gunner HE traverse left, steady on, five hundred, fire five for effect."[33]

The Sherman bucked back as it shot forth five high explosive shells toward Bourgaltroff. After firing the five shells, Williams peeked his head out of the turret, looked over, and saw Ted Weston on the back of his disabled tank manning his .50cal gun. It was spitting out shells. An infantryman climbed up on Williams' Sherman, seeing him in the turret, and yelled in his ear. Colonel Lyons wanted the tanks to pull back and take up defensive positions now.

Williams keyed the microphone, yelling for Hammond and Rivers to come in. He repeated his radio call again and again for his forward tank sections to respond, but there was no answer. He threw the mic down and shouted, "Damnit!"

Then Williams radioed Ted Weston's disabled tank. He told Weston to get to A-17 right away. Weston arrived within a minute, and Williams told him to take over and keep up the fire; he would go find out about Rivers and Hammond.

Weston assured him that if they sent the whole damn German Army that they ain't getting through. Williams jumped off the back of the tank and saw Big Tit coming toward him, his face anguished. "They got knocked out all of 'em D.J.," he said and continued that some of them were with the medic now in the church.

Williams and Big Tit headed straight there and were met by a buck Sergeant, Henry Conway, with tears streaming down his cheeks. Conway informed them Rivers had been killed, and he thought Lt. Hammond had been as well. Williams demanded to know where Robertson, their medic, was. Conway responded that he had headed up to Rivers' tank with stretcher-bearers.

Williams turned to Big Tit and said they were going up there as well; there could be more wounded. He ordered Tit to get four men and more stretchers and follow him. Big Tit was off in an instant, and Conway also agreed to join them.

Williams was able to crawl up to PFC Vinton E. Hudson's disabled tank with the stretcher-bearers. They retrieved Hudson, whose leg was missing just below his mid-thigh. They got them back safely to the medical area and were met by Ray Robertson, whose face confirmed the worst.

Robertson told Williams that Rivers was dead, and he also believed that Lt. Hammond and Cpl. Ewing, the other tankers in Rivers' section, had been killed. He was just about to head out to them. Williams told Robertson to take the red cross flag with them. Williams found out later that Colonel Lyons had also been struck, hit by German mortars.

Williams stepped away from his medic and saw Big Tit helping with the wounded. Williams went behind the church and let the tears flow. He could not stop them; everything had crashed together in a sickening crescendo of death. His blood moved like sludge in his veins, and he grasped for answers as he became numb.

At that moment, he didn't care whether he lived or died. And worst of all, he blamed himself for not ordering Rivers to leave the battlefield. The man could have gone home with the Silver Star. He had done his duty. Somehow, someway, Williams had to make this right. He headed back to his tank as the battlefield fell silent. Williams, exhausted, caught some shut-eye, but his mind still burned with anguish and torment.

The following day dawned as bright and clear as the previous one. Williams navigated the labyrinth of broken equipment, strewn German and American helmets, and the ever-present rotting bodies to grab some coffee, more out of habit than anything else. He was still numb and awaiting word of whether the battalion would pull Able Company back.

Just as he had that thought, Colonel Hollis Hunt, who'd taken over battalion command for the wounded Colonel Bates, pulled up and emerged from a half-track outside headquarters. The commander's uniform was immaculate, and his steel helmet gleamed in the sun. He looked clean-shaven and wore a scarf. His nostrils flared at the overwhelming stench surrounding him. Williams approached and saluted the commander, remaining stone-faced. Hunt's first words stated the obvious: "you've had quite a battle around here I see."

Williams reported to him his dead and wounded, and the Colonel responded with impatience and indifference. Col. Hunt informed him that Able Company was being relieved, and they were to pull back to Obreck with the battalion. As the Colonel turned away, Williams stepped forward to him and said he wanted to put Sgt. Rivers in for the Medal of Honor.

Col. Hunt responded with surprise, "What?"[34]

Williams continued that Rivers had already received the Silver Star and that the Colonel could put it through channels. The Colonel pursed his lips and adjusted his scarf as Williams provided even more details of Rivers' leg wound and how his tanker refused to evacuate. Hunt remained expressionless.

Several days later, on November 23, Williams went formally to Colonel Hunt's office and presented him with a typed document listing the reasons Ruben Rivers should be awarded the Medal of Honor. Colonel Hunt lifted the page and glanced over it and sighed and said it was not so easy but he would try. But Williams knew his recommendation would not be acted upon; he knew no black soldiers were being recommended for the Medal of Honor. It would be forgotten about and ignored, and he made a promise that day: if he survived the war, he would not let this stand.

Captain Williams commanded Able Company through the remainder of 1944 until he and Big Tit were wounded in a firefight in early January. Both survived and were evacuated on January 7, 1945 after a tearful goodbye to their company. Both Big Tit and

David Williams were carried out of the Belgian Ardennes in an ambulance together.

Fifty-two years later, Williams made good on the promise he had made to himself in Colonel Hunt's office; Rivers would be honored for his heroic actions in Able Company. On January 13, 1997, David Williams attended the White House ceremony with Grace Wilfork, Rivers' sister, when she accepted the country's highest medal for valor, the Medal of Honor, on Rivers' behalf.

RUBEN RIVERS, MEDAL OF HONOR CITATION

For extraordinary heroism in action during 15–19 November 1944, toward Guebling, France. Though severely wounded in the leg, Sergeant Rivers refused medical treatment and evacuation, took command of another tank, and advanced with his company in Guebling the next day. Repeatedly refusing evacuation, Sergeant Rivers continued to direct his tank's fire at enemy positions through the morning of 19 November 1944. At dawn, Company A's tanks began to advance towards Bourgaltroff but were stopped by enemy fire. Sergeant Rivers, joined by another tank, opened fire on the enemy tanks, covering company A as they withdrew. While doing so, Sergeant Rivers' tank was hit, killing him and wounding the crew. Staff Sergeant Rivers' fighting spirit and daring leadership were an inspiration to his unit and exemplify the highest traditions of military service.

PART SEVEN

John Fox

Chapter 19

Transfer Student

The middle-aged college counselor with glasses slung low on his nose leaned back behind his desk perplexed. He believed the eager 19-year-old student across from him was making a grave mistake that he would only regret in years to come; leaving Ohio State University.

John Fox from Woodlawn, Ohio, had listened politely to the counselor's arguments that the number of credits lost transferring to Wilberforce University would set him back perhaps a year. Further, students typically transfer *in* from Wilberforce, not *out* from one of the most prestigious institutions in the country to Wilberforce. It made no sense to the administrator.

Fox's mind and heart, however, were already made up. He had decided on a vocation that few in the late 1930s considered – a military career. America was not at war, and there were hopeful signs that President Roosevelt's social and monetary policies were easing the worst of the Great Depression. Still, Fox felt a calling that he could not deny and believed the transfer was worth it.[1]

Wilberforce University, the oldest private African American University in the United States, was founded in 1856. The school was only one of three institutions in the country that offered the Reserve Officers' Training Corps (ROTC) program to black Americans.

Perhaps what attracted Fox was the ROTC program's proud heritage. The military science department at Wilberforce had been started in 1894 by newly appointed Lieutenant Charles Young, the third black graduate of West Point and the only African American commissioned officer in the entire US Army at the time. Young was also the first African American to rise to the rank of Colonel. Fox transferred into the ROTC program at Wilberforce during his sophomore year and never looked back.

The ROTC at Wilberforce was commanded during Fox's tenure by a highly decorated black World War I veteran, Captain Aaron R. Fisher, recipient of the Distinguished Service Cross for conspicuous gallantry and the Croix de Guerre with a gold star from France. "Cap" Fisher, as he was referred to by the cadets, was legendary for his booming voice and strict adherence to discipline. Graduates from the program felt he instilled toughness in them and a deep reservoir of resilience.

Becoming part of the military in the ROTC, Fox blossomed. He had always been an active, outgoing young man but now wore a proud, confident smile. He attracted admirers effortlessly and formed many lasting friendships in the ROTC. One of those friendships was with Jefferson Jordan, a young man from Georgia who became part of Fox's inner circle.

Jordan taught Fox how to play poker, a card game that was easy to learn but difficult to master. It was all in the psychology, Jordan explained, in outsmarting your opponent, and in all circumstances, whether winning or losing, a player should remain calm and relaxed.* Fox was a natural at the game, and it taught him how to think clearly and be decisive in all situations.

Between drills and studying for his degree, Fox earned extra money training and exercising horses at a local stable. Although he had grown up in a suburb of Cincinnati, his family had lived for a time in rural Ohio. That's when Fox had developed a love for horses and riding. He also became an avid hunter.

---

* Jefferson Jordan would later find his card-playing psychological skills helpful as a successful attorney in Detroit.

Both Fox and Jordan graduated from Wilberforce University in 1940 and were commissioned as 2nd Lieutenants on June 13. Their careers in the service would follow very different tracks, but their paths would cross again.

The Army summoned Fox to Fort Devens near Ayer, Massachusetts, with the activation of the all-black 366th Infantry Regiment on February 10, 1941. At Devens, he began artillery training in an antitank unit. The 366th was exceptional in that all the officers were black except for its first commander, who was white. The black officers principally came from either the Wilberforce or Howard University ROTC units. Of the 132 officers, 128 were college graduates. Several possessed master's degrees, and two were PhDs. No man in the enlisted ranks had less than an eighth-grade education.[2]

The 366th was the only regiment that a black Colonel would command in a theater of operation during World War II. Colonel Howard D. Queen, who would take over in January 1943, wielded power through quiet authority and was not characterized as a "tough guy." He didn't need to be; he had risen from Private up through the ranks to become a commanding officer, and the men respected him greatly.

In the late spring of 1941, the 366th sent Fox to Fort Benning, Georgia, where he trained in rifle and heavy weapons tactics. He graduated Officer Candidate School (OCS) there on August 15, 1941 and returned to Massachusetts.

In addition to his duties in the 366th with antitank M Company, Fox was often assigned on weekends as Cadre Officer to train incoming recruits. In top physical condition, Fox would lead the men on 40-mile hikes carrying 35lb packs. It was an ordeal to keep the new, underfit men moving. Some could barely complete the task.

The duty assignment Fox enjoyed most was being placed in charge of the regiment's MPs in Boston. In Boston, the 366th's Military Police presence was due to a riot in the city caused by the 369th Coast Artillery and the 372nd Infantry. The police had difficulty quelling the riot, and local authorities brought in the 366th temporarily for extra security. The Boston assignment got Fox off base on weekends. He took advantage of his time off-duty when he indulged in his passion for riding at Franklin Park Riding Stables in Dorchester, Massachusetts.

One Saturday afternoon in August 1941, when Fox was preparing to ride at Franklin Park Stables, he met the woman who would become his wife. Fox was saddling his black colt in the stable, and a pretty, petite woman caught his eye, Arlene Marrow. Fox noticed her entering the adjacent paddock cooling her horse down from a ride. So he paused and walked over to the stable entrance to get a closer look.

Arlene had grown up around horses as her father and grandfather owned stables that rented horses around the city, and she was a natural equestrian. Arlene noticed Fox and glared at him, thinking he was brash for staring at her, but Fox simply smiled. Arlene blushed at the confidence Fox exuded and coyly rode over to him. Admiring Arlene's chestnut mare, Fox said she sure was a beauty, although Arlene knew the compliment was meant for her.

Arlene thanked him and mentioned she'd never seen him around the stables. While noting her thick Cape Cod accent, Fox replied that he was on a duty assignment from Fort Devens, but he hoped to be coming by more often now. Arlene blushed once again and pulled the reins of her horse to guide it toward the stables. Fox shared his full name, and Arlene replied with hers and said she hoped she'd see him again, calling him "Mr. Fox."

A romance blossomed, and Arlene and Fox went horse riding often. They also took long walks in the park and enjoyed rowing on Scarboro Pond, getting to know each other. Arlene was attracted by Fox's confident smile and outgoing and honest nature and thought him very handsome.

Within several months they were engaged and intended to marry in the spring of 1942 in Brockton, where Arlene's parents had just moved. The couple wanted to have a large wedding to coincide with Arlene's father's birthday, but the attack on Pearl Harbor disrupted their plans dramatically. Fox was determined to marry before he shipped out, but he was uncertain of when that would be.

Fox and Arlene decided to have a small ceremony, nothing elaborate, in January in the chapel at Fort Devens. Fox's numerous friends, though, had other plans. They arranged to have a formal military ceremony and reception with an honorary saber arch. When Fox and Arlene exited the chapel, they were stunned to see Fox's friends standing at attention with their sabers crossed and held aloft.

A rainbow appeared as they exited the church, adding to the day's magic, which many in attendance said meant the marriage was blessed. Three months later, the newlyweds had settled in a home in Ayer, Massachusetts, and were indeed "blessed" with the announcement that Arlene was expecting a child.

With the arrival of spring 1942, Fox with M Company deployed to Brownsville Junction, Maine. Subsequently, the entire 366th Infantry was dispatched to 80 different places in New England to provide civilian security and prevent sabotage. More than 200 acts of enemy sabotage had struck civilian targets in the United States during World War I, such as rail lines and manufacturing plants.

One of the most notorious was in Vanceboro, Maine, in 1915 on the US-Canadian border. A lone German soldier, Werner Horn, acting on orders of Franz von Papen, the military attaché of the German Embassy in Washington DC, planted a suitcase of dynamite on the Vanceboro Bridge rail crossing. The timed explosive caused minor damage to the rail line, but the incident haunted US military planners for years.

Fox with M Company left Fort Devens on April 20 and arrived in Bangor, Maine, one day later, then traveled 50 miles north to remote Brownsville Junction. Making the most of his time in the wilderness of central Maine, Fox befriended an older man who took him out fishing. Being an outdoorsman, Fox loved the pastime and tried to convince Arlene to take up the sport. After several trips and numerous mosquito bites, Arlene hung up her rod and reel, saying she'd go dancing with Fox anytime but fishing, never again.

Fox's unit stayed in Brownsville Junction until May 22, when it redeployed to provide security to Dow Field in Bangor through early July. Fox had performed well while on deployment, and his superiors had taken notice. Fox was promoted to 1st Lieutenant in a ceremony in August 1942.

The following month, an officer arrived at Fort Devens who would become one of Fox's closest friends. Otis Zachary, born in

Puerto Rico, hailed from Spanish Harlem in New York City. He was dark-skinned and wiry with a pencil-thin mustache. His Latin background mixed with his Manhattan upbringing conspired to create a fast-talking, quick-witted dynamo who excelled in everything he chose to take on. Zachary had arrived as a newly commissioned 2nd Lieutenant in late September from Officer Candidate School at Fort Benning, Georgia, and joined Fox's antitank company.

With the onset of winter, Fox and Arlene focused on the arrival of their child as they entered the final month of 1942. December began colder than average, and a series of snowstorms blanketed the Nashoba Valley. Just days after one major storm dumped more than two feet of snow, Arlene went into labor with the roads still unplowed. It was the middle of the night, and Fox, instead of panicking, sprang into action.

Just past two o'clock in the morning, Fox arrived at the Fort Devens barracks on foot, looking for his friend Zachary. Waking him, he asked if he knew how to drive a tractor; Zachary didn't but knew someone who did. So they both ran to the maintenance depot on the base. The lone soldier on duty, hearing a knock at his door in the middle of the night, almost spilled his full cup of coffee. The maintenance soldier was startled to see Fox and Zachary, whom he knew. The pair convinced him of the need to borrow a tractor.

In short order, Fox with Zachary arrived back at his home atop a military tractor with the maintenance soldier behind the wheel. The tractor had a heavy-duty snowplow attached. Fox shuffled Arlene into their black '40 Ford coupe, a former police pursuit vehicle, and followed the commandeered snow plow five miles to Community Memorial Hospital. With the birth of their daughter, Sandra Marie, later that morning on December 15, 1942, John Fox became a proud and doting father.

After Fox enlisted Zachary's help with the tractor, their friendship grew. Fox outranked him as a 1st Lieutenant, and he jokingly told Zachary his ROTC training gave him the upper hand. Not to be outdone, Zachary had already spent three years in the Army before OCS plus attended ROTC in high school. Zachary told Fox his training with *real* weapons carried much more weight.

Fox, however, could always knock Zachary down a peg when he affectionately called him "shrimp" due to the man's 5ft 7in. stature. The good-natured ribbing continued through their nine months of training into their deployment overseas.

In late January 1943, Colonel Howard Queen took up his position as commander of the 366th, making the outfit one of only four Army regiments with all black officers. For Colonel Queen, it was a "dream realized" as he had been qualified to assume the position for eight years. The Army, however, had continually passed him over.

Higher command's original intention had, of course, been to replace the departing white commander with another one. Still, pressure from civic and political groups and the black press eventually forced the Army brass to change their minds.[3]

Queen was one of the original cavalry Buffalo soldiers and had served in the Mexican Campaign of 1916. Considered by the men as "tough but fair," he commanded with quiet authority and did not suffer fools. A stickler for army regulations, Queen soon crossed paths with Fox's friend Zachary. The Colonel was displeased with Zachary's long hair and had the base barber give him a close-cropped flat-top haircut popular in the Marines. During the 366th's weekly Friday haircuts, no one else received Zachary's extreme military cut. Fox laughed when he saw the result and called Zachary "Flat-top." In fact, Zachary became so associated with his new hairstyle that his artillery call sign became Flat Top 8.

"Flat Top" soon grew on Colonel Queen as they shared an interest in the Bible, and the Colonel would have Zachary read Bible passages aloud often when the outfit gathered for meetings. Zachary frequently told Queen that he believed himself destined for the priesthood. Colonel Queen, suppressing his laughter at the officer's blatant lie, would respond that it was said that with God, *all* things are possible, even a miracle such as that.

In mid-1943, Fox's antitank M Company became Cannon Company, constituting the 366th's primary organic indirect fire support. A cannon company during World War II was usually equipped with a total of six M3 105mm towed short-range howitzers in three cannon platoons. Personnel totaled five officers and between 109 and 118 enlisted men with four attachments. Targets for a cannon company included automatic weapons, antitank guns, mortars, infantry howitzers, troop concentrations, roadblocks, pillboxes, strongly fortified buildings, and armored vehicles.[4] Through the summer into the fall, Fox and his men trained on the new guns and learned their roles well.

The 336th was ordered to Camp Atterbury, Indiana, in early fall 1943 for further infantry training. First, however, higher command relocated them to an Army facility 500 miles to the south in Bowling Green, Virginia. A.P. Hill Military Reservation, named after a Confederate General who took part in the Battle of Gettysburg, had a maneuver area spread out over nearly 80,000 acres. The 366th sent an advance officer team south to prepare the way for the arrival of 3,232 officers and men and all their equipment on October 14, 1943.

When the 366th arrived, however, nothing was prepared, no dining or training facilities or even sleeping quarters. In fact, on the first night of the regiment's arrival, they had to pitch tents in a field for a place to sleep. Colonel Queen was furious that nothing had been prepared by the officers who had preceded them. Plus, the Colonel had nearly 3,500 starving irritated men on his hands, who had traveled ten hours in 6 x 6 trucks, that he needed to calm down. The Colonel gathered several officers and MPs, broke into a supply warehouse, and carried out enough food so his men could eat that evening. It was certainly an inauspicious welcome to the south.

The following morning, a more disturbing "welcome" came when Bowling Green residents discovered thousands of armed black soldiers had descended upon their town. The mayor, city council, and a group of angry townspeople met and expressed outrage that they hadn't been informed. They all decided that the black soldiers had to leave. The citizens' group led by the mayor lodged a protest with the garrison commander Lieutenant Colonel Elmer F. Munshower that day, threatening to take their case all the way to the Pentagon if necessary.[5]

The Lieutenant Colonel commanded the 1336th Service Unit, which oversaw the A.P. Hill Reservation, and he assured irate citizenry the 366th's assignment to A.P. Hill was temporary. The unit would be moving along shortly.

The 366th had less than a month of combat readiness training at the Military Reservation before they had to pack up and head west to Camp Atterbury, Indiana, just south of Indianapolis. However, their departure did not occur until the well-maintained trucks they'd arrived in were exchanged for battered, poorly maintained ones. The A.P. Hill Military Reservation supplied trucks badly in need of repairs which then broke down en route through the snowy West Virginia mountains, and needed to be towed through the bitter cold.

By this time in late 1943, in letters home to Arlene, Fox expressed frustration that they might not ever see combat. The 366th was well trained and rated "combat-ready." The men, in fact, were over-trained and being shuffled from one military facility to another, which was dampening morale.

The one aspect that provided hope was the constant outcry from black churches, civil rights groups, and the black press to put African Americans into combat service overseas alongside white soldiers. Fox and other black soldiers considered papers such as the *Pittsburgh Courier* and the *Chicago Defender* their allies in their campaign to be deployed. However, President Roosevelt's FBI Director, J. Edgar Hoover, believed the black newspapers were enemies of the state and labeled them seditious.

Hoover orchestrated hearings before a select committee of Congress on the dangers of the black press. In 1942, Hoover presented Attorney General Francis Biddle with lengthy reports on what he saw as seditious activity by the African American press.[6] He demanded Biddle indict a group of black publishers for treason.[7] The publisher of the *Chicago Defender*, John Sengstacke, getting wind of the potential shutdown of his newspaper and possible imprisonment, asked to meet with Biddle.

The two met at the Justice Department in Washington DC, and Sengstacke held his ground, stating they were just as American as every other citizen and protected by the right to free speech. Biddle relented, and the two came to an extraordinary agreement dictating that if Sengstacke representing the entirety of the black press agreed to "not escalate the campaign for equality" during the war, the papers could continue operating and would not be prosecuted under the Espionage Act.[8] Although clearly not the best of resolutions, it averted a total shutdown of the black media and the African American voice in the nation at the time.

The 366th arrived at Camp Atterbury around Thanksgiving in November 1943 and settled into infantry training. The commanding officer overseeing the facility was Colonel Welton M. Modisette, who set out to make their lives difficult in every way possible. Modisette had spent a lifetime in the military, entering the Army in 1912. Places he had been posted included the Alcatraz Disciplinary Barracks and serving as Executive Officer of the Disciplinary Barracks at Camp Stanley, Texas.

Modisette created separate rules for the 366th. Officers and enlisted men could only attend the post theater during certain hours and were not allowed to enter the Post Exchange at all. Camp Atterbury was one of the stateside military facilities which housed German prisoners of war, and Colonel Queen noted that those prisoners were granted more privileges than his men. He filed a formal complaint with the Inspector General, which rectified the situation immediately.

Escaping on leave for the holidays from the prison-like atmosphere created by Modisette, Fox was able to return home to Ayer, Massachusetts, in time to celebrate his daughter Sandra's first birthday on December 15, 1943. It was family time that Fox treasured the most, and his baby daughter was the apple of his eye.

The day after Christmas, with his thoughts miles away from the war, the phone rang in the Fox household. Fox, who was watching Arlene feed Sandra in her highchair, got up to answer it. The smile disappeared from his face as the 366th's S-3 informed him the regiment had gotten orders to prepare to head overseas, and Fox needed to return to Atterbury by week's end.

Putting the receiver down, Fox decided not to tell Arlene the news right away but instead suggested a spur-of-the-moment trip to visit Arlene's parents in Brockton to surprise them. Arlene was confused but agreed. Fox wanted to tell Arlene about the deployment at her parents' home, hoping the news would be easier to handle, surrounded by family. The trip to Brockton would be the last time Fox ever saw Arlene or Sandra.

Chapter 20

Shipping Out

Upon Fox's return to Camp Atterbury, he learned that the 366th had been scheduled a month of map-reading training in the countryside. The additional time gave rise to the hope he'd have one last visit on leave with his family.

Fox, anguished, called Arlene in late January telling her that Colonel Queen denied his and another married man's request for a couple of days' leave, which was traditionally granted to soldiers with families. Fox tried to ease the pain of not getting home by telling Arlene he'd be back sooner than she expected. Indeed, Fox believed he'd be back before the year was out. The war was going well in Europe, which is where he hoped they were being sent. Arlene remained strong and upbeat on the phone, but when she hung up, emotion overwhelmed her. She retreated to her bedroom in tears while Sandra was down for a nap.

In late March 1944, the 366th traveled east to Camp Patrick Henry, Virginia, for embarkation on the 27th. Emotions within the outfit ran the gamut from excitement to dread; they still didn't know their final destination. Colonel Queen gathered his officers together in the Recreation Hall on Avenue A at Camp Henry as rain poured down in sheets outside. At this pre-embarkation meeting, he impressed upon them that this was not a vacation cruise and order and discipline were to be upheld; they represented the 366th, and he would hold them accountable for the behavior of their men.

The officers were anxious, nervous anticipation filled the room, but Queen lightened the mood by asking "Father Zachary" to close out the meeting with a passage he'd chosen from the Bible, First Chronicles 19:13.

Zachary smiled as he pulled a small Bible from his jacket, telling the Colonel that "he knew this one," eliciting an eyebrow raise from Col. Queen and laughter from fellow officers as they bowed their heads.

Zachary began, "Be of good courage, and let us behave ourselves valiantly for our people, and for the cities of our God: and let the LORD do that which is good in his sight."

✳✳✳

The colossal USS *General William Mitchell*, commanded by Joseph W. Sensing, sat hulking adjacent to Pier 4 at Hampton Roads, Virginia, as the 366th waited in formation under a cavernous dockside steel shelter. A pounding rain on the structure's metal roof drowned out almost every other sound. It was only the second Atlantic crossing for the 622-foot troopship newly commissioned on January 19, 1944. The ship could hold 5,289 personnel, and the 366th along with a separate antitank unit met that capacity.

The ten-day Atlantic crossing was uneventful, but the men made good use of their time. Zachary, now one of Col. Queen's favorite subordinates, was frequently Officer of the Day, overseeing everyone and handling any daily issues. Onboard there was a platoon of Puerto Ricans, whom Zachary often chatted with, and 40 Tuskegee Airmen* bound for Sicily.

Fox kept busy playing poker, a game at which he now excelled. He would often borrow money from Zachary, whom he paid back with interest at the end of the sea crossing. It was a lighthearted,

* Tuskegee Airmen refers to the primarily African American pilots (fighter and bomber) as well as support crew who served during World War II.

almost innocent time for Fox and the men in the 366th. Still unexposed to combat, they possessed a joie de vivre, and no one allowed themselves to believe they would not be returning home.

The USS *Mitchell* reached the port of debarkation on April 6 at Casablanca, Morocco; 48 hours later, the 366th loaded onto flat rail cars for the American military facility at Oran in Algeria, North Africa. At Oran, Colonel Queen received a copy of a letter sent to Washington DC from the USS *Mitchell*'s Captain, Joseph Sensing. The commander wrote that "the 366th has set an example of discipline and attention to duty while on this ship. The morale of your unit has been higher than any similar unit observed by me in the past."[9]

The 366th spent three weeks at Oran, and while there, the enlisted men were constantly harassed by white officers and MPs from other units. When soldiers of the 366th were out in the town's marketplace window shopping, white officers made a habit of coming up behind them, tapping them on the shoulder, and telling them they'd failed to salute. At Colonel Queen's headquarters outside Oran, he suddenly started receiving numerous delinquency reports due to the white officers filing charges. The Colonel finally had to secure a deuce and a half with seats that he utilized almost every day of the week to retrieve his enlisted men from jail.[10]

During this time, Fox, who was usually optimistic by nature, became disillusioned with the treatment they all received. He wrote a revealing letter home to Arlene expressing his deep frustration.

He wrote, "I wanted the experience; I'm really getting it. Segregation at every turn, and I mean in the worst kind of way. Some of these rotten dogs I have to work around are worse now than they were in the States. I have even come to honestly hate some of them, and I don't bite my tongue about it either. They are so unfair."[11]

On April 29, the 366th was again aboard ships and sailing from Oran to Naples, Italy, in an armada of two American, three French, and one British ship. The troop transports were escorted by two flanking American destroyers on the five-day voyage to Italy.

The arriving seafaring convoy found Naples blocked by wreckage in the choked-off harbor. Ships destroyed by the Germans lay capsized, protruding out of the ocean at every angle imaginable.

The same destruction would greet Medal of Honor recipient Lt. Vernon Baker and the 370th later that summer. Army engineers had constructed a ship-to-ship gang-plank causeway, which allowed the men to disembark. However, a departure from the vessel was delayed several hours as German planes had been spotted in the area. This first visage of war subdued the men and left them circumspect.

Upon disembarking, they found the city deserted and bleak. The detritus of war-torn Naples seemed to engulf them. The 366th bivouacked just north of the harbor at Bagnoli in a dust-swept crater, while Colonel Queen and several aides found rooms at one of the few hotels left standing in Naples.

After a week, Col. Queen and the 366th relocated 140 miles northeast to San Severo in the Province of Foggia, Italy, where Queen established his regimental headquarters. Although the men were in peak physical condition, combat-ready, and expecting to be placed on the front lines, the 366th was instead broken up into battalions, separated, and assigned to non-combat security duty. There was nothing Colonel Queen could do. The well-trained infantry regiment now walked the perimeters of fences guarding numerous airfields, ammunition dumps, and other military facilities. Morale plummeted, and this rear-echelon assignment began their deterioration as a cohesive fighting unit.

Fox and Zachary and 138 enlisted men in Cannon Company were assigned to guard the 15th Air Force in Manfredonia, 40 miles east of San Severo on the Adriatic Sea. The site included an ammunition dump and fuel storage for the aircraft. They made their camp adjacent to the beach, and some men took advantage of a daily swim as the weather warmed.

One afternoon Fox and fellow officer Frank Cloud had been tasked to pick up a crate of dynamite and blasting caps near Foggia. Cloud dreaded the trip, not because of the danger of transporting explosives, but for riding shotgun in a jeep with Fox. Fox had gained a reputation for speed in the outfit after he'd given several soldiers at Fort Deven a lift to auxiliary training off-base in his '40 Ford coupe. The automobile was so fast police forces used it extensively at the time. One soldier, after the white-knuckle ride to the training, took a separate car back to Devens. Fox loved to drive fast no matter what the vehicle.

By the time Fox and Cloud returned with the dynamite, Cloud could barely exit the jeep; he was so shaken. Zachary came through the camp, saw Fox and Cloud arrive back, and ran to help with the explosives. Cloud, seeing Zachary approach, asked "Flat Top" if he'd ever seen his life flash before his eyes. Zachary hadn't, but Cloud said he had about a million times on the trip to get the dynamite with Fox.

June brought word of the successful invasion of Normandy on the 6th. The Allied attack lifted spirits that the war on all fronts might be over sooner than anyone expected. Gains were also being made in the Mediterranean theater. Rome fell to the Allies just a day before the landings in France, and the Germans began a retreat north. It appeared to the 366th scattered all over Italy that they would serve in their posts on security detail for the remainder of the war. On July 30, Fox took the time to respond to a letter from Arlene that reflected his homesickness.

I'll pray a prayer for you and ask God to bring me back to you very soon. Hold Sandra tight and tell her Daddy said, "Kiss Mommie for Daddy." Darling, all I need is you. You ask if I want anything. Yes, I do very much – my family. It is really hard at times to keep from going to pieces under the mental strain a man has to bear with while being away from those who are honestly dear to him.[12]

Changes were on the horizon in the fall of 1944, and one change would have a profoundly personal impact on Fox in late September. He received a telegram at Manfredonia that his mother, Myrtle, had passed away on September 20. She had been in poor health, but she was relatively young at 54. Fox's immediate thoughts were of the impact on his two sisters, Myrtle, 28, and Jane, not yet 18. His father had left the family years earlier, and Fox felt responsible for his siblings' welfare. Myrtle, he believed, could hold her own as she was a teacher and entirely independent, but Jane was another story. Fox contacted Arlene immediately about inviting Jane over to visit and help her get through this difficult time. Arlene agreed and took Jane in for a time in early October.

Also, in October, Colonel Queen went down with typhus, an infection caused by bacteria transmitted via bites from fleas, mites, or ticks. Untreated typhus can lead to severe complications and is potentially fatal. Queen partially recovered by early November in time to receive word to gather up the 366th and report to the commander of the 92nd Division, General Almond, in the Po Valley in northern Italy. The 92nd did not have a replacement depot or "repple depple" pool of combat soldiers as it was called in Italy to draw from; the 366th were to be it.

When the Germans retreated after the fall of Rome, they dug in along the Gothic Line on high ground, which ran through rugged terrain in the Pisan Hills and other mountainous areas. The defensive line was a 170-mile front and a nearly impenetrable concrete wall that bogged down the Allied push north. Overall German commander in the Mediterranean theater, Generalfeldmarschall Albert Kesselring, had employed more than 15,000 Italians as slave-laborers. They worked over nine months to construct a series of well-fortified machine gun nests, casemates, bunkers, observation posts, and artillery-fighting positions to repel any attacks. It was Hitler's line in the sand in Italy.

Col. Queen, though appreciative about being summoned by the 92nd into action, became alarmed that his regiment had lost their combat readiness in six months of rear-echelon duty. Queen submitted a request to General B.O. Davis, Sr. and General Jacob L. Davis asking that his troops be immediately withdrawn from guard duty and given 30 days of training to strengthen combat readiness. Colonel Queen heard nothing back on his request for days.

On November 4, the 366th was officially assigned to the 92nd as combat soldiers. Fox and Cannon Company and other units of the 366th headed north in the second week of November and converged on an area just south of Pisa.

General Almond sent word back to Colonel Queen stating that the 366th would be given 15 days, not 30 days as requested. By the time of the entire regiment's and Colonel Queen's arrival just before Thanksgiving on November 23, those 15 days had shortened to five.

Thanksgiving for John Fox and the 366th was a dreary affair as heavy rains confined the regiment to their tents. A soggy turkey dinner was provided in a mess tent to celebrate the day, but the men were surrounded by starving Italians holding out buckets, hoping for a handout. Many men shared their meals, but the atmosphere was anything but celebratory.

On the evening of December 1, Fox, Zachary, and the soldiers in the 366th were welcomed to the combat zone personally by General Almond. The speech Almond gave to the 366th in Barga still invokes controversy and debate today. Almond, a South Carolinian who had graduated from Virginia Military Institute (VMI), was an avowed racist. Almond didn't appreciate the political pressures that had caused the Army to bring black troops to the front lines.

General Almond unceremoniously began his speech saying, "I did not send for you, your Negro newspapers, Negro politicians, and white friends have insisted on your seeing combat, and I shall see that you get combat and your share of the casualties."[13]

The reaction in the ranks was what one would expect – outrage. One Sergeant in the 366th, Willard Williams of Tennessee, who kept notes of his experiences during the war, vividly summed up the men's reaction to Almond's words: "he let us know he didn't give a hoot about having us, but since we were there, he would make use of us as cannon fodder."[14]

Colonel Queen composed a request to be relieved from command of the 366th the following day. He wrote in part:

> The treatment the regiment and myself have received during attachment to the 92nd Division has been such as to disturb me mentally and has not been such as is usually given to an officer of my grade and service. To keep my record clear and up to normal expectations, before I break under the present strain, as I am now physically and mentally exhausted.[15]

The writing was on the wall; Colonel Queen had become a figurehead. The commander knew he would not be allowed to lead the men he'd trained into battle, plus he was still recovering from his illness. Colonel Queen's request was granted, and he left the Mediterranean theater on December 11, 1944.

Sergeant Willard Williams, reflecting from his notes about the departure of Colonel Queen, summed up the feeling of the men: "My personal feeling and the feeling of many others in the 366th was Colonel Queen was too strong a man to head up an all-Negro unit as far as the whites were concerned. He kept their feet to the fire from the time we left Fort Devens until we arrived in the Po Valley."[*,16]

Lieutenant Colonel Alonzo Ferguson, a World War I veteran, replaced the outgoing Col. Queen as commander of the 366th on December 15. He was well-liked and gained the nickname "Cotton Top" because of his white hair. However, he was no pushover, but similar to Queen, he had very little responsibility at the front beyond logistical duties with the regiment.

On December 9, Fox and Cannon Company relocated from south of Pisa to rejoin the rest of the 366th in Loppia opposite the Gothic Line. They were now attached to the African American 598th Field Artillery Battalion (FAB) commanded by white Lieutenant Colonel Robert C. Ross. Lt. Col. Ross was pleased to have Cannon Company under his command, and he was well-liked by the men. Ross made a point of getting to know the new unit and appreciated their esprit de corps and expertise.

Due to the heavy rain that month, when Cannon Company arrived on the 9th and attempted to emplace their guns, one of their trucks got hopelessly mired in mud. The truck's location blocked other military traffic on the road and did not make a great first impression. Fox and Frank Cloud, and several other men, eventually freed the truck and set the guns as night fell.

---

* Howard D. Queen retired as a Colonel from the US Army. He passed away in 1978 and is buried at Arlington National Cemetery.

Chapter 21

Give 'em Hell

"Fire It! There's more of them than there are of us.
Give 'em hell!"

JOHN FOX

NEAR BARGA, ITALY

DECEMBER 14, 1944

In October 1944, the Germans planned for a vigorous offensive against the left (western) wing of the American Fifth Army. This enemy sector of the Gothic Line was under the command of Generalleutnant Walter Jost of the 42nd Jäger Division. The area was considered a quiet sector, and the Germans were fully aware of the arrival of the untested black infantry troops within the 92nd Division.

Their grand attack plan comprising 40,000 men – two Italian divisions and one German division – with ample tank, artillery, and air support never got off the ground. There were neither tanks nor aircraft nor enough fuel to support the attack. The Allies controlled the skies over Italy, and any movement of what little armor the Germans had would be discovered and destroyed.

The ambitious plan was scaled back and refocused by Italian General Carloni and Otis Fretter-Pico, the German commander of the 148th Infantry Division. The new plan called for a limited local attack along a narrow front, between Sommocolonia (east of Serchio River) and Mount Pania Secca (west of the Said River).

A crucial component of the attack with 4,600 men was that it could be launched without the need for reinforcements. The goal of the planned offensive named Operation *Wintergewitter* (Winter Thunderstorm) was to improve the Axis defensive position in Garfagnana and restrict the movement of American forces and capture vital supplies, including weapons, ammunition, and food. A secondary goal was to boost the flagging morale of the Italian fascist forces.

As the Christmas holiday approached, Zachary was ordered to rotate into forward observation (FO) duty on December 17 in Sommocolonia. Fox prepared to begin three days of intense forward observer training on the 20th with Survey Sergeant William Wyatt at the 598th FAB. Fox was typically assigned to FDC (Fire Direction Center). He was considered the best they had as he was highly skilled at math and could calculate firing coordinates backward and forwards.

A week before heading over to forward observer training, Fox, on December 14, took the time to write a "Christmas letter" home to Arlene.

Fox wrote, "Combat is hell on earth, and I don't mean maybe. I'm taking the best possible care of myself, considering the conditions under which we have to live. But, I'll make it out – anyway, I hope so. Those damn Germans are hell – I know. As yet I received only Sandra's cake – am saving it for Xmas day – I'll try not to cry when I eat it."[17]

Sommocolonia, where Zachary was now stationed as Forward Observer, was a small windswept village high in the Apennine Mountains overlooking Barga in Tuscany. His radio operator was fellow Puerto Rican Bartolome Malavet, and his jeep driver, Herbert Williams.

Residents were welcoming to the Americans, and Zachary in his short duration there gained many admirers. One friend, local priest Don Fredianelli, called him "Puerto Rico." When Zachary's FO duties were complete Fredianelli gave him a small prayer card with a reproduction of Sommocolonia's Santa Maria del Carmine printed on the back in remembrance of his church attendance.

Frank Cloud took over Zachary's forward observation post in the village on the 18th. Cloud was surprised that Zachary had secured an almost brand-new jeep that he gave Cloud for his use. Cloud didn't ask where he'd gotten the vehicle. Zachary also loaned Cloud his driver, Williams, and radio operator, Malavet. Zachary conveyed that the area was pretty quiet with not much activity, but to stay alert.

By this time, just past mid-December 1944, the Allies had intelligence to indicate that the Germans were planning an attack in the area. Intelligence reported the 148th Infantry Division and the Italian Monte Rosa and San Marco Marine Divisions were in the area, and the 157th Gebirgsjäger Division might have been moving there as well. The 92nd had been planning its own attack for Christmas day. The 92nd decided to wait to determine whether to proceed with their assault until the 24th.

With the observation post in Sommocolonia needing to be manned over the holiday, Fox decided to volunteer for the extended four-day Christmas posting. Others could have been assigned, but he volunteered. Perhaps he wanted to test his new FO skills, or maybe he wanted time alone. Sommocolonia was known to be a lonely assignment.

Fox met Frank Cloud outside Barga near the Command Post (CP) just past 0830 hours on the 23rd. He asked to borrow a fresh uniform; he'd only brought his dress greens and didn't want to wear them out in the field. Cloud went to fetch his spare uniform as Zachary came out of FDC to wish Fox a Merry Christmas. Zachary did so and added that FO duty was a terrible way to spend the holiday.

Fox smiled, saying it'd be okay; he'd make the best of it. Fox shared that Arlene had sent him Sandra's birthday cake. His daughter had made it all by herself as a Christmas gift for him.

Zachary betrayed genuine emotion, telling Fox that the war seemed worse during Christmas, really rotten, especially for family men like him. Fox frowned in agreement. Zachary changed the subject asking if Fox remembered how they'd snagged that tractor to get Arlene to the hospital with the baby. Fox smiled, remembering, and said, how could he forget. The two shook hands on that cold winter morning as they parted, believing they would remain lifelong friends.

Fox, Malavet, and Williams arrived in Sommocolonia just after 0900 hours in San Rocco Piazza. The town appeared deserted. Malavet suggested they drop their gear at the forward observer post where he'd been with Cloud and Zachary, on the second floor of a house in town. Fox, however, decided to survey the area first to determine the best location. Fox found it in La Rocca tower.

The 46-foot tall, three-story stone tower had been built in the tenth century as a fortress and had survived many centuries of war; it seemed the perfect location. Fox and his men occupied the top floor, a 25-foot-square open room with thick chestnut ceiling beams and a brick floor. The room had a couple of mattresses and a wooden table with a few chairs.

The same day Fox established his FO post, American troops began concentrating in and around Sommocolonia, preparing for the 92nd's planned Christmas day attack on Lama. The tiny hamlet was a mile and a half north of the village. The attack was purely diversionary as the 92nd's main assault was to take place at Bologna. The 366th's 2nd Battalion held the town of Barga on the American right flank, while the 370th held Gallicano, west of the Serchio River. The 370th's 2nd Battalion (less G Company) with two companies from the 366th attached moved into Sommocolonia on the morning of Christmas Eve.[18]

That day General Almond called off his attack. Italian partisans had passed intelligence to Almond's headquarters for weeks regarding a significant buildup of German troops north of Barga and Sommocolonia. The 92nd decided to prepare to fend off an Axis offensive which they expected would be launched on December 27.

With Sommocolonia receiving only sporadic enemy mortar, artillery, and small arms fire, the day of Christmas Eve, the 2nd Battalion of the 370th withdrew under cover of darkness at midnight, leaving only one platoon of the 366th's F Company and a platoon of H Company to defend the town. In total, this was approximately 72 men.[19]

Christmas day dawned sunny and warmer than usual in Sommocolonia. Fox was entering the third day of his four-day forward observer assignment. Taking some time out of the tower to partake of the turkey dinner brought up to the troops, he encountered his old friend from Fort Devens, 1st Lieutenant Graham Hervey Jenkins of Philadelphia. Jenkins, who went by the name of Hervey, commanded 366th's H Company weapons platoon of machine gunners.

Jenkins and Fox spotted each other in the chow line and came together shaking hands. Both joked that it was crazy they'd ended up in this tiny village on Christmas together. Fox pulled a recent photo of Sandra from his wallet that Arlene had mailed and shared it with his friend. Fox knew Jenkins could see the pride in his face. The two separated, wishing each other a Merry Christmas once Fox had his food, although he'd left Malavet on watch in the tower.

A Christmas mass was held in the village's 12th-century church by Father Fredianelli at 1600 hours so the villagers could retreat early to the safety of their basement shelters for the night. In the waning light, Fox opened the bakery box, which held Sandra's cake. He shared the vanilla cake with chocolate frosting with Malavet and Williams. Although the frosting was now crusty, all enjoyed the Christmas treat. Fox noted an increase in enemy mortar fire as he later grabbed an hour of sleep. It was concerning, but the day had been quiet for the most part.

At 0450 hours on the 26th, a German mortar struck the 12th-century church bell tower less than 50 feet from Fox's location on the third floor of La Rocca tower. A heavy artillery barrage immediately followed this clanging first strike. Shells fell, exploding throughout the town as Fox jumped on the radio calling in artillery support from the 598th.

It was still dark, and his coordinates were the German positions he had given them a day earlier on a nearby hill. The 598th's counter-battery volley pounded the nearby hill. As the echoes of the American artillery explosions died away, an eerie silence settled over the village. There was no answering enemy fire.

Fox paced, knowing what this possibly meant – an infantry attack. Suddenly at 0518 hours, an enemy machine gun close by pierced the morning silence.

Fox again called for artillery fire as he peered out into the darkness through field glasses. Malavet, his radio operator, sat with his back against the wall, passing the handset back and forth to Fox. Williams held a lighter over a map rolled out on Fox's lap.

At 0540 hours, Fox and his men heard explosions from land mines the partisans had laid on the north road leading to Lama. These mine explosions confirmed Fox's fears of an enemy infantry advance, and they came as a deadly surprise to the 3rd Company of the 4th Hochgebirgsjäger Battalion. Below in the village, the two platoons of the 366th set up a defensive perimeter, but amidst the echoing rifle fire, it was difficult to tell from which direction the attack was coming.

From the tower, in the brightening morning light, Fox could now make out figures scrambling on the hillock just north of town, and he heard a call on the radio from Italian partisans defending that sector. They requested immediate artillery support.

Soon the 366th mortar platoon commanded by Lieutenant Louis Flagg was saturating that area with 60mm shells. Fifteen minutes later, the rifle fire stopped. Williams, Malavet, and Fox looked at one another. Perhaps that was it, a limited attack, maybe a patrol? All breathed a momentary sigh of relief as dawn started to break through on the 26th.

Fox and his men in the tower did not know that Axis infantry was repositioning, splitting up to attack Sommocolonia from two directions. The 4th Hochgebirgsjäger Battalion, wearing their distinctive berets with eagle's head crests, ascended from the north on the Lama path reinforced by a squad of machine gunners.

On the cemetery path, the Austro-German Alpine Mittenwald Battalion was also advancing toward the village from the east. Both these units were a mixture of German and Austrian soldiers and attached to the 148th Infantry Division. They were young, well trained, and highly motivated. The battalions had crossed the Radici Pass in a heavy snowstorm two days earlier, arriving just north of Sommocolonia on Christmas morning.

The hour between 0600 and 0700 was tense and deathly quiet, then suddenly all hell broke loose. An intense barrage of enemy artillery, mortar, and machine gun fire lit up the village like none of the defending soldiers had ever experienced. Fox was on the radio back to Zachary at FDC calling for fire on the eastern path where the Mittenwald Battalion was advancing.

Overwhelmed at 0735 hours, Hervey Jenkins, commander of H Company's weapons platoon, radioed for reinforcements. The battalion ordered a platoon of E Company to Sommocolonia, when perhaps they should have ordered the entire company. Jenkins reported house-to-house fighting and requested mortar and artillery fire. The S-2 back at the CP recorded in the 366th's 2nd Battalion journal that Jenkins informed them, "Don't worry about anything, his men would hold."

Unfortunately, the platoon of reinforcements from E Company would never reach Jenkins in Sommocolonia. They were repulsed at 1020 hours by German snipers and machine gunners who had the route well covered leading into town.

Fox could look across from his tower outpost at the German forces swarming through the village; some were engaged in hand-to-hand fighting with the 366th. A partisan sniper, Torello Tonnarelli, hidden in one of the homes, was picking many of the enemy off. The Italian sniper was credited with shooting more than 20 German soldiers that day.

Fox continued to call in artillery strikes beyond the town to stem the tide of advancing enemy infantry. He could not direct fire onto the village itself for fear of hitting his own men. Earlier that morning at 0830 hours, Sgt. William Wyatt at the 598th battery in an excited voice on the radio confirmed that Fox's coordinates had blown apart a mule train. It had been attempting to resupply the attackers with ammunition.[20]

The enemy even noted Fox's skill at directing the artillery fire. An Austrian soldier, Hans Burtscher, non-commissioned officer, 2nd Company of the 4th Hochgebirgsjäger Battalion of Kampfgruppe IV Hoch Pioneers present at the battle wrote in his diary:

> The artillery observer of the enemy has to be on top of the upper tower, in our opinion. He is guiding the artillery splendidly to our damage. The artillery shells are now striking

very nearby, near the groups lying behind us. The biggest
danger is the shells bursting near trees.[21]

Burtscher went on to record in his battle diary how Fox became a
marked man:

> Our marksmen, experienced soldiers, mostly from Steiermark,
> Salzburg, and Karnten (regions of Austria) are given the
> command to finish off the enemy artillery observer in the tower.[22]

Even though American reinforcements were not reaching the
besieged men, they tenaciously held on, putting up one hell of
a fight. Assessing their deteriorating situation, the Germans,
by mid-morning, pulled Mittenwald soldiers from Bebbio and
Scarpello to aid in the stubborn battle at Sommocolonia. With
the additional troops, the attacking Austro-German force totaled
270 men, almost three times the number of soldiers defending the
village; two platoons of the 366th plus approximately 25 Italian
partisans.

Fox knew Jenkins had requested reinforcements as he'd heard
his radio call earlier that morning, but Fox saw none had arrived.
Suddenly below in the town, shouts and gunfire intensified. Fox and
his men peered down, alarmed to see what looked like hundreds of
Germans swarming into town from all directions.

The radio crackled to life, and Fox heard Jenkins call back to his
cousin, Lt. Arthur Fearing, in the 366th mortar platoon in Ponte
di Catagnana conveying the grim situation:

> Cuz, it looks like they're coming after us. Please, when you get
> back to the States, tell my wife and my kid and my mother and
> all that I love them because I just don't feel I'm gonna make it
> through this.[23]

Fox dropped his head into his hands, whispering a desperate
prayer, then jumped back on the radio, calling in coordinates
closer to the village. As he returned to look down at the streets,

he could see Jenkins rushing from one wounded man to another, trying to pull them back to safety behind a stone wall, all the while returning fire.

As Jenkins rushed back to the last wounded man in the street, he was struck down by machine gun fire. Fox watched his old friend crumple to the road in a pool of blood. Jenkins would be awarded the Silver Star posthumously for his gallant actions that morning attempting to save the men in his platoon.

Fox became grave with tears in his eyes; he turned to Malavet and Williams and told them it was time for them to go. They protested, but Fox made it an order and told them to get the hell off the mountain any way they could. He'd made up his mind to stay. The men's eyes locked a moment, then Williams and Malavet dashed down the tower stairs out into the firestorm. Williams was killed seconds later; Malavet was captured, and spent the remainder of the war in Stalag VII-A Moosburg Bavaria, Germany. He was liberated on May 23, 1945.

Fox looked down at his map. He circled his tower position then looked over to the phone connected to the 598th. He grabbed the handset shortly before 1100 hours. Sgt. Wyatt answered at the 598th battery, and Fox conveyed that the situation was beyond hopeless; the platoons had been overrun. Fox provided Wyatt with new coordinates. Silence came back on the line, then Wyatt said, "John, that's your position."

Fox was focused and resolute, saying the Germans would take his position any minute, and there were only a few of their men left but hundreds of the enemy. Fox repeated his request to fire on the coordinates he provided. Fox added that after the HE (high explosive) rounds had fired to wait ten minutes, then lay down smoke so any of the 366th left alive could escape.

Wyatt refused; he did not have the authority to fire on his own men, but he would connect Fox with Colonel Ross to determine what to do. The call transferred over to FDC, and Zachary picked it up.

Fox heard Zachary's voice answer and shouted, "Flat Top put everything you got on my location, on the tower!"

Zachary leaned forward in shock and shouted, "Hell no, I can't do that, John."

Fox reiterated, "We're overrun. There's no time. Here's the coordinates."

As Zachary scribbled them down, Col. Ross entered, and Zachary handed him the phone, saying it was Fox and he wanted fire on his position.

"Fox, what's going on?" Ross demanded.

"We're overrun, sir. You gotta fire on the coordinates I just gave Flat Top."

Ross picked up the paper with the coordinates Zachary wrote down and then quickly confirmed the location on a map, "John, that's your position."

"I know how to read a damn map. I know."

Ross shouted for an aide who came running. Ross scribbled an urgent note and instructed the subordinate to take the request immediately to General Truscott. Ross told Fox that he'd get him an answer from higher up.

The aide returned within minutes. Zachary broke into tears as the aide frowned, nodding his head, the order was approved, and he passed the signed confirmation back to Ross.

Ross picked up the handset and told Fox that they would honor his request but asked him one last time if he was sure about what he was doing.

Fox, out of patience and out of time, shouted into the phone, "Yes, damn it. Fire it. Give 'em hell!"[24]

Col. Ross put the receiver back on the field telephone and directed Zachary to punch in the coordinates. Zachary's hand trembled as he put in the numbers for all three batteries of the 598th in Loppia to fire as Ross had ordered. These were the 598th A and B batteries with 155mm howitzers and the 366th's attached Cannon Company, Fox's own unit with its 105s.

Wyatt, per procedure, fired a single round and waited for adjustment from Fox. Fox radioed back that the shell was 100 yards above and 75 yards wide of the target.

Wyatt adjusted and fired one more round.

The shell rocked the tower, falling just 25 yards short. Fox's ears rang as he grabbed the radio, telling Wyatt it was short by 25 yards. Fox told him to make the final adjustment and fire for effect.

Wyatt conveyed the adjustment to Zachary at FDC. Zachary punched in the revised coordinates but froze.

Ross shouted, "Damnit, Lieutenant, give the order to fire."

Zachary yelled, "Fire mission. Converge sheath. All guns fire for effect!"

Then he closed his eyes. Ross ordered a second salvo, and it roared forth with the additional smoke rounds that Fox requested. Tears cascaded down Zachary's face that he could not stop. Silence hung over the FDC as Ross rubbed his face with his hands then yelled, "Okay. Listen up! We're going to have a minute of silence in honor of Lieutenant Fox. All guns, all personnel."[25]

The order was transmitted to all batteries in the field, and all stood at attention. One officer and only 17 enlisted men out of 72 in the two platoons of the 366th in Sommocolonia were able to escape. The remainder were casualties or became prisoners of war.

The German offensive ran out of steam, and the Americans recaptured the area around Sommocolonia by December 30. After New Year's Day, the 92nd sent a Graves Registration and body recovery team into the village. Two men testifying in separate interviews positively identified the body of John Fox.

Remarkably both men had a connection to him. Cleveland Wells, a medic from Ohio with the 370th Graves Registration team, in an interview with author Solace Wales in 2010, reported his findings from the time. In Wells' examination of the yet unidentified body of John Fox, he discovered in Fox's pockets two photographs, one of Fox's sister Jane whom Wells knew as she frequented a drug store where he had previously worked. A second photo was of Fox and Jane's aunt Mary Willie Morning, Cleveland Wells and Jane's 5th-grade teacher.[26]

The second man who identified Fox's body had a closer relationship; in fact, they were old friends. As part of the Graves Registration team, 2nd Lt. Jefferson Jordan, attached to the 371st, traveled into Sommocolonia with Wells, his subordinate. In an interview he gave in the mid-1970s he recalled identifying Fox's body before Cleveland Wells found the photographs in Fox's pockets:

> The crew called me concerning the identification of one of the bodies. There was nothing on the body to use for identification, and they wanted to know how to list the man. While I stood there looking at the cadaver, deciding what should be done, it occurred to me that I knew this man despite the fact that his face was battered. It was John Fox.[27]

One can only imagine his emotions on that January morning in 1945, standing over his deceased friend whom he hadn't seen since graduating with him in ROTC at Wilberforce.

✳✳✳

In early 1945 Brigadier General William H. Colburn, the 92nd Division's artillery commander, endorsed Lt. Fox's name for the Distinguished Service Cross. The General confirmed his submission of the DSC for Fox in an interview on July 2, 1945.[28] It is unclear when General Almond first learned of Fox's heroic act, but what is confirmed is he knew no later than March 4, 1945, when he received back a report requested from the 370th Infantry Regiment about events in the Serchio Valley. That report described Fox's actions in detail.[29]

Why Almond took no action in forwarding Fox's name for the DSC to Fifth Army is unclear. Perhaps it was because he considered the mission at Sommocolonia a monumental failure. Or possibly he was angered by the recent poor infantry performance, in his estimation, of a week-long February offensive in 1945 involving the 366th. We may never know the answer. However, Almond did approve the Silver Star (posthumous) for Lt. Graham H. Jenkins in 92nd Division General Order 18 on May 6, 1945.

Fox's heroic act of valor went unrecognized for decades until his cause was taken up by Dr. Hondon B. Hargrove, an author, and veteran of the 92nd Division's service in Italy. Hargrove spearheaded an exhaustive investigation with the help of Arlene Fox and many others and submitted his report to the Department of the Army, which agreed with his findings.

Lt. John Fox was awarded his long-overdue Distinguished Service Cross at Fort Devens on May 15, 1982. Arlene Fox was on hand at the ceremony to receive the honor. Fifteen years later, she and Otis Zachary attended the White House Medal of Honor ceremony together in January 1997. Arlene, with tear-filled eyes, accepted the country's highest medal for valor from President Bill Clinton on Fox's behalf.

JOHN FOX, MEDAL OF HONOR CITATION

For conspicuous gallantry and intrepidity at the risk of his life above and beyond the call of duty: First Lieutenant John R. Fox distinguished himself by extraordinary heroism at the risk of his own life on 26 December 1944 in the Serchio River Valley Sector, in the vicinity of Sommocolonia, Italy. Lieutenant Fox was a member of Cannon Company, 366th Infantry, 92d Infantry Division, acting as a forward observer, while attached to the 598th Field Artillery Battalion. Christmas Day in the Serchio Valley was spent in positions which had been occupied for some weeks. During Christmas night, there was a gradual influx of enemy soldiers in civilian clothes and by early morning the town was largely in enemy hands. An organized attack by uniformed German formations was launched around 0400 hours, 26 December 1944. Reports were received that the area was being heavily shelled by everything the Germans had, and although most of the U.S. infantry forces withdrew from the town, Lieutenant Fox and members of his observer party remained behind on the second floor of a house, directing defensive fires. Lieutenant Fox reported at 0800 hours that the Germans were in the streets and attacking in strength. He called for artillery fire increasingly close to his own position. He told his battalion commander, "That was just where I wanted it. Bring it in 60 yards!" His commander protested that there was a heavy barrage in the area and the bombardment would be too close. Lieutenant Fox gave his adjustment, requesting that the barrage be fired. The distance was cut in half. The Germans continued to press forward in large numbers, surrounding the position. Lieutenant Fox again called for artillery fire with the commander protesting again, stating, "Fox, that will be on you!" The last communication from Lieutenant Fox was, "Fire It! There's more of them than there are of us. Give them hell!" The bodies of Lieutenant Fox and his party were found in the vicinity of his position when his position was taken. This action, by Lieutenant Fox, at the cost of his own life, inflicted heavy casualties, causing the deaths of approximately 100 German soldiers, thereby delaying the advance of the enemy until infantry and artillery units could be reorganized to meet the attack. Lieutenant Fox's extraordinarily valorous actions exemplify the highest traditions of the military service.

Epilogue

THE REST OF THE STORY

All of the Medal of Honor recipients in this book have passed away. Four of the men died as a result of their gallant actions. One, George Watson, was lost at sea but is memorialized in the American Battle Monument Cemetery in Manilla. The three others were laid to rest at cemeteries around the world. John Fox is buried in Whitman, Plymouth County, Massachusetts, near Brockton at Colebrook Cemetery in a family plot. Ruben Rivers is buried at Lorraine American Cemetery and Memorial in Saint-Avold, Departement de la Moselle, Lorraine, France. Willy James Jr. is buried at Netherlands American Cemetery and Memorial in Margraten, Eijsden-Margraten Municipality, Limburg, Netherlands.

The remaining Medal of Honor recipients who survived the war, Vernon Baker, Edward Carter Jr., and Charles Thomas, all adjusted as best as they could to civilian life and a country where prejudice remained the norm. All gave interviews reflecting on their service after the war. Vernon Baker has several hours of videotaped interviews posted with the Veterans History Project at the Library of Congress, which you can watch online. I recommend it highly.

CHARLES THOMAS

Thomas retired from the military with the rank of Major on August 10, 1947. He married Bertha Mae Thompson on July 22, 1949. They had two children, Michael Charles Thomas and Linda Camile

Thomas. Linda passed away from cancer prior to her 12th birthday and Michael died in 2020. Thomas had a long career working as a computer programmer for the IRS in Michigan.

Thomas was received and treated as a war hero in Detroit after the war. Many men who had served with him in Europe felt "they had seen a ghost" when they saw Thomas and his father out on the street; they couldn't believe he had survived his many wounds. In interviews after the war, Thomas showed his humility but also a grasp of the situation he found himself in:

> They say men under stress can do unusual things. I imagine this was true in my case. I know I hung onto one thought, deploy the guns and start firing or we're dead. Thinking back on it, I knew if the job could be done, these men could do it because they could and would fight; they were proud, and they were good. Training and discipline were key, and they had plenty of both. No doubt my men seeing me hurt and still doing my job pushed them to even greater effort. You have to adjust to living with death in war, but don't let anyone tell you you are not afraid.
>
> As to the high number of illiterates, one thing they learned was to fight and fight well. For many, the 614th was their first outside attachment from the rural south, and they were proud of their unit. These were not ignorant men by any means; they were unschooled. Need I say I was proud to serve with them.[1]

Charles Thomas died at the age of 59 on February 15, 1980 and was laid to rest at Westlawn Cemetery in Wayne County, Michigan. His wife Bertha passed away in January of 1989.

VERNON BAKER

Vernon Baker remained in Italy after the war until orders arrived in late 1946, sending him back home. He left Italy on February 7, 1947 on the transport ship USS *Henry P. Stevens* bound for England then America.

Back in the States, Baker briefly considered college and taking advantage of the GI Bill. His officer commission was due to expire in several months, and he needed a college degree to maintain it. But in the end, with the prodding of his sister, Baker decided against college. Instead, he reenlisted upon the expiration of his commission as a 1st Lieutenant.

He briefly became an Army photographer and a Master Sergeant in the Signal Corps, but the Army was actively recruiting a new black airborne division with higher pay. Baker, though he wasn't keen on jumping out of airplanes, decided to sign up.

He finished jump school at Fort Bragg in Fayetteville, North Carolina, and graduated as a 1st Sergeant from NCO (non-commissioned officer) school at the top of his class. He joined K Company of the 3rd Battalion of the 505th Infantry Regiment in the 82nd Airborne Division.

With the outbreak of the Korean War in 1950, Baker decided to apply for active duty and transferred to the 11th Airborne at Fort Campbell, Kentucky. However, the Chief of Staff of the 11th told Baker that they weren't sending any Distinguished Service Cross recipients to Korea. Baker was too valuable, he told him, as a morale booster. Baker knew they had sent white DSC recipients to Korea, but black DSC recipients were few and far between. He figured he was a valuable commodity to them as the airborne wanted to demonstrate an inclusive outlook.

Although the 11th Airborne kept Baker stateside, with the passage of the bill eliminating discrimination in the armed forces on September 10, 1951, he rose from platoon leader to company commander. Baker, with this promotion, became one of the first black NCOs to command an all-white company.

With the end of the Korean conflict, Baker decided against reenlisting in the 11th Airborne. He had had his fill of Army politics and chose instead to return to the Signal Corps as a photographer in the NCO ranks at Fort Huachuca. There, he met Fern Brown, a divorced swimming instructor with young daughters, and they were married in June 1953, and soon, another daughter, LaVerne

Baker, arrived in late December 1954. The family adopted one more daughter, nine-year-old Larise from Korea, while Baker was temporarily stationed there for a year.

Baker remained in the Army, returning to the airborne serving as a Company 1st Sergeant. He transferred to Germany with his family in 1967 during the Vietnam War. With only three years to reach 30 years of service, Baker decided the situation in Germany was untenable. The anti-war sentiment and rampant drug use of the soldiers unnerved him to such a degree that he feared being mugged and began carrying a .45-caliber pistol at all times.

In the end, he felt it was best to leave the service. He jumped out of his last airplane at 48 and mustered out of the Army at Fort Hamilton, New York, a week later in August 1968. His military career was over, but he carried on in a service career as he went to work for the Red Cross, which he stayed with for the next 20 years.

Baker and Fern relocated to Seaside, California, in the 1970s. In January 1986, Fern began having chest pains and was rushed to the hospital, where she deteriorated rapidly, falling into a coma. She passed away a week after entering the hospital. Fern and Baker had been together 39 years.

With the memories too much to bear in the home, Baker decided that he needed a change. One of the places he loved was Idaho, where he'd made many hunting trips with his buddies. He located a cottage and decided to move to Coeur d'Alene, Idaho, in May 1987. The area reminded him of the hills of Italy and his boyhood in Cheyenne.

Two years later, while on a stopover at the Spokane, Washington airport, Baker met an interior designer, Heidy Pawlik, who had moved to the States from Germany. Although noting her German accent, Baker fell in love with her and they relocated to Idaho where they were married. Baker would often joke afterward that "he married the enemy."

Baker, happier than he'd been in a long time, loved the fact that people in Idaho left him alone, and no one knew of his service in the war. Here he found the peace and quiet with his wife, Heidy, that he had sought his entire life.

That was until he was contacted in March of 1994 by Professor Daniel Gibran at Shaw University in Raleigh, North Carolina. The Army had commissioned a new study to determine why no black service members from World War II had been awarded the Medal of Honor.

Baker was skeptical at first. He felt he had received his due with the Distinguished Service Cross and didn't relish the aspect of reliving the hell his men had gone through at Castle Aghinolfi, when their commander left them to die. Baker, however, reluctantly agreed because he felt that the country should know the odds he and his men had faced and receive the recognition they had been denied.

On January 13, 1997, Baker stood alone as the only surviving recipient of the seven black soldiers from World War II chosen to be awarded the Medal of Honor. He was tearful at the ceremony but thankful that he was among the seven men to receive the overdue recognition. In remarks afterward, he said, "The only thing that I can say to those who are not here with me is, 'Thank you, fellas, well done. And I will always remember you.'"[2]

His legacy is best summed up in his own words:

We were Buffalo soldiers; we had to fight to the last man to retain any shred of dignity. We did the best we could – and a hell of a lot better than anyone believed we could. We fought fiercely and proudly for a country that shunned us, and we kept fighting because we knew the price of allowing Nazi fascism to rule was far greater than even what we endured.

War, however, is the most regrettable proving ground. For the sake of my nineteen comrades, I hope no man black, white, or any color ever again has the opportunity to earn the Medal of Honor. War is not honor. Those who rush to launch conflict, and those who seek to create heroes from it, should remember war's legacy. You have to be there to appreciate the horrors. And die to forget them.[3]

Vernon Baker passed away on July 13, 2010 at the age of 90 and was laid to rest at Arlington National Cemetery in Virginia.

EDWARD CARTER JR.

Edward Carter reached the rank of Sergeant First Class in 1949. His postwar life was a story of continued discrimination, frustration, false accusations but ultimate redemption mainly driven by the efforts of his tenacious daughter-in-law, Allene Carter. She co-wrote with Robert Allen the book *Honoring Sergeant Carter: Redeeming a Black World War II Hero's Legacy*.

Edward Carter was a born soldier, it was his profession and first love, and his transition to civilian life was complicated. Discrimination after the war was widespread, and many black veterans had trouble securing employment, including Carter. He applied but was turned down for a VA (Veterans Affairs) loan to launch a painting business and eventually landed as the Director of Public Relations for the Eastside Chamber of Commerce in Los Angeles. He became chairman of the Chamber's Veterans Bureau and attempted to form an interracial veterans committee. He saw it as a way black and white veterans could work together to set an example to improve race relations. Unfortunately, the committee never got off the ground.

Frustrated, he returned to the life he knew best and reenlisted in the military. Carter was assigned to Camp Lee, Virginia, in the First Service Group, but it was only temporary. His combat experience was needed, and he became an instructor on loan from the Army in the California National Guard and transferred west to Sacramento. Carter served successfully at different posts across the state. In the late 1940s, however, it came to light that he had been under investigation and surveillance by the Army Counterintelligence Corps (CIC) for suspected communist sympathies. The investigation stemmed from his service with the Abraham Lincoln Brigade in Spain.

In 1948 Carter was abruptly removed from the National Guard post without explanation and reassigned to the Military Police

Provost Detachment in Fort Lewis, Washington. Here he was well respected and successful but still under investigation.

In the spring of 1949, he relocated his family from Los Angeles to Tacoma and was promoted to Sergeant First Class. His future was looking bright, and he announced he planned on reenlisting when his tour was up in September of that year.

The Army, however, had other plans. They decided to bar his reenlistment, even though Carter was held in high regard by his superior officers in the Detachment at Fort Lewis. Higher command made this decision, and Carter, being the warrior, decided to fight against it and defend his honor. Two days after getting the letter of denial for reenlistment, he traveled to the Pentagon in Virginia to plead his case.

He asked the Army Inspector General for a hearing but was refused. Army Intelligence also declined to meet with him. Carter even appealed to President Harry Truman in a letter that October declaring his loyalty to the United States, but it was all to no avail.

Carter returned to Tacoma and moved his family to a small farm in Orting, Washington. He taught his boys, "Buddha" and Redd, all about farm life and how to shoot, while he picked up odd jobs here and there, but his family continued to struggle.

After seven months of fighting and getting nowhere, Carter decided in desperation to return his Distinguished Service Cross to President Truman via an attorney, Herbert Levy, with the American Civil Liberties Union (ACLU) in New York. Carter had lost two civilian jobs as word was getting around that he had been kicked out of the Army for being a communist. Levy held onto the medal and decided to continue a letter-writing campaign, which was ineffective.

By 1954 Carter wrote to Levy that he was forced to concede defeat. He asked for the return of his papers and the DSC. Upon receiving the medal back, he told Mildred that "he almost broke down and cried. That Army deal I took harder than anything I ever had to. You'll never realize how tough it was on me."[4]

The family returned to Los Angeles, but Carter joined them later after working several jobs in Tacoma trying to pay off their bills.

When he finally returned to the family, he was a changed man who had grown quiet and despondent. His relationship with Mildred suffered; they'd grown apart. As a result of the turmoil, Carter's health deteriorated, and he was diagnosed with lung cancer. His condition worsened rapidly, and on January 30, 1963, Sergeant Edward Carter died at the age of just 46.

For over 30 years, that remained the end of the story for Sergeant Carter until he was recognized deservedly with the nation's highest military honor for valor in 1997, the Medal of Honor. Fortunately, this proud man's story did not end there. His daughter-in-law, Allene Carter, who attended the 1997 ceremony with President Clinton in Washington, pressed his case further.

She recognized that the military had done a terrible wrong to the legacy of a proud soldier who only sought to serve his country.

Allene went on a crusade to correct the record of Carter's military service and clear his name. Through the Freedom of Information Act, she requested all of Carter's associated military records and those of the intelligence agencies. Allene discovered a long campaign to smear an innocent man's name, which had begun when Carter was at Fort Benning in 1942. She read report after report stating there was no evidence to support the suspicion that Edward Carter was a communist. His investigation was finally closed.

With binders of materials in hand, Allene enlisted the help of the media to clear her father-in-law's name. She contacted reporter Joe L. Galloway at *US News and World Report*, who had penned the *New York Times* bestseller *We Were Soldiers Once and Young*, with Colonel Hal Moore. Galloway and his editorial board were stunned with the material Allene Carter had uncovered. On Memorial Day weekend 1999, two years after Carter's Medal of Honor was awarded, the news magazine decided to make Edward Carter's story the lead with Sergeant Carter's picture on the cover.

The damning article began "about how a battlefield hero could be broken by the country he served." The exposé and public outcry prompted a letter of apology shortly thereafter from President Clinton and a new investigation by the Board of Correction for Military Records. Not only did the board find medals that Carter was supposed to have received, but they issued a new discharge certificate for his second enlistment for the period 1946–1949 that removed any statement of restriction on his ability to reenlist.

In the conclusion of their written report, the Board of Correction for Military Records stated that:

> The denial of reenlistment at the conclusion of the former service member's second enlistment was unjust. The allegations of interests by the former service member in conflict with those of the United States are determined to be unfounded based on a review of all the evidence available. The denial of reenlistment should be rescinded with apologies.

Subsequently, on November 10, 1999, in the Pentagon's Hall of Heroes with Carter's former commander, Russell Blair, present, the Army made an official public apology. General John Keane, Army Vice Chief of Staff, apologized on behalf of the US Army for the banishment of Sergeant Edward Carter. The proud soldier's name was officially cleared at last.

Afterword

The men you have just read about undoubtedly deserved to receive the Medal of Honor shortly after World War II for their gallant actions above and beyond the call of duty. Not only is the awarding of the military's highest honor for bravery an uphill battle at any point in time but it was a goal that was utterly beyond reach for all black soldiers in 1941–1945. Most of these men's commanders knew this, so they submitted paperwork for the second-highest award for valor, the Distinguished Service Cross.

Captain David Williams was the stubborn exception as he pressed his superior officers on awarding the Medal of Honor to Ruben Rivers and would not settle for anything less. That is why Rivers holds the distinction of being the only man who did not have his Distinguished Service Cross elevated to the Medal of Honor as he had been awarded the Silver Star. For some, even receiving their DSC was an arduous task, as in the case of John Fox, who received his posthumously in 1982 after an intense campaign on his behalf by Hondon Hargrove.

The delay of more than 50 years for all these men to be finally awarded their proper recognition can be attributed in large part to systematic racism within the military hierarchy and then to the glacial speed of the United States government to finally not only recognize but admit the wrong.

Courageous and persistent individuals did press the issue for decades with the government, including David Williams. Still, it took a catalyst to get the wheels of government turning in these men's favor.

According to author and NYU professor Dr. Jeffrey Sammons, the impetus was awarding the Medal of Honor to World War I soldier Freddie Stowers on April 24, 1991, prompted in part by African American military historian Leroy Ramsey. In 1986 Ramsey contacted the office of New York Republican Congressman Joseph J. DioGuardi, armed with volumes of research on black World War I and World War II soldiers whose brave combat actions qualified them for the Medal of Honor.

Congressman DioGuardi found Ramsey's research meticulous and the absence of recognition alarming. He sought bipartisan support from Texas Congressman and head of the Congressional Black Caucus, Democrat Mickey Leland, to help look into the matter.[1] Leland agreed to help, and together they pressed for an independent Defense Department study into the absence of Medals of Honor for deserving black soldiers.

Funding for the undertaking was approved at $320,585, and the Pentagon awarded a contract to Dr. Daniel K. Gibran at Shaw University in Raleigh, North Carolina, one of the nation's historically black universities.[2]

Before the investigation formally commenced, however, the Army stumbled across a misplaced file on Corporal Freddie Stowers, which revealed his superiors had in fact recommended him for the Medal of Honor. Since no action had been taken to deny him the medal, according to Congressman DioGuardi, it was not legally necessary to open the statute of limitations. The Defense Department reopened his case in November of 1990, with his medal being awarded the following year by President H.W. Bush.

Until that time, no black soldier from World War I had been awarded the country's highest military honor. Subsequently, it would take another 24 years for an additional black soldier from World War I, William Henry Johnson, to be awarded the Medal of Honor in 2015 during the Obama administration.

Meanwhile the formal study at Shaw University had gotten underway in May 1993. Dr. Gibran's team interviewed hundreds of eyewitnesses, including families of potential recipients and candidate Vernon Baker himself. The investigators also sifted through countless archival military documents. They found startling evidence; no surviving documentation that any black soldier from World War II was ever recommended for the Medal of Honor.[3]

"It was an unwritten thing," Dr. Gibran said of the attitude at the time. "It was a concerted effort on the part of white officers not to give this award to a black guy."[4]

Additionally, Gibran reported that "they'd found statements pertaining to the fact that white commanders had repeatedly said the Medal of Honor would not be for a black soldier in this war."

The exhaustive 200-page study, *Exclusion of Black Soldiers from the Medal of Honor in World War II*, authored by Dr. Gibran, Elliot V. Converse III, John A. Cash, Robert K. Griffith Jr., and Richard H. Kohn, focused on the six Distinguished Service Crosses known to have been awarded to black soldiers in the Army during the war. The study uncovered another three. The final list of DSC recipients included Vernon Baker, Edward Carter Jr., John R. Fox, Willy F. James Jr., Charles L. Thomas, George Watson, Leonard E. Dowden, Robert J. Peagler, and Jack Thomas.[5] The investigators' reasons for choosing the DSC as the benchmark for consideration of elevation to the Medal of Honor was based on two precedents. First was General John J. Pershing's order after the end of World War I that all DSCs be reevaluated for consideration of the Medal of Honor. By Armistice Day, only four had been approved. Second, in 1943, General Eisenhower asked his Fifth Army commander in North Africa to do the same. As a result, in both cases, the number of Medals of Honor significantly increased.

The only anomaly in the Shaw study was Silver Star recipient Ruben Rivers, whom the authors added in their final recommendations to the Army. They wrote:

> Therefore this study recommends that the army evaluate, for
> elevation to the Medal of Honor, the Distinguished Service
> Crosses earned by black soldiers during World War II and,
> in addition, consider whether Staff Sergeant Ruben Rivers,

who may have been officially recommended for the Medal for his heroic acts in battle in 1944 and who in any case died unrecognized for acts of valor that resulted in his death, also merits the award.[6]

I am convinced that Rivers' inclusion was as a result of Captain David Williams' unflagging tenacity to see his fearless fighter from Oklahoma honored as he originally intended. Williams was interviewed extensively for the Shaw University study and even supplied the authors with photographs of Rivers from the war.

In the end, the Army had the final say and chose the men you have read about in this book, including, of course, Ruben Rivers. At the White House ceremony in 1997, David Williams accompanied the Rivers family to see the honor bestowed. Interviewed afterward, he spoke of the bond between soldiers, and for him, color never entered into the equation.

"You have to understand. In battle, you fight for each other. The pride in the unit. You have a cohesion," Williams said, then paraphrased Shakespeare's Henry V, "When men fight shoulder to shoulder and bleed and die for a just cause, they become brothers."[7]

About the long campaign he waged on behalf of Rivers, Williams said he believed God kept him alive for one reason: To see that Ruben Rivers was awarded the Medal of Honor. In tears at the close of the White House ceremony, Williams proudly proclaimed himself a "Black Panther" and said, "We did win, didn't we. God can take me at this moment because the deed is done."[8]

***

There are two leading and active petitions at this writing to award the Medal of Honor to two more black soldiers from World War II: Corporal Waverley Woodson and Messman Third Class Doris "Dorie" Miller. Both men acted "above and beyond the call of duty" on two of the most harrowing days in the history of the war: December 7, 1941 and June 6, 1944.

During the Japanese attack on Pearl Harbor, Dorie Miller from Waco, Texas, was aboard the USS *West Virginia* when it was struck during the surprise attack. Miller, a physically commanding presence, was the ship's heavyweight boxing champion, and he used that strength to carry several wounded men to safety, including the ship's Captain, Mervyn S. Bennion.

After securing the Captain, Miller returned to the sinking ship and saw an unmanned .50-caliber Browning antiaircraft machine gun; he immediately jumped on it. He had never touched or fired the weapon prior to this time. Over 15 minutes it was estimated he was able to shoot down three to four Japanese dive bombers.[9]

When asked how he was able to accomplish such a feat, Messman Miller responded, "It wasn't hard. I just pulled the trigger, and she worked fine."[10] His actions saved the lives of hundreds of sailors. Miller was subsequently awarded the Navy Cross, while an incapacitated Captain Bennion whom Miller carried to safety received the Medal of Honor. Miller died nearly two years later in late November 1943, when a Japanese torpedo struck his ship, the USS *Liscome Bay*, taking the lives of 644 sailors, including Miller.

On June 6, 1944, Waverly "Woody" Woodson was serving as a medic with the 320th Barrage Balloon Battalion and went ashore at Omaha Beach. He was immediately wounded by shrapnel in the groin area. Ignoring his injury, he went to work treating dozens and dozens of men while under intense enemy fire.

Over the next 30 hours, until he collapsed, Woodson was credited with attending to the wounds of over 200 men.[11] It was gallant conduct under fire, which his commanding officer cited as "extraordinarily brave." Although Woodson was later awarded the Bronze Star and the Purple Heart for his actions, it was recently discovered by journalist and author Linda Hervieux when she unearthed an Army memo that Woodson had, in fact, been recommended for the Medal of Honor in 1944.

Both Dorie Miller and Waverly Woodson clearly deserve the nation's highest military honor. They acted courageously above and beyond the call of duty, and I urge all Americans to voice their support and add their names to the current petitions. It is what these soldiers deserve. Let this be an act that moves us beyond the darkness of the past to a better world for our children and future generations – a world that Dr. Martin Luther King Jr. envisioned in 1963:

> *I have a dream that my four little children will one day live in a nation where they will not be judged by the color of their skin but by the content of their character.*

Acknowledgments

Not a writer I know would pen an acknowledgment section at the beginning of a book; it is only done at the end, after the journey, when there is a moment to reflect. And this book has certainly been a journey, perhaps one of a lifetime.

I am so sincerely grateful that this trip was not undertaken alone. Many people helped in this herculean effort. They opened their hearts and archives to us, most specifically the families and descendants of the seven immortal heroes you have read about in this book.

Every one of these people has made this book possible. Allow me to tell you a little about them. First, I must thank my primary historian and researcher, Arthur Collins Jr. He has been invaluable throughout this effort from the very first day when we discussed the idea for this book. I have known Art for over a decade. He literally "came to my rescue" when I needed African American World War II reenactors for my *Wereth Eleven* film and later for a movie on the American Revolution. He has an outstanding organization and website at 5thplatoon.org.

Also, in the research area, I must thank Tommy McArdle for his historical vetting of the manuscript. Tommy, a military veteran, served as a historical advisor on several of my films, and he was instrumental along with visionary producer Joe Small in introducing me to Captain Dale Dye, who helped on another one of my films.

I also must thank the people who believed in this book and brought it to the world: my literary agent, Greg Johnson at

WordServe Literary, who instantly supported the book, saying it was a book whose time had come, and, of course, my editor at Osprey, Kate Moore. Kate has been a tireless champion for this book through the difficult days of the pandemic lockdown in the UK, getting her team together to give this undertaking the green light.

A great deal of research went into this book, as you can imagine, and one of the genuinely outstanding writers and researchers out there who helped in this effort was Solace Wales and her book *Braided in Fire*. Solace spent more than 30 years digging into the story of John Fox and the Italian partisans who helped the American effort in the battle of Sommocolonia. The reason Fox's story is so accurate in this book is due to Solace. She has a dogged determination to get the history factually correct. She also introduced me to Sandra Fox, John Fox's daughter, whom I have to thank. Sandra was gracious enough to allow us to use the family photo of John, which has only appeared in print once. Staying with the family members, I also must thank Sandra Holliday, Charles Thomas's niece, for her assistance with information regarding his children. Willie Rivers, Ruben Rivers' youngest brother, also helped in allowing us permission to use the Rivers family photos. Margaret and Johnny Pender, the niece and nephew of Willy James Jr., must also be thanked.

One of the first people to get us in direct touch with the men's families was Laura Jowdy, Archivist and Historical Collections Manager at the Congressional Medal of Honor Society, and I must thank her. She provided invaluable contact information and textual archival materials, which enhanced the accuracy of the stories. The same goes for Molly Randolph, Curator at Charles H. Coolidge National Medal of Honor Heritage Center in Chattanooga, Tennessee. She offered and provided reference images and assistance, for which I am grateful. I am also indebted to Joe Wilson Jr., author of *The 761st Black Panther Tank Battalion in World War II: An Illustrated History of the First African American Armored Unit to See Combat*. Joe provided the photos of Captain David Williams, which have never previously been published. Joe and David were good friends, and he assisted David's effort in securing the Medal of Honor for Ruben Rivers.

I have saved perhaps my most significant appreciation to anyone on a project to Allene Carter, Sergeant Edward Carter's daughter-in-law. I set her apart. She does not take "no" for an answer, especially from the military, and Allene single-handedly got the government to apologize publicly to Sergeant Carter for their treatment of him during the Cold War. Allene also had the government agree to reinter Sergeant Carter at Arlington National Cemetery the day after his Medal of Honor ceremony.

Allene provided the majority of the irreplaceable photos in this book. Most, if not all, have never been published before. She is the living "ambassador" for the seven Medal of Honor families, and she is staunchly protective of the men's legacy. Allene also understood what we were trying to accomplish, and I will be forever grateful to her for her help. She is one of a kind.

***

I must close by thanking you, the reader, for taking this journey and seeking to know more about these extraordinary soldiers. They sacrificed for all of us, and we all owe them a debt of gratitude.

Robert Child

Appendix

Full Roster of 3rd Platoon, Company C, 614th Tank Destroyer Battalion

3rd Platoon, Charles Thomas's platoon, was the first black unit to be awarded the Presidential Unit Citation.

Mitchell, George W. 1st Lt.	Smith, Dave Pvt.
Cannon, Robert S/Sgt.	Robertson, Roosevelt Sgt.
Harris, Robert W. T/5	King, Plato Pvt.
Smith, Henry J. T/5	Brown, Barnett W. PFC
Phipps, William H. PFC	Childs, Jack PFC
Shinhoster, Benjamin W. PFC	James, Daniel Cpl.
Nesby, James E. Pvt.	Jeffries, Odell T/5
Solomon, Silvester V. Pvt.	Johnson, Linwood Pvt.
West, Walter Sgt.	Higgs, Vernon W.
Spell, Blease Cpl.	Booker Dillard L. T/5
Evans, Vandy Jr. Pvt.	Bullock, Robert L. T/5
Kenneth, Howard PFC	Gordon, Willie J. Pvt.
McKnight, Hayward Pvt.	Glasco, Delmon B. PFC
Rattler, Charlie B. Pvt.	Speight, Jessie L. Pvt.
Tabron, William L. Sgt.	Sturvident. Jesse T. PFC
Murph, Shelton Cpl.	Williams, Samuel Pvt.
Hester, Charlie PFC	Green, Robert Pvt.
Milis, Walter H. Jr. PFC	Cooper, John Pvt.
Moore, Luther Jr. PFC	Riley, Lucius Pvt.
Perry, James A. T/5	Swindell, Burnie Pvt.

Simmons, Peter Cpl.	Detiege Eugene J. Pvt.
Phillips, Thomas J. Sgt.	Whitlow, Lennon L. Cpl.
Hockaday, Al Jr. Cpl.	Jones, Reed Jr. Pvt.
Knight, Whit L. PFC	Wheeler, Leonard Pvt.
Modlin, Willie PFC	Welch, Wilbert Pvt.
McDaniel, Thomas C. Pvt.	Harrington, Silvester S/Sgt.
Parrack, Sam Pvt.	Tobin, Leon Pvt.

Notes

PART ONE: CHARLES THOMAS

1 "Pearl Harbor Radio Broadcast from December 7, 1941: Free Borrow & Streaming." *Internet Archive*, Dec. 7, 1941, https://archive.org/details/ccoro_000063.

2 Brevitz, Colin. "Fort Custer during World War II." *Military History of the Upper Great Lakes*, October 12, 2015, https://ss.sites.mtu.edu/mhugl/2015/10/11/fort-custer-during-world-war-2/.

3 Thompson, James G. Letter. *Pittsburgh Courier*, January 31, 1942.

4 "World War II Operational Documents." *Ike Skelton Combined Arms Research Library (CARL) Digital Library*, https://cgsc.contentdm.oclc.org/digital/collection/p4013coll8/id/3060.

5 "The Tank Killers." *Fortune Magazine*, November 1942.

6 "World War II Operational Documents."

7 Bureau of Public Relations, War Department documentary film, 1943 "Tank Destroyers" Training at Camp Hood, sponsored by the Santa Fe Railroad.

8 Cohen, Warren. "Task Force Blackshear 'Recognizing Valor: Profile of Charles Thomas, African-American World War II Hero.'" *Michigan History Magazine*, 1997, http://don.genemcguire.com/Task_Force_Blackshear.htm.

9 Quoted in Bailey, J.R. "Bill." "1941 WWII Louisiana Maneuvers." *Military Trader/Vehicles*, Jan. 7, 2009, www.militarytrader.com/militaria-collecting-101/1941-louisiana-maneuvers-the-big-one.

10 "Remembering Camp Shanks." *Hudson Valley Magazine*, Nov. 27, 2019, https://hvmag.com/life-style/history/remembering-camp-shanks/.

11 "HMS Jervis Bay." *The Bay Ships War Service – HMS Jervis Bay*, https://hmsjervisbay.com/Story.BayShips_2.php.

12 Richard, C.J., Captain F. A. Adjutant. Headquarters 614th Tank Destroyer Battalion. Unit History and Supporting Documents, "Narrative Report December 1944 614th Tank Destroyer Battalion." January 20, 1945.

13 Motley, Mary Penick. *The Invisible Soldier: The Experience of the Black Soldier, World War II*. Wayne State University Press, 1987.

14 Lee, Ulysses. *The Employment of Negro Troops*. Center of Military History, United States Army, 1990.

15 Papa's War Part 3, http://www.pierce-evans.org/pwpart3.htm.

16 Motley. *The Invisible Soldier*.

17 The 411th Infantry Unit Journal, Declassified by NARA March 16, 2011, 103rd Infantry Division World War II Association, Dale Center for the Study of War & Society, University of Southern Mississippi.

18 Motley. *The Invisible Soldier*.

19 Motley. *The Invisible Soldier*.

20 Blackshear, Lt. Col. John P., 411th Infantry, EO. "Letter of Certification of the actions of Taskforce Blackshear 14 December 1944," written December 20, 1944.

21 Martin, Sgt. Ralph. Stars & Stripes Correspondent. "Negros in Combat." *Yank Magazine*, Issue: February 23, 1945.

22 Martin. "Negros in Combat."

PART TWO: VERNON BAKER

1 Olsen, Ken. "World War II Hero Vernon Baker Dies." *The Spokesman-Review*, July 22, 2010, www.spokesman.com/stories/2010/jul/14/world-war-ii-hero-vernon-baker-dies/.

2 Baker, Vernon J. and Ken Olsen. *Lasting Valor*. Bantam, 1999.

3 Baker and Olsen. *Lasting Valor*.

4 Olsen. "World War II Hero Vernon Baker Dies."

5 "Liberation of Rome." *Europe Remembers*, https://europeremembers.com/destination/liberation-of-rome/.

6 Atkinson, Rick. *The Day of Battle: The War in Sicily and Italy, 1943–1944*. Henry Holt and Company, 2007.

7 Baker and Olsen. *Lasting Valor*.

8 Baker, Vernon. "Vernon Baker Collection." *Veterans History Project* (American Folklife Center, Library of Congress), Jan. 1, 1970, https://memory.loc.gov/diglib/vhp/bib/loc.natlib.afc2001001.89614.

9   Lee, Ulysses. *The Employment of Negro Troops*. Center of Military History, US Army, 1994.

10 Gibran, Daniel K. *The 92nd Infantry Division and the Italian Campaign in World War II*. McFarland, 2001.

11 Baker and Olsen. *Lasting Valor*.

12 Gibran. *The 92nd Infantry Division and the Italian Campaign in World War II*.

13 Baker and Olsen. *Lasting Valor*.

14 Baker and Olsen. *Lasting Valor*.

15 Baker and Olsen. *Lasting Valor*.

16 Baker and Olsen. *Lasting Valor*.

17 Baker. "Vernon Baker Collection."

PART THREE: WILLY JAMES JR.

1   US Army Center of Military History. *Chapter XXII: Volunteer Infantry Replacements*, https://history.army.mil/books/wwii/11-4/chapter22.htm.

2   Letter, Gen. Davis to Chief GI Sec, Hq ETO USA, 5 Mar 45, GI Sec Rpt 33, ETO AG 333-1.

3   Radeska, Tijana. "Walt Disney Produced Propaganda Films for the US Government during WWII." *The Vintage News*, Aug. 2, 2016, www.thevintagenews.com/2016/08/02/disney-produced-propaganda-films-u-s-government-world-war-ii/.

4   Hoegh, Leo A. and Howard J. Doyle. *Timberwolf Tracks: The History of the 104th Infantry Division, 1942–1945*. Infantry Journal Press, 2004.

5   HQ Staff 413th IR, History of the 413th Infantry Regiment, GEN. 949.5421 H6292. Copyright 1946.

6   Hoegh and Doyle. *Timberwolf Tracks*.

7   Hoegh and Doyle. *Timberwolf Tracks*.

8   Simkin, John. *Spartacus Educational*, Spartacus Educational, https://spartacus-educational.com/2WWstringerA.htm.

9   Hoegh and Doyle. *Timberwolf Tracks*.

10 In a May 7, 1996 article in the *Kansas City Star*, G Company 2nd Lieutenant, Donald R. Weishaupt, who was at the battle of Lippoldsberg and took over commanding the platoon after the death of Lt. Armand Serrabella, told reporter Mary Sanchez unequivocally, "there was not a single machine gun fired by the

Germans that day." The issue of whether the citation accurately lists the German weaponry used in no way diminishes James's actions.

PART FOUR: EDWARD A. CARTER JR.

1 *New York Times*, March 1, 1932.
2 Nelson, Cary, and Jefferson Hendricks. *Madrid 1937: Letters of the Abraham Lincoln Brigade from the Spanish Civil War*. Routledge, 2013.
3 Convery, David. "There's a Valley in Spain … Commemorating the Battle of Jarama." *The Dustbin of History*, Dustbin of History, February 20, 2013. Feb. 26, 2021, https://thedustbinofhistory. wordpress.com/tag/xiv-international-brigade/.
4 Carter, Allene G., and Robert L. Allen. *Honoring Sergeant Carter: A Family's Journey to Uncover the Truth about an American Hero*. Amistad, 2004.
5 Convery. "There's a Valley in Spain."
6 Gnam, Carl, et al. "A Sergeant in the 12th Armored Division." *Warfare History Network*. July 17, 2020, https://warfarehistorynetwork. com/2018/12/26/a-sergeant-in-the-12th-armored-division/.
7 Gnam, Carl, et al. "A Sergeant in the 12th Armored Division."
8 Carter and Allen. *Honoring Sergeant Carter*.
9 Carter and Allen. *Honoring Sergeant Carter*.

PART FIVE: GEORGE WATSON

1 "Sharecropping in Mississippi." *PBS*, Public Broadcasting Service, www.pbs.org/wgbh/americanexperience/features/emmett-share cropping-mississippi/.
2 LaFosta, Alex. "Racism in the 1920s & 1930s." *The Classroom: Empowering Students in Their College Journey*, Jan. 10, 2019, www.theclassroom.com/racism-1920s-1930s-23783.html.
3 "Rosenwald School." *Wikipedia*, Wikimedia Foundation, https:// en.wikipedia.org/wiki/Rosenwald_Sc.
4 "The New KKK." *Mental Floss*, Nov. 26, 2015, www.mentalfloss. com/article/71720/wwi-centennial-new-kkk.
5 "Greenville, Mississippi Rejects the Ku Klux Klan." *PBS*, Public Broadcasting Service, www.pbs.org/wgbh/americanexperience/ features/flood-greenville/.

6 Louise Wood, Amy. "Ku Klux Klan." *Mississippi Encyclopedia*, Center for Study of Southern Culture, May 1, 2018, https://mississippiencyclopedia.org/entries/ku-klux-klan/.

7 "Mississippi State University." *Wikipedia*, Wikimedia Foundation. https://en.wikipedia.org/wiki/Mississippi_State_University.

8 Government Printing Office, US Federal Census, 1930.

9 Sher, David. "Would You Buy a Pickle from Vulcan?" *Comeback Town*, June 7, 2016, http://comebacktown.com/2016/06/08/would-you-buy-a-pickle-from-vulcan/.

10 Government Printing Office, US Federal Census, 1930.

11 "B. O. Hargrove." *Bhamwiki*, www.bhamwiki.com/w/B._O._Hargrove.

12 *Quartermaster School History WWII*, https://qmmuseum.lee.army.mil/WWII/qm_school.htm.

13 *Quartermaster School History WWII*.

14 *Quartermaster Corps*, www.u-s-history.com/pages/h1714.html.

15 "What Was Hygiene Like For US Soldiers In WWII?" *Weird History*. https://www.youtube.com/watch?v=GCHUgiaitxk.

16 *General MacArthur Takes Command of Australia's Defence*, www.pacificwar.org.au/battaust/MacArthurinAustralia.html.

17 "MacArthur Leaves Philippines to Defend Australia." *World War 2.0*, Mar. 27, 2017, https://blogs.shu.edu/ww2-0/1942/03/27/macarthur-leaves-philippines-in-attempt-to-defend-australia/.

18 *General MacArthur Takes Command of Australia's Defence*.

19 "World War II – Asiatic-Pacific Theater Campaigns." *World War II – Asiatic-Pacific Theater Campaigns*. US Army Center of Military History, https://history.army.mil/html/reference/army_flag/ww2_ap.html.

20 "MacArthur Leaves Philippines to Defend Australia."

21 Shindo, Hiroyuki. "Japanese Air Operations over New Guinea." *Journal of the Australian War Memorial*, Issue No. 34, June 2001.

22 Staff Writer. "Pvt. Watson, Negro Solider, is Given DSC Posthumously," *The Birmingham News*, August 15, 1943.

PART SIX: RUBEN RIVERS

1 "Seminole Oil Boom." *American Oil & Gas Historical Society*. April 29, 2014. https://aoghs.org/petroleum-pioneers/seminole-oil-boom/.

2 *Earlsboro, Pottawatomie County, Oklahoma*, https://sites.rootsweb.com/~okpcgc/towns/earlsboro.html.

3 Farris, David. "The Oklahoma Terror, Aka Pretty Boy Floyd." *Edmond Life & Leisure*, https://edmondlifeandleisure.com/the-oklahoma-terror-aka-prettyboy-floyd-p15753-76.htm.

4 White, Lamar, et al. "The Beginning of Hell." *Bayou Brief*, www.bayoubrief.com/2019/09/17/the-beginning-of-hell/.

5 Lengel, Ed. "The Black Panthers Enter Combat: The 761st Tank Battalion, November 1944: The National WWII Museum: New Orleans." The National World War II Museum, www.national ww2museum.org/war/articles/black-panthers-761st-tank-battalion.

6 Williams, David J. *Hit Hard*. Bantam Books, 1983.

7 Gnam, Carl, et al. "Patton's Panthers: The Story of the 761st Tank Battalion." *Warfare History Network*, https://warfarehistorynetwork. com/2017/06/21/pattons-panthers-the-story-of-the-761st-tank-battalion/.

8 Network, Warfare History. "Operation Torch: Why Did America Fight French Forces in 1942?" *The National Interest*, The Center for the National Interest, Jan. 18, 2021, https://nationalinterest. org/blog/reboot/operation-torch-why-did-america-fight-french-forces-1942-176489.

9 Abdul-Jabbar, Kareem, et al. *Brothers in Arms: The Epic Story of the 761st Tank Battalion, WWII's Forgotten Heroes*. Recorded Books, 2004.

10 Williams. *Hit Hard*.

11 Abdul-Jabbar. *Brothers in Arms*.

12 Gnam. "Patton's Panthers."

13 Williams. *Hit Hard*.

14 Gnam. "Patton's Panthers."

15 Williams. *Hit Hard*.

16 Lengel. "The Black Panthers Enter Combat."

17 Williams. *Hit Hard*.

18 Staff, HistoryNet. "How Patton's All-Black Tank Battalion Took the Fight to the Nazis." HistoryNet, www.historynet.com/black-panther-battalion-backed-by-patton-took-the-fight-to-the-nazis.htm.

19 Williams. *Hit Hard*.

20 Williams. *Hit Hard*.

21 Williams. *Hit Hard*.

22 Gnam. "Patton's Panthers."

23 Staff, HistoryNet. "How Patton's All-Black Tank Battalion Took the Fight to the Nazis."

24 Williams. *Hit Hard.*
25 Staff, HistoryNet. "How Patton's All-Black Tank Battalion Took the Fight to the Nazis."
26 Gnam. "Patton's Panthers."
27 Staff, HistoryNet. "How Patton's All-Black Tank Battalion Took the Fight to the Nazis."
28 Williams. *Hit Hard.*
29 Williams. *Hit Hard.*
30 Williams. *Hit Hard.*
31 Williams. *Hit Hard.*
32 Williams. *Hit Hard.*
33 Williams. *Hit Hard.*
34 Williams. *Hit Hard.*

PART SEVEN: JOHN FOX

1 Ackerman, Cory M. "'I Did Not Send For You' – John Fox and the Medal of Honor." *The National Medal of Honor Museum*, https://mohmuseum.org/john-fox-and-the-medal-of-honor/.
2 Motley, Mary Penick. *The Invisible Soldier: The Experience of the Black Soldier, World War II.* Wayne State University Press, 1987.
3 Motley. *The Invisible Soldier.*
4 "US Army Infantry Cannon Company (1943–45)." *Battle Order*, www.battleorder.org/usa-1943-cannonco.
5 Pratt, Dr. James. "The 366th Infantry Regiment in World War II" (video lecture at Fort Devens), 2014.
6 "The Black Press: Soldiers Without Swords: Transcript." *PBS*, Public Broadcasting Service, www.pbs.org/blackpress/film/fulltranscript.html.
7 "The Black Press: Soldiers Without Swords: Transcript." *PBS.*
8 "The Black Press: Soldiers Without Swords: Transcript." *PBS.*
9 Motley. *The Invisible Soldier.*
10 Motley. *The Invisible Soldier.*
11 Wales, Solace. *Braided in Fire: Black GIs and Tuscan Villagers on the Gothic Line.* Knox Press, 2020.
12 Wales. *Braided in Fire.*
13 Ackerman. "'I Did Not Send For You.'"
14 Motley. *The Invisible Soldier.*
15 Wales. *Braided in Fire.*

16 Motley. *The Invisible Soldier.*

17 Wales. *Braided in Fire.*

18 Lee, Ulysses. *The Employment of Negro Troops.* Center of Military History, United States Army, 2001.

19 Lee. *The Employment of Negro Troops.*

20 Wales. *Braided in Fire.*

21 Wales. *Braided in Fire.*

22 Wales. *Braided in Fire.*

23 Wales. *Braided in Fire.*

24 Wales. *Braided in Fire.*

25 Wales. *Braided in Fire.*

26 Wales. *Braided in Fire.*

27 Motley. *The Invisible Soldier.*

28 Lee. *The Employment of Negro Troops.*

29 Lee. *The Employment of Negro Troops.*

EPILOGUE

1 Motley, Mary Penick. *The Invisible Soldier: The Experience of the Black Soldier, World War II.* Wayne State University Press, 1987.

2 Boone, Rebecca. "Medal of Honor Hero Vernon Baker Dies at Age 90." *NBCNews.com*, NBCUniversal News Group, July 15, 2010, www.nbcnews.com/id/wbna38251927.

3 Baker, Vernon J., and Ken Olsen. *Lasting Valor.* Bantam, 1999.

4 Carter, Allene G., and Robert L. Allen. *Honoring Sergeant Carter: Redeeming a Black World War II Hero's Legacy.* HarperCollins e-Books, 2009.

AFTERWORD

1 DioGuardi, Joseph J. "Remembering Overlooked Black Soldiers." Roll Call, Dec. 13, 2019, www.rollcall.com/2016/05/30/remembering-overlooked-black-soldiers/.

2 Thompson, M. Dion. "A Matter of Honor Medals: Thanks to a Battle by Veteran Vernon J. Baker and an Army-Assembled Team of Historians, Seven Black Soldiers Join the Ranks of World War II's Heroes." *Baltimoresun.com*, Oct. 22, 2018, www.baltimoresun.com/news/bs-xpm-1997-01-14-1997014150-story.html.

3   Thompson. "A Matter of Honor Medals."

4   Thompson. "A Matter of Honor Medals."

5   Converse, Elliott Vanveltner, and Julius W. Becton. *The Exclusion of Black Soldiers from the Medal of Honor in World War II: The Study Commissioned by the United States Army to Investigate Racial Bias in the Awarding of the Nation's Highest Military Decoration.* McFarland & Co., 2008.

6   Converse and Becton. *The Exclusion of Black Soldiers.*

7   Thompson. "A Matter of Honor Medals."

8   Thompson. "A Matter of Honor Medals."

9   Warbirds. "Pearl Harbor Attack Facts – Doris Miller, Hero At Pearl Harbor." *Pearl Harbor Warbirds*, 18 Aug. 2016, https://pearlharborwarbirds.com/pearl-harbor-attack-facts-doris-miller-hero-at-pearl-harbor/.

10   Warbirds. "Pearl Harbor Attack Facts – Doris Miller, Hero At Pearl Harbor."

11   Doyle, Dan. "This Man's Unmatched Heroism On Omaha Beach, Normandy, Saved Hundreds." *The Veterans Site News*, 7 Feb. 2020, https://blog.theveteranssite.greatergood.com/waverly-woodson/.

Bibliography

Abdul-Jabbar, Kareem, et al. *Brothers in Arms: The Epic Story of the 761st Tank Battalion, WWII's Forgotten Heroes.* Recorded Books, 2004.

Ackerman, Cory M. "'I Did Not Send For You' – John Fox and the Medal of Honor." *The National Medal of Honor Museum,* https://mohmuseum.org/john-fox-and-the-medal-of-honor/.

Atkinson, Rick. *The Day of Battle: The War in Sicily and Italy, 1943–1944.* Henry Holt and Company, 2007.

Bailey, J.R. "Bill." "1941 WWII Louisiana Maneuvers." *Military Trader/Vehicles,* Jan. 7, 2009, www.militarytrader.com/militaria-collecting-101/1941-louisiana-maneuvers-the-big-one.

Baker, Vernon J. and Ken Olsen. *Lasting Valor.* Bantam, 1999.

Baker, Vernon. "Vernon Baker Collection." *Veterans History Project* (American Folklife Center, Library of Congress), Jan. 1, 1970, https://memory.loc.gov/diglib/vhp/bib/loc.natlib.afc2001001.89614.

Blackshear, Lt. Col. John P., 411th Infantry, EO. "Letter of Certification of the actions of Taskforce Blackshear 14 December 1944," written December 20, 1944.

Boone, Rebecca. "Medal of Honor Hero Vernon Baker Dies at Age 90." *NBCNews.com,* NBCUniversal News Group, July 15, 2010, www.nbcnews.com/id/wbna38251927.

"B. O. Hargrove." *Bhamwiki,* www.bhamwiki.com/w/B._O._Hargrove.

Brevitz, Colin. "Fort Custer during World War II." *Military History of the Upper Great Lakes,* Oct. 12, 2015, https://ss.sites.mtu.edu/mhugl/2015/10/11/fort-custer-during-world-war-2/.

Bureau of Public Relations, War Department documentary film, 1943 "Tank Destroyers" Training at Camp Hood, sponsored by the Santa Fe Railroad.

California Newsreel. "The Black Press: Soldiers Without Swords." https://newsreel.org/transcripts/soldiers.html.

Carter, Allene G., and Robert L. Allen. *Honoring Sergeant Carter: A Family's Journey to Uncover the Truth about an American Hero.* Amistad, 2004.

Carter, Allene G., and Robert L. Allen. *Honoring Sergeant Carter: Redeeming a Black World War II Hero's Legacy.* HarperCollins e-Books, 2009.

Cohen, Warren. "Task Force Blackshear 'Recognizing Valor: Profile of Charles Thomas, African-American World War II Hero.'" *Michigan History Magazine*, 1997, http://don.genemcguire.com/Task_Force_Blackshear.htm.

Converse, Elliott Vanveltner, and Julius W. Becton. *The Exclusion of Black Soldiers from the Medal of Honor in World War II: The Study Commissioned by the United States Army to Investigate Racial Bias in the Awarding of the Nation's Highest Military Decoration.* McFarland & Co., 2008.

Convery, David. "There's a Valley in Spain … Commemorating the Battle of Jarama." *The Dustbin of History*, Feb. 20, 2013. https://thedustbinofhistory.wordpress.com/tag/xiv-international-brigade/.

DioGuardi, Joseph J. "Remembering Overlooked Black Soldiers." Roll Call, Dec. 13, 2019, www.rollcall.com/2016/05/30/remembering-overlooked-black-soldiers/.

Doyle, Dan. "This Man's Unmatched Heroism On Omaha Beach, Normandy, Saved Hundreds." *The Veterans Site News*, Feb. 7, 2020. https://blog.theveteranssite.greatergood.com/waverly-woodson/.

Earlsboro, Pottawatomie County, Oklahoma, https://sites.rootsweb.com/~okpcgc/towns/earlsboro.html

Farris, David. "The Oklahoma Terror, Aka Pretty Boy Floyd." *Edmond Life & Leisure*, https://edmondlifeandleisure.com/the-oklahoma-terror-aka-prettyboy-floyd-p15753-76.htm.

General MacArthur Takes Command of Australia's Defence, www.pacificwar.org.au/battaust/MacArthurinAustralia.html.

Gibran, Daniel K. *The 92nd Infantry Division and the Italian Campaign in World War II.* McFarland, 2001.

Gnam, Carl, et al. "A Sergeant in the 12th Armored Division." *Warfare History Network.* July 17, 2020, https://warfarehistorynetwork.com/2018/12/26/a-sergeant-in-the-12th-armored-division/.

Gnam, Carl, et al. "Patton's Panthers: The Story of the 761st Tank Battalion." *Warfare History Network*, https://warfarehistorynetwork.com/2017/06/21/pattons-panthers-the-story-of-the-761st-tank-battalion/.

Government Printing Office, US Federal Census, 1930.

"Greenville, Mississippi Rejects the Ku Klux Klan." *PBS*, Public Broadcasting Service, www.pbs.org/wgbh/americanexperience/features/flood-greenville/.

"HMS Jervis Bay." *The Bay Ships War Service – HMS Jervis Bay*, https://hmsjervisbay.com/Story.BayShips_2.php.

Hoegh, Leo A. and Howard J. Doyle. *Timberwolf Tracks: The History of the 104th Infantry Division, 1942–1945*. Infantry Journal Press, 2004.

HQ Staff 413th IR, History of the 413th Infantry Regiment, GEN. 949.5421 H6292. Copyright 1946.

LaFosta, Alex. "Racism in the 1920s & 1930s." *The Classroom: Empowering Students in Their College Journey*, Jan. 10, 2019, www.theclassroom.com/racism-1920s-1930s-23783.html.

Lee, Ulysses. *The Employment of Negro Troops*. Center of Military History, United States Army, 1994.

Lengel, Ed. "The Black Panthers Enter Combat: The 761st Tank Battalion, November 1944: The National WWII Museum: New Orleans." The National World War II Museum, www.nationalww2museum.org/war/articles/black-panthers-761st-tank-battalion.

Letter, Gen. Davis to Chief GI Sec, Hq ETO USA, 5 Mar 45, GI Sec Rpt 33, ETO AG 333-1.

"Liberation of Rome." *Europe Remembers*, https://europeremembers.com/destination/liberation-of-rome/.

Louise Wood, Amy. "Ku Klux Klan." *Mississippi Encyclopedia*, Center for Study of Southern Culture, May 1, 2018, https://mississippiencyclopedia.org/entries/ku-klux-klan/.

"MacArthur Leaves Philippines to Defend Australia." *World War 2.0*, Mar. 27, 2017, https://blogs.shu.edu/ww2-0/1942/03/27/macarthur-leaves-philippines-in-attempt-to-defend-australia/.

Martin, Sgt. Ralph. Stars & Stripes Correspondent. "Negros in Combat." *Yank Magazine*, Issue: February 23, 1945.

"Mississippi State University." *Wikipedia*, Wikimedia Foundation, https://en.wikipedia.org/wiki/Mississippi_State_University.

Motley, Mary Penick. *The Invisible Soldier: The Experience of the Black Soldier, World War II*. Wayne State University Press, 1987.

Nelson, Cary, and Jefferson Hendricks. *Madrid 1937: Letters of the Abraham Lincoln Brigade from the Spanish Civil War*. Routledge, 2013.

Network, Warfare History. "Operation Torch: Why Did America Fight French Forces in 1942?" *The National Interest*, The Center for the

National Interest, Jan. 18, 2021, https://nationalinterest.org/blog/reboot/operation-torch-why-did-america-fight-french-forces-1942-176489.

Olsen, Ken. "World War II Hero Vernon Baker Dies." *The Spokesman-Review*, July 22, 2010, www.spokesman.com/stories/2010/jul/14/world-war-ii-hero-vernon-baker-dies/.

Papa's War Part 3, http://www.pierce-evans.org/pwpart3.htm.

"Pearl Harbor Radio Broadcast from December 7, 1941: Free Borrow & Streaming." *Internet Archive*, Dec. 7, 1941, https://archive.org/details/ccoro_000063.

Pratt, Dr. James. "The 366th Infantry Regiment in World War II" (video lecture at Fort Devens), 2014.

Quartermaster Corps, www.u-s-history.com/pages/h1714.html.

Quartermaster School History WWII, https://qmmuseum.lee.army.mil/WWII/qm_school.htm.

Radeska, Tijana. "Walt Disney Produced Propaganda Films for the US Government during WWII." *The Vintage News*, Aug. 2, 2016, www.thevintagenews.com/2016/08/02/disney-produced-propaganda-films-u-s-government-world-war-ii/.

"Remembering Camp Shanks." *Hudson Valley Magazine*, Nov. 27, 2019, https://hvmag.com/life-style/history/remembering-camp-shanks/.

Richard, C.J., Captain F. A. Adjutant. Headquarters 614th Tank Destroyer Battalion. Unit History and Supporting Documents, "Narrative Report December 1944 614th Tank Destroyer Battalion." Jan. 20, 1945.

"Rosenwald School." *Wikipedia*, Wikimedia Foundation, https://en.wikipedia.org/wiki/Rosenwald_Sc.

Sanchez, Mary. *Kansas City Star*, Issue: May 7, 1996.

"Seminole Oil Boom." *American Oil & Gas Historical Society*. April 29, 2014, https://aoghs.org/petroleum-pioneers/seminole-oil-boom/.

"Sharecropping in Mississippi." *PBS*, Public Broadcasting Service, www.pbs.org/wgbh/americanexperience/features/emmett-sharecropping-mississippi/.

Sher, David. "Would You Buy a Pickle from Vulcan?" *ComebackTown*, June 7, 2016, http://comebacktown.com/2016/06/08/would-you-buy-a-pickle-from-vulcan/.

Shindo, Hiroyuki. "Japanese Air Operations over New Guinea." *Journal of the Australian War Memorial*. Issue No. 34, June 2001.

Simkin, John. *Spartacus Educational*, https://spartacus-educational.com/2WWstringerA.htm.

Staff Writer. "Pvt. Watson, Negro Solider, is Given DSC Posthumously," *The Birmingham News*, August 15, 1943.

Staff, HistoryNet. "How Patton's All-Black Tank Battalion Took the Fight to the Nazis." HistoryNet, www.historynet.com/black-panther-battalion-backed-by-patton-took-the-fight-to-the-nazis.htm.

The 411th Infantry Unit Journal, Declassified by NARA March 16, 2011, 103rd Infantry Division World War II Association, Dale Center for the Study of War & Society, University of Southern Mississippi.

"The Black Press: Soldiers Without Swords: Transcript." *PBS*, Public Broadcasting Service, www.pbs.org/blackpress/film/fulltranscript.html.

"The New KKK." *Mental Floss*, Nov. 26, 2015, www.mentalfloss.com/article/71720/wwi-centennial-new-kkk.

"The Tank Killers." *Fortune Magazine*, November 1942.

Thompson, James G. Letter. *Pittsburgh Courier*, January 31, 1942.

Thompson, M. Dion. "A Matter of Honor Medals: Thanks to a Battle by Veteran Vernon J. Baker and an Army-Assembled Team of Historians, Seven Black Soldiers Join the Ranks of World War II's Heroes." *Baltimoresun.com*, Oct. 22, 2018, www.baltimoresun.com/news/bs-xpm-1997-01-14-1997014150-story.html.

US Army Center of Military History. *Chapter XXII: Volunteer Infantry Replacements*, https://history.army.mil/books/wwii/11-4/chapter22.htm.

"US Army Infantry Cannon Company (1943–45)." *Battle Order*, www.battleorder.org/usa-1943-cannonco.

Wales, Solace. *Braided in Fire: Black GIs and Tuscan Villagers on the Gothic Line*. Knox Press, 2020.

Warbirds. "Pearl Harbor Attack Facts – Doris Miller, Hero At Pearl Harbor." *Pearl Harbor Warbirds*, Aug. 18, 2016, https://pearlharborwarbirds.com/pearl-harbor-attack-facts-doris-miller-hero-at-pearl-harbor/.

"What Was Hygiene Like For US Soldiers In WWII?" *Weird History*. 2021, https://www.youtube.com/watch?v=GCHUgiaitxk.

White, Lamar, et al. "The Beginning of Hell." *Bayou Brief*, www.bayoubrief.com/2019/09/17/the-beginning-of-hell/.

Williams, David J. *Hit Hard*. Bantam Books, 1983.

"World War II – Asiatic-Pacific Theater Campaigns." *World War II – Asiatic-Pacific Theater Campaigns*. US Army Center of Military History, https://history.army.mil/html/reference/army_flag/ww2_ap.html.

"World War II Operational Documents." *Ike Skelton Combined Arms Research Library (CARL) Digital Library*, https://cgsc.contentdm.oclc.org/digital/collection/p4013coll8/id/3060.

Index